BEST PRACTICES IN SUSTAINABLE DEVELOPMENT GOALS

About the Editors

Professor (Dr) Sujit Kumar Paul is working as a Professor of Rural Development and Management in the Department of Lifelong Learning and Extension, Visva-Bharati (A Central University and an Institution of National Importance), Santiniketan, West Bengal, India. He is also a development practitioner, researcher and resource person in the field of rural development and management. He has conducted several research projects funded by national and international agencies. Professor Paul is engaged in teaching, research and guiding PhD scholars. As prolific writer, he has published more than 100 research papers on various developmental issues in the national and international journals of repute. He authored eleven books on various development issues. He also edited four issues of the *International Journal of World Education*, published by the AWE (International). Professor Paul has visited different countries for academic and research and extension activities. He is closely associated with various government and non-government organizations, societies and associations in different capacities. Professor Paul is the AWE UN Representative and has been serving as Vice-President of AWE International – an international organization that holds "Consultative Status" with the Economic and Social Council (ECOSOC) in the United Nations for the last twenty-two years.

Dr K Gireesan is performing as Head, Department of Public Administration, Rajiv Gandhi National Institute of Youth Development (Institute of National Importance), Ministry of Youth Affairs and Sports, Government of India, Regional Centre, Chandigarh. He has obtained Postgraduate Degree and Doctoral degree in Public Administration from Panjab University, Chandigarh. His areas of research interest are: Empowerment of Local Government Institutions; Mainstreaming Youth in Governance; Youth and Political Leadership; Constituency Management; and Sustainable Development.

BEST PRACTICES IN SUSTAINABLE DEVELOPMENT GOALS

Edited by

Sujit Kumar Paul

K. Gireesan

CONCEPT PUBLISHING COMPANY PVT. LTD.
NEW DELHI - 110 059

ISBN: 978-93-6344-911-4

First Published 2025

Published and Printed by

Concept Since 1974

Concept Publishing Company Pvt. Ltd.
A/15-16, Commercial Block, Mohan Garden
New Delhi-110059 (India)
T: +91-11-41101460
E: publishing@conceptpub.com, *W*: www.conceptpub.com

Cataloging in Publication--Courtesy: D.K. Agencies (P) Ltd. <docinfo@dkagencies.com>

Best practices in sustainable development goals / edited by Sujit Kumar Paul, K. Gireesan.
pages cm
Contributed articles.
Includes bibliographical references and index.
ISBN 9789363449114

1. Sustainable development--India. 2. Sustainable development. 3. Community development--Government policy--India. 4. Community development--Government policy. 5. India--Economic policy--21st century. 6. India--Social policy--21st century. I. Paul, Sujit Kumar, 1970- editor. II. Gireesan, K., editor.

LCC HC435.4.B47 2025 | DDC 338.954 23

सत्यमेव जयते

राज्यपाल पश्चिम बंगाल
Governor of West Bengal
রাজ্যপাল, পশ্চিমবঙ্গ

17.01.2025

MESSAGE

Humanity is on the fast track path to achieving the sustainable development goals by 2030. It is said rightly that we have not inherited the Earth from our forefathers. We have borrowed it from our children. What we borrow from our children we are bound to repay, if possible, with interest.

Mahatma Gandhi's observations hold water now. He said, "The Earth has enough resources for everyone's need, not everyone's greed. " Rachel Carson, in her momentous book 'Silent Spring,' which first exposed the evils men have committed on Mother Nature, starts with a quotation from Albert Schweitzer. "Man has lost the capacity to foresee and to forestall; he will end by destroying the world."In this context, any attempt, anywhere in the world, to create awareness among human beings about the need for sustainable development is more than welcome.

I see the present book, 'Best Practices in Sustainable Development Goals', edited by Dr. Sujit Kumar Paul and Dr. K. Gireesan, in this global context. The purport of the book is the message, "A stitch in time saves nine." I am sure this book will serve as an eye-opener for anyone who is interested in the future of mankind, the future of the environment, and the future of Mother Nature. I wish the book all the very best.

Dr C.V. Ananda Bose

RAJ BHAVAN
KOLKATA

Foreword

As global challenges intensify, the urgency for sustainable development has never been clearer. The concept of "sustainable development", first introduced by the World Commission on Environment and Development (WCED) in 1987, seeks to meet present needs without compromising the ability of future generations to meet their own. At the core of sustainable development is the balancing act between ecological, human, and economic well-being, with an emphasis on stewardship of the planet's finite resources. This forward-thinking principle requires us to act responsibly, ensuring that the earth's resources are preserved for future generations.

This *Best Practices in Sustainable Development Goals* as an edited book highlights successful models, approaches, and experiences from various regions around the world. It brings together contributions from institutions, organizations, and individuals dedicated to sustainable development. This book emphasizes that achieving the SDGs is a collective effort requiring commitment, adaptability, and resilience from all stakeholders. It calls for a steadfast belief in the potential for creating a sustainable, equitable, and prosperous future for both people and the planet. This book urges readers to adopt an ecosystem-based approach in their daily lives and stresses that the time for action is now, with limitless possibilities for a better future.

The United Nations' adoption of the Sustainable Development Goals (SDGs) in 2015 represents a global commitment to address issues like poverty, inequality, climate change, peace, and prosperity by 2030. The SDGs are a call for global collaboration and urgent action across nations to eradicate poverty, protect the environment, and create equitable societies. However, achieving these goals requires innovative strategies, accelerated action, and partnerships that span across governments, businesses, civil society, and individuals.

This book provides a valuable compilation of best practices, transformative models, and lessons from diverse communities striving toward sustainable development. It highlights not only global initiatives but also local projects and grassroots efforts that exemplify the power of inclusive development, gender equality, peace, and environmental sustainability. One such example is Rabindranath Tagore's "Sriniketan Experiment", which presents a model for holistic rural development. Tagore's vision emphasizes education, health care, agricultural reforms, and vocational training, all of which align closely with the SDG agenda, particularly in terms of empowering marginalized communities.

Youth empowerment and education for peace-building also play a central role in achieving the SDGs. As the world faces increasing socio-political tensions, the youth are emerging as catalysts for change, fostering understanding in a divided world. Their engagement is essential to achieving global peace, justice, and equality, all of which are integral to the SDGs. This book underscores the importance of education as a means of nurturing leadership, critical thinking, and social responsibility among young people.

Additionally, the book delves into the role of indigenous knowledge and practices in sustainability, particularly through the lens of academic perspectives such as those offered by sociologist Andre Beteille. His argument that sociology, like sustainability, must be rooted in indigenous knowledge is especially pertinent in today's global context. Emphasizing indigenous ways of life fosters more contextually relevant and culturally sensitive approaches to development, which are crucial to the SDGs.

Women's leadership is another key focus of this collection. Gender equity is not only an SDG in itself but also a foundational element for achieving other SDGs. Women, especially in leadership roles, bring unique insights that can drive transformative change. Empowering women at the local level is critical for advancing sustainable and equitable development. When women are involved in decision making and leadership, they contribute to broader community development, including improvements in education, health, and economic participation.

The articles within this volume provide practical insights into overcoming development challenges through both innovative projects and lived experiences of communities facing unique struggles. From the Solar 2002 project in Belgium, which incorporates renewable energy and ecologically intelligent building techniques, to India's push for inclusive social security, the chapters emphasize context-specific solutions for sustainable development. These contributions explore the challenges faced by marginalized farmers in India's border regions, the sociocultural livelihood of the Santhal tribe, and the impact of microfinance in lifting communities out of poverty.

These diverse case studies highlight that sustainable development is not a one-size-fits-all solution. Each community faces distinct obstacles that require tailored approaches, whether it's the impact of climate change on agriculture, the role of social security systems in poverty reduction, or the empowerment of indigenous populations through cultural preservation and economic opportunities. The importance of considering local contexts and involving communities in the decision making process is underscored throughout the collection.

Ultimately, this volume reinforces the idea that true sustainability can only be achieved when no one is left behind. Whether addressing poverty, environmental degradation, or social inequality, the SDGs call for a comprehensive, inclusive approach to development. This collection is not just an academic reflection on sustainable development but a call to action for policymakers, practitioners, and communities to engage with the complexities of global development challenges and work toward innovative solutions. By embracing diversity and inclusion in our approaches to the SDGs, we can create a more equitable, sustainable, and peaceful world for future generations.

This book will remain a seminal work in this field of development management. I congratulate the authors and the editors Professor Sujit Kumar Paul and Dr K. Gireesan.

Dr W.G. Prasanna Kumar
Former Chairman
Mahatma Gandhi
National Council of Rural Institute (NCRI)
Ministry of Human Resource Development
Government of India

Preface

The Sustainable Development Goals (SDGs), adopted by all United Nations member states in 2015, represent a comprehensive framework aimed at fostering peace, prosperity, and sustainability for people and the planet. With seventeen interlinked goals encompassing a wide range of social, economic, and environmental dimensions, the SDGs provide a roadmap for governments, institutions, agencies, and individuals to navigate through the complexities of sustainable development.

Over the years, different countries have shown considerable success with vast number of development initiatives and interventions by the state and non-state actors. The innovative approaches, strategies, experiences and practices lead to sustainability in reaching out to the most marginalized sections of the society. Considering the significance of these initiatives and their importance as replicable models, it is pertinent to formulate a compendium of case studies, success stories and best practices in SDGs.

This book *Best Practices in Sustainable Development Goals* serves as an important resource for academicians, researchers, professionals, administrators, practitioners and students committed to advancing sustainable development. It synthesizes innovative approaches, successful strategies and diverse experiences from different sectors and drawn from different countries. This book captures some of the case studies, success stories, and best practices highlighting the significance and application of SDGs.

The different chapters in this book have been classified into four parts. Each chapter of this book delves into specific goals, illustrating how diverse actors, from grassroots organizations to multinational corporations, are implementing effective strategies. Readers will encounter case studies that reflect a broad spectrum of initiatives, including community-led conservation efforts, innovative educational programmes, and sustainable business practices. These narratives not only provide insight into what works but also offer practical guidance for those seeking to replicate or adapt these initiatives in their own contexts.

Furthermore, the book emphasizes the significance of partnerships. The SDGs are built on the premise that sustainable development requires collective action across sectors and borders. The authors explore the role of public-private partnerships, civil society engagement, and international cooperation in achieving these ambitious goals. Through collaborative efforts, stakeholders can leverage resources, knowledge, and expertise, amplifying their impact and fostering a shared commitment to a more sustainable future.

In the face of mounting global challenges, the time for action is now. The SDGs represent not only a framework for addressing pressing issues but also a call to envision a better world for future generations. As one embark on this exploration of best practices, the authors encourage readers to engage critically with the material, reflect on their own role in this transformative journey, and consider how they can contribute to the realization of the SDGs in the community and beyond.

Let this book serve as a source of inspiration, a practical guide, and a catalyst for action as one work together to achieve the SDGs for all. It is essential to recognize the diverse perspectives and voices that shape our understanding about sustainable development. I do hope that the book *Best Practices in Sustainable Development Goals* will contribute towards enhancing better understanding of the approaches, experiences and practices on sustainable development.

We express our sincere gratitude to all the contributors round the globe for their contribution to this volume. We are extremely grateful to Dr W.G. Prasanna Kumar, Former Chairman, National Council of Rural Institute (NCRI), Ministry of Human Resource Development, Government of India for writing the Foreword for this edited volume. Finally, we express our appreciation to the publisher in bringing the book on time.

Sujit Kumar Paul
K. Gireesan

Contents

Part II

Part III

List of Contributors

Allan Furth, Co-Founder and Retired Founding Director, Cobscook Institute, Trescott Township, Maine, USA.
Email: alan@cobscookinstitute.org; www.cobscookinstitute.org

Arkadeep Goswami, Research Associate,Centre for Inclusive Development Charitable Trust, West Bengal, India.
Email: arkadeep220195@gmail.com

Asmaa Sleem, Vice-President, Association for World Education and Content Strategist and professional trainer/facilitator; Creative Leadership/Caux Initiatives of Change Foundation; and, Educator and founder of Lifelong learning talks, Egypt.
Email: Asmaa.ahmed.sleem@gmail.com; asmaasleem84@yahoo.com

Banasree Das, District Support Specialist, Technical Support Unit, Water For People India, Kolkata, West Bengal, India.
Email: b.x.das@waterforpeople.org

B.K. Pandey, Professor of Practice, Arun Jaitley National Institute of Financial Management, Faridabad, Haryana, India.
Email: bkpandey@nifm.ac.in

Devashree Desai, Master's Student, Department of Clinical Sciences, Dr Vishwanath Karad MIT World Peace University, Pune, Maharashtra, India.
Email: 1102220023@mitwpu.edu.in

Ganesh Mane, PhD Scholar, Department of Public Health, Dr Vishwanath Karad MIT World Peace University, Pune, Maharashtra, India.
Email: ganesh.mane@mitwpu.edu.in

Guido-Henri De Couvreur, Senior Member, Association for World Education and President, Mondo vcw, Belgium.
Email: guido@mondo.be

Heenakshi Bhansali, Assistant Professor, Department of Clinical Sciences, Dr Vishwanath Karad MIT World Peace University, Pune, Maharashtra, India.
Email: heenakshi.bhansali@mitpwu.edu.in

Inbarasan K.G., Research Wing Lead, Institute of Grassroots Governance, Tamil Nadu, India.
Email: inba.science09@gmail.com

Jacob Erle, Director, International Academy for Education and Democracy, Copenhagen K, Denmark.
Email: je@iaed.info ; www.iaed.info

Jaya Bhalla, Associate Professor (SG), Arun Jaitley National Institute of Financial Management, Faridabad, Haryana, India.
Email: jaya@nifm.ac.in

K. Gireesan, Head, Department of Public Administration, Rajiv Gandhi National Institute of Youth Development (Institute of National Importance by the Act of Parliament), Ministry of Youth Affairs and Sports, Government of India, Regional Centre, Chandigarh, India.
Email: gireesan.decentralisation@gmail.com

Manju Singh, Professor, Department of Humanities and Social Sciences, Malaviya National Institute of Technology, Jaipur, Rajasthan, India.
Email: manjus.hum@mnit.ac.in

Mark Tappan, Professor of Education, Emeritus, Colby College, Waterville, Maine, USA.
Email: mark.tappan@colby.edu

May Rendon-Cinco, Former Senior Trainer of the Education for Life Foundation (ELF); Director, Distance Learning

Programme ELF; Freelance Grassroots Educator, Adult Learning and Education advocacy of the Civil Society Network for Education Reforms (E-Net Philippines).
Email: may.cinco@gmail.com

Moumita Sarkar, Senior Regional Director, Programs, IPAS Development Foundation, New Delhi, India.
Email: sarkarm@ipas.org

Niels Larsen, Regional Centre of Expertise for Education for Sustainable Development (RCE), Denmark and Kijani Institute, Kenya.
Email: niladk5@gmail.com

Prabagaran M., Training and Implementation Wing Lead, Institute of Grassroots Governance, Tamil Nadu, India.
Email: prabagaranlg@gmail.com

Raisuyah Bhagwan, Professor, Department of Community Health Studies, Durban University of Technology. South Africa.
Email: bhagwanr@dut.ac.za

Ramanuj Ganguly, Professor, Department of Sociology, West Bengal State University, Barasat, Kolkata, West Bengal, India.
Email: rg.wbsu@gmail.com

Ravikant Kumar, Knowledge Management Specialist, Water For People India,Kolkata, West Bengal, India.
Email: kumar@waterforpeople.org

Riya De, Treasurer and Field Coordinator Centre for Inclusive Development Charitable Trust, West Bengal, India.
Email: riyade90@gmail.com

Saibal Paul, Deputy Director, and Lead-Policy, Member Development and Sector Building Department, Sa-Dhan, the National Association of Impact Finance Institutions; SRO designated by Reserve Bank of India; NSO designated by NRLM.
Email: saibalpaul@sa-dhan.org

Sanjoy Karmakar, Postgraduate Student, Department of Geography, Visva Bharati University, Santiniketan, Birbhum, West Bengal, India.
Email: sanjoygeography@gmail.com

Shamim Mohammad, Associate Professor, Department of Clinical Sciences, Dr Vishwanath Karad MIT World Peace University, Pune, Maharashtra, India.
Email: Shamim.mohd@mitwpu.ed.in

Soumen Sarkar, AGM and Regional Operations Manager, IDBI Bank, Mumbai, Maharashtra, India.
Email: soumensarkr@gmail.com

Sreyasi Ray, Assistant Professor, The Heritage Academy, Affiliated to the Maulana Abul Kalam Azad University of Technology, Kolkata, West Bengal, India.
Email: sreyasri.ray@gmail.com

Sujata Tripathy, State Lead West Bengal, Water For People India, Kolkata, West Bengal, India.
Email: stripathy@waterforpeople.org

Sujit Kumar Paul, Professor of Rural Development and Management, Department of Lifelong Learning and Extension, Institute of Rural Reconstruction, Visva-Bharati (A Central University), Sriniketan, Birbhum, West Bengal, India.
Email: skpaulrd@gmail.com; sujitkumar.paul@visva-bharati.ac.in

Sulagna Dutta, Research Scholar, Department of Lifelong Learning and Extension, Institute of Rural Reconstruction, Visva-Bharati (A Central University), Sriniketan, Birbhum, West Bengal, India.
Email: sulagnavb@gmail.com

Titas Ghosh, Senior Co-ordinator, Programs, IPAS Development Foundation, New Delhi, India.
Email: ghosht@ipas.org

Vinoj Manning, Chief Executive Officer, IPAS Development Foundation, New Delhi, India.
Email: manningv@ipas.org

Wafa Singh, PhD Scholar, Department of Community Health Studies, Durban University of Technology, South Africa.
Email: wafasingh86@gmail.com

Introduction

Sujit Kumar Paul and *K. Gireesan*

The World Commission on Environment and Development (WCED) defined sustainable development as "development that meets the needs of the present without compromising the ability of future generations to meet their own needs" in its 1987 Brundtland report. Sustainable development is the "organizing principle for meeting human development goals while simultaneously sustaining the ability of natural systems to provide the natural resources and ecosystem services on which the economy and society depend". Countries all over the world envision suitable practices that support ecological, human and economic health and vitality. Sustainability presumes that resources are finite and should be used wisely and optimally with a view to long-term priorities. In simplest term, sustainability is about our children, grandchildren, and the world that we will leave for them.

All member states of the United Nations adopted the Sustainable Development Goals (SDGs) in 2015. Also known as the "Global Goals", it as a global call of action to eradicate poverty, safeguard the environment, and guarantee that everyone lives in peace and prosperity by 2030. Global partnerships are expected to strengthen the combined actions for achieving the goals. Achievement of the SDGs are envisioned by several countries and mainstreaming the SDGs in national development strategies and programme are attempted by international organizations, international funding agencies and the countries themselves, in order to make a remarkable progress in this direction. Countries are adapting several programmes and initiatives that would directly contribute to advancement of the SDG agendas. Progress is being made in many places and countries, but overall action to meet the goals is not yet advancing at the required speed or scale.

Over the years, different countries have shown notable success with vast number of developmental interventions by different stakeholders, especially the governments and civil society organizations. They have demonstrated creative methods, successful tactics, enduring influence, and sustainability in interacting with the most marginalized segments of society. Given the significance of these programmes and their value as trustworthy reference models, a compilation of the best SDG practices shall be created, documenting case studies on diverse aspects and from different regions. In line with the principle of cooperative federalism and devolution of funds to the local government institutions, all spheres of government are key stakeholders in realizing the SDGs. In this regard, specific, innovative and best practices for achieving SDGs from different parts of the world are documented here.

Here, the primary goal is to showcase the models, approaches, practices and experiences that are unique, sustainable, and replicable by making suitable variations along with synthesizing lessons for the future to improve quality of life of the community. It can be viewed as a sourcebook to provide information regarding the approaches and practices for achieving SDGs all over the world. In the progress of SDGs, every single contribution of the government, local government institutions, civil society organizations, corporates, including the individuals, in spite of its magnitude and scale, is valuable. Underlining the significance of the subject, academicians, researchers, professionals, administrators, and practitioners were requested to contribute the best practices, field initiatives, case studies, experimented models and perspectives, contributing towards the SDGs. This edited book captures the status of SDGs and its practices from the global, the regional, the national and the local, with inputs from number of institutions, organizations and individuals who are "working with and working for sustainable development".

I

The SDGs are designed to address interconnected global challenges by recognizing that progress in one area can impact progress in others. They aim at a wide range of objectives, including ending poverty and hunger, promotion of health and education, gender equality, environmental sustainability, etc. By integrating these goals through acknowledging the interdependencies between social, economic, and environmental factors, it aims to promote holistic and sustainable development worldwide. Prioritizing progress for those who are left behind, especially among marginalized communities in remote rural areas, is crucial for achieving the SDGs. In India, these commitments involve addressing various forms of inequality, discrimination, and exclusion, particularly targeting vulnerable and marginalized groups such as Scheduled Tribes, minorities, women, and girls residing in rural areas where people living in poverty and those affected by conflict or disaster. Rabindranath Tagore's "Sriniketan Experiment" exemplifies a proactive approach towards addressing the challenges faced by rural communities, reflecting the broader aim of SDGs. Tagore, being a humanist, recognized the profound suffering endured by the villagers living in conditions of acute poverty, malnutrition, ill-health, and illiteracy. Through the Sriniketan Experiment initiated in 1922 within Visva-Bharati, Tagore aimed to uplift and empower the villages focused on holistic development, encompassing aspects such as education, health care, agricultural reforms, vocational training, and cultural enrichment. Similar to the SDG objectives and approaches, Tagore's "Sriniketan Experiment" sought to cultivate self-reliance, community engagement, and sustainable practices, fostering a sense of dignity and well-being among the villagers. **Professor Sujit Kumar Paul and Sulagna Datta** in their article "Tagore's Sriniketan Experiment: An Ideal Model for Achieving Sustainable Development Goals" tried to investigate

Rabindranath Tagore's Sriniketan Experiment as a paradigmatic example of sustainable development practices and how it is proven to be an ideal model for achieving the SDGs. Through a rigorous scrutiny of historical records, scholarly literature, and contemporary approaches, the study aims to demonstrate how Sriniketan Experiment embodies the principles and objectives of the SDGs. This research also contributes to the discourse on sustainable development by elucidating the practical implications of Tagore's vision for contemporary global challenges.The paper emphasizes the importance of integrating localized approaches like the Sriniketan Experiment into broader strategies for achieving SDGs worldwide.

The 2030 Agenda for Sustainable Development stands as a beacon, advocating for rigorous efforts across nations to address pressing global challenges. At its core lies a fundamental thing that peace and sustainable development are intrinsically intertwined. The 2030 Agenda's statement, "Without peace, there's no sustainable development, and without sustainable development, there's no peace", really hits home, showing how these things rely on each other. It's like a wake-up call, urging us to work together to tackle issues like violence, insecurity, and other problems that hold back progress. As we strive for a world that's fairer, more just, and more peaceful, it is very important to look at the best ways to make progress on goals like peace, justice, and ensure everyone gets a good education. Thus, it is imperative to explore the best practices and strategies that can push us towards realizing these interconnected aspirations. In a world increasingly polarized, where opinions clash and divisions deepen, the youth emerge as catalysts for change, weaving threads of understanding through the fabric of controversy. **Asmaa Sleem** in her article "Fostering Growth and Well-being: Best Practices for SDGs, Leadership, Peace Education, Inner Development, and Lifelong Learning" tried to explore the pivotal role and the best practices of youth education for peace building, as part of peace education, SDGs and inner development goals. Shedding light on the integral role of peace education and the involvement of youth in peace building illuminates the pathways to achieve the SDGs. And In the pursuit of a more equitable and prosperous world and within the framework of the 2030 Agenda for Sustainable Development lies a profound acknowledgement of the deep relationship between peace, justice, and quality education.

Sreyasi Ray and Professor Ramanuj Ganguly in their paper "Sustainability: An Alternative Approach—Andre Beteille's Thoughts on Developing Sustainable Sociology", tried to understand sustainability on Andre Beteille's perspectives. Andre Beteille, with his inquisitiveness to ensure sustainability of the discipline of sociology, developed an interest to comprehend sociology, its nature and significance through his academic endeavours. Generally, the word "sustainability" is associated with environment and natural resources. It also stands as the quality of being able to continue over time. Beteille found that delving into research and study of subjects related to current affairs has gained tremendous parlance in sociology. However, to sociologists like Beteille, "interest in current affairs can stimulate sociological enquiry and investigation". But the "long-term growth of an intellectual discipline becomes distorted and even jeopardized when it allows itself to be driven entirely by the interest in current affairs to the exclusion of all other interests". Over dependency on the Western methods and lack of innovation of indigenous methods to study our own society are some of the flaws that have engulfed the subject. He further mentioned that turning away of sociologists from the concepts, methods and data in the long run, will impoverish and affect the enrichment of sociology in India. Beteille suggested that researches getting influenced by government and NGOs should not restrict themselves to provide immediate practical solutions only. It is certainly true that research with its attention in current affairs at the cost of theory will impact its sustainability. To Beteille, it is this increasing concern with current affairs that has led to the development of myopic view to study the fundamental features of Indian society and sociology, thereby impacting the sustainability of the subject.

"Role of Women Leaders at the Local Level to achieve the Sustainable Development Goals" by **Dr K. Gireesan** is an attempt made to achieve the SDGs highlight the role of women leaders at the local level by analysing the economic, social, and environmental dimensions. It is viewed that identifying, analysing and practising various practical and strategic functions with a gender perspective could contribute significantly towards addressing the existing gender gaps and achieving the SDGs at a faster pace. The author puts forward a number of suggestions that could be considered by the leadership, especially by the women leaders at the local level, towards achieving the SDGs. The author advocates that policy formulation in multiple domains shall be made for meeting the needs of future generations with due thrust and weightage on diverse demographic segments, keeping in view the principles of "equity" and "empowerment".

II

Professor Mark Tappan, Jakob Erle and Alan Furth in their article "Trauma Responsive Equitable Education: A Model for Communities Seeking to Bring the UN's Sustainable Development Goals to Life" described an innovative and empowering education programme, Trauma Responsive Equitable Education (TREE). It enables the ideas and issues that are in the minds of students, including early elementary school students, to make school life attractive and relevant to them. The authors assert that a local initiative such as TREE, with its impacts and approach, are strengthened and compounded when they understand them and stitch them effectively to the SDGs. The TREE project contributes to the achievement of the national obligations of the SDGs, especially in education.The integrated agenda of the SDGs gives the scope for learning and reflection for educators, students, families, and communities to understand their work in the context of the world they live in. At the same time, it provides a framework for dialogue on why learning environments, as exemplified by TREE, are needed to cope with and shape our hyper-complex world.

Advancing indigenous peoples education contributes greatly to break the historic discrimination, marginalization and inequalities experienced by indigenous persons. Providing them context-based basic literacy and leadership formation, equal opportunity to quality and culturally-sensitive formal education and alternative learning systems, recognizing and respecting their indigenous knowledge systems and practices are fundamentals to enhance their full potentials and uplift their self-esteem. From this point of view, **May Rendon-Cinco** in her article "LAKAS High School in the Philippines: Advancing Indigenous People's Education toward Sustainable Development" tried to explore the LAKAS High School (LHS) Model for sustainable development of the indigenous people. As the education system discriminates and marginalize the indigenous persons, advancing indigenous people's education is a pathway to empower them. This was shown in the experience of the Aeta, the indigenous people around Mt. Pinatubo in the Philippines. Through the collective effort of their elders and leaders of their organization called LAKAS, the indigenous persons were able to negotiate with the government's Department of Education to build their own school which they named LHS. Thus, it becomes an institution of mainstreaming the Aeta knowledge systems and practices in the basic formal education. In this context, sustaining other forms and modes of learning to enrich their life and environment that meet the development of the Aeta at present without compromising the needs of the future generation of their tribe becomes significant.

Dr Heenakshi Bhansali, Dr Shamim Mohammad, and Devashree Desai in their article "Accessibility and Affordability of Mental Health Services in India" tried to explore the current landscape of mental health services in India, with a focus on the challenges associated with accessibility and affordability. Despite increased awareness of mental health issues, a significant proportion of the Indian population continues to experience difficulties to receive adequate mental health care. This chapter analyses the socio-economic, geographical, and cultural variables that contribute to the limited availability of mental health services, particularly in remote rural and marginalized populations. Affordability emerges as a critical concern, as a considerable segment of the population struggles to bear the financial burden associated with mental health treatment. The 2015-16 National Mental Health Survey (NMHS), that was done in twelve states, exposes India's massive burden of mental health disorders. According to the report's findings, the proportion of mental health issues to the country's total disease burden doubled between 1990 and 2017. One in seven Indians, were thought to be affected with mental illnesses of varying severity, the most common being depression and anxiety. This chapter examines the existing mental health infrastructure, public policies, and initiatives aimed at addressing these challenges. It also examines the effectiveness of current interventions in promoting accessibility and affordability. The authors analysed data gathered from mental health professionals, policymakers, and individuals with lived experiences on the economic implications and regional disparities in utilization of mental health services. They highlighted number of technological advancements and the role of telemedicine in bridging the accessibility gap. Despite the efforts made by the governments to provide universal and affordable mental health care shortage of mental health specialists, inadequate infrastructure, and stigma still remain as the major reasons for the huge treatment gaps for majority of disorders. The findings highlight the need for a multi-faceted approach that includes policy reforms, community engagement, and increased public awareness campaigns. Recommendations for enhancing mental health education, integrating mental health into primary health care, and developing innovative financial models for affordability are presented. The article highlights how critical it is to address these issues in order to develop an Indian mental health care system that is more responsive and accessible.

Moumita Sarkar, Titas Ghosh, and Vinoj Manning in their paper "Enhancing Agency of Young Women and Girls for Improved Sexual and Reproductive Health and Rights" presents the findings and insights gained from a project aimed at enhancing agency and improving young women's sexual and reproductive health (SRH) outcomes in selected districts of Jharkhand and West Bengal. The primary goal of the project was to help achieve the "SDG-3.7 (Universal access to sexual and reproductive health services and information) and SDG-5.6 (Ensuring universal access to sexual and reproductive health and rights, under gender equality)". Recognizing the diverse challenges faced by this demographic segment, the project adopted a comprehensive approach towards building a sustainable SRH ecosystem supporting the rights of adolescents and young women. This involved engagement not only with adolescent girls and young women but also engaged a diverse array of stakeholders, encompassing male partners, family members, and community influencers. To enhance the provision of SRH services, the intervention focused on strengthening youth-friendly SRH services within public health facilities. A mixed-method evaluation design was used to assess the outcomes of the intervention. The assessment focused on understanding the barriers and facilitators that influence SRH decision making, access to SRH information and services, and the agency of adolescents and young women.

Ganesh Mane and Dr Shamim Mohammad in their article "Eradication of Hunger and Malnutrition: Practices and Approaches in Malnutrition Reduction in India" discusses the relevant SDGs, measurement indices and methods, policy and legal aspects and community practices to reduce the hunger and malnutrition across India. Hunger is a major concern in developing countries and SDG2 exclusively deals with the eradication of hunger. It covers the different macro and micro indices used to measure the progress across the globe on hunger, food security, and malnutrition. The chapter analyses India's position on these indices which continue to be a serious cause of concern. India's ranking on the Human Development Index (HDI) was 131 out of 191 countries in 2021-22; Global Multidimensional Index (MDI) was 66 out of 109 countries in 2021, and Global Hunger Index (GHI) was 111 out of 125 countries in 2023. At micro level, the chapter deals with anthropometric nutritional status measurement such as Weight, Height, Mid Upper Arm Circumference (MUAC), Head Circumference, BMI, and Waist Hip Ratio. In SDGs' ranking, India (112) continues to be far behind from its neighbouring countries like Sri Lanka (83) and Bangladesh (101). Stunting (35.5%) and wasting (19.3%) in children and anemia in women of reproductive age (57%) continues to keep India behind in all possible measurement indices. Interventions like Community Based Management of Acute Malnutrition (CMAM) are needed to facilitate across the country. The authors advocate for a multisectoral approach, bringing stakeholders from health care, agriculture, water and sanitation, land reforms, PDS system, etc. is required to address this multifaceted issue comprehensively.

Dr Banasree Das, Ravikant Kumar, and Sujata Tripathy in their article "Water for People India: Assessing Interventions and Aligning with Sustainable Development Goal 6" focused on the interventions by Water for People India (WFPI) in its mission to provide sustainable water and sanitation solutions, aligning with the SDG-6. The paper aims to ensure the availability and sustainability of water and sanitation for all, by proper management. The Millennium Development Goals (MDGs) concluded in 2016, ushering in the Agenda of Sustainable Development, which includes total seventeen SDGs by including every field of development. Out of this, SDG-6 focuses on clean water and sanitation facility accessibility for all. In India, significant challenges remain, particularly in rural areas where water contamination and inadequate sanitation persist, the WFPI aligns its mission with SDG-6, promoting sustainable water and sanitation solutions. Since 2007, the WFPI has implemented community-driven programmes across several states, enhancing access to water and sanitation, fostering local ownership, and addressing climate resilience. Innovative approaches like leveraging local art for behaviour change have proven effective in promoting WASH practices. Scaling efforts and integrating climate adaptation strategies are crucial for achieving long-term impact and reaching 100 million people by 2030. Through partnerships, technological innovations, and community engagement, the WFPI continues to make significant strides towards SDG-6 in India. The paper highlights the effectiveness of community-based approaches, infrastructure development, and capacity-building programmes. This paper puts forward suggestions to achieve significant improvements in water accessibility and sanitation coverage, contributing to enhanced health outcomes and socio-economic development.

III

Contemporary India is faced with the co-existence of critical and unsustainable developmental challenges (such as environmental degradation, socio-economic disparities, gender-based violence, etc.), which have underscored the *status-quo* approaches to human development, will no longer suffice. This scenario demands for a deviation from the business-as-usual approach, from all institutions and sectors, especially Higher Education Institutions (HEIs), who are recognized as public institutions. Its research function is expected to be "more engaged" with social issues, in being able to address the developmental challenges, while also helping HEIs to fulfil their social responsibilities. Although HEIs have traditionally contributed to knowledge creation through their research function, the contemporary, multi-level, varied and cross-sectoral challenges call for an innovative approach to research. This new approach is expected to be responsible, engaged and result in the production of "new knowledge"; one which transcends disciplinary boundaries, is co-produced and has the potential to address the challenges of unsustainability. In lieu of this, it is essential that HEIs embrace a renewed and responsible approach to research, and one of the ways to do so is to adopt the practice of "Community Based Participatory Research (CBPR)". **Wafa Singh, Professor Raisuyah Bhagwan, and Professor Manju Singh** through this chapter entitled "Adopting Community Based Participatory Research for Advancing Sustainable Development: Lessons from Indian Higher Education Institutions" explores the conceptual framework of CBPR, while shedding light on its practices and positioning in the Indian higher education landscape. The chapter complements this exploration by capturing some of the institutional best practices in CBPR, and closes with concrete reflections on the potentials, promises, and way forward in this area of work, for attaining the global goals of sustainable development.

Technical and vocational education and training (TVET) plays a key role in providing the workforce with knowledge, skills, and competencies to facilitate the transition to a greener economy and engage with the complexity to trasnsform into a more sustainable and greener societies. The paper entitled "Practical Partnership between TVET in Denmark and Kenya" by **Dr Niels Larsen** is about a partnership between three vocational centres in Denmark and one in Kenya working with co-learning within the umbrella of SDG and the subject of carpentry and joinery woodwork. The aim was to get more experiences and reflection on how it was possible to work cross culturally between the Global North and the Global South and to develop a didactical model for this kind of work.

Local government institutions, such as municipalities and panchayats, are instrumental in advancing specific SDGs. They are responsible for various essential services and development projects that align with the SDG targets, including clean water supply, waste management, and sustainable urban planning. The vast and diverse socio-economic, cultural, and environmental landscape of India necessitates a tailored approach to SDG localization. This process involves adapting global objectives to address specific local challenges and opportunities. Localization is crucial for effectively addressing multidimensional poverty and inequality, and it requires a comprehensive, whole-of-society approach. Key elements of successful localization include effective multi-level governance, inclusive decision making, and active participation of sub-national governments. Local governments are pivotal in the effective localization and implementation of SDGs, bridging global policies with local realities. Through this paper entitled "Role of Local Governments in Accelerating Sustainable Development

Goals in India: Achievements, Challenges, and Strategic Actions", **Dr Jaya Bhalla, and Dr B.K. Pandey** examined the critical role of local governments in India in achieving and accelerating the SDGs by 2030. It explores the impact of local governments on SDGs, highlights key successes, identifies challenges faced, and provides actionable strategies for enhancing local government contributions to meet the SDG targets.

Participatory structures have existed at the grassroots level in India since ancient times, in the form of local assemblies known as *sabha*s and *samiti*s. These structures were later found in the medieval history as village assemblies called *mahasabha*. Endowed with the constitutional status, the *grama sabha* could prepare developmental plans at the grassroots level, fostering self-governance within their area of jurisdiction. The SDGs play a vital role to ensure the developmental gaps are noticed and addressed at various levels. SDG-16 (Peace, Justice and Strong Institutions) is an important goal that focuses on promoting inclusive societies, building effective, accountable and inclusive institutions at all levels along with promoting peace and justice for all. This case depicts the impact of various participatory structures as democratic institutions in a village panchayat. **Prabagaran M. and Inbarasan K.G.** through their article "Impact of Participatory Structures at the Grassroots: A Case Study from Prathabaramapuram Village Panchayat, Nagapattinam, Tamil Nadu" delves into the significance of various participatory structures, including *gram sabha*s and other *sabha*s such as the Ward Sabha, Women's Sabha (Magalir Sabhai), Sabha for the Differently Abled (Matruthiranali Sabhai), and Children's Sabha (Balar Sabhai). It discusses about the decentralized decision making through various *sabha*s in the Prathabaramapuram Village Panchayat, Keelaiyur Panchayat Union, Nagapattinam district, which can serve as a developmental model.

IV

Solar 2002 is a demonstration project in Belgium that serves both as a visitor and educational centre. It aims to promote alternative and sustainable techniques in secondary education and demonstrate the possibility of ecologically and intelligently designed buildings. The project emphasizes the importance of renewable energy and the need to raise awareness among various stakeholders. Solar 2002 incorporates innovative techniques such as moisture-regulating thermal insulation, heat recovery, water extraction from rainwater, waste water treatment, and efficient use of solar energy. It focuses on reducing primary energy consumption and achieving a zero balance on secondary energy. The project highlights the relations/linkages between human actions and their global impact, encouraging a shift toward harmonious living with nature. **Guido-Henri De Couvreur,** in his paper titled "A Solar Realization with Connections to SDGs" provides insights into the technical aspects and priorities for rational energy consumption. Overall, Solar 2002 represents a case study of a bio-ecological house striving for energy efficiency and environmental responsibility.

The SDGs are largely attained in developing countries like India by providing adequate social security coverage to the underprivileged. For a long time since Independence, the biggest obstacle to the country's inclusive development has been the large rural population's exclusion from social security coverage. The two most important steps India has taken in the last ten years to achieve the SDGs are its push for financial inclusion and its integration with social security programmes. In order to claim its progress towards the SDGs, the union and state governments shall jointly develop a strong social security system for inclusive progress throughout the nation and among all groups. The paper "Significant Approaches Towards Social Security Leading to Sustainable Development Goals in India: A Study" by **Dr Soumen Sarkar** looked at the traditional methods for categorizing social security systems and tried to address the origins and fundamental ideas of social security from a global viewpoint. Based on the review of related literature, the limitations of implementing social security have been discussed. In order to provide a clearer understanding of their goals, the author attempted to group all these activities under particular headings.

The important steps taken by the Union government to advance the nation's social security programme were discussed in the paper. It highlighted a wide range of projects, their shortcomings, and their efficacy in promoting sustainable development in society, and put forward suggestions.

Farmers living along the international border face tough restrictions. They are not allowed to grow crops taller than 3 ft, and they can't easily access their own lands for farming. And, they have to rely on the BSF personnel to open the gates in the fencing whenever they need to work on their land. Adding to these challenges, there is a lack of irrigation system in the border areas, making it even harder to the farmers for agricultural practices. Coupled with the issues of climate change, the weather in places like Cooch Behar has become highly unpredictable, making farming even more difficult. SDG-1 aims to eliminate poverty in all its manifestations worldwide. It seeks to eradicate extreme poverty globally, ensuring universal access to essential needs such as food, water, shelter, health care, and education. However, human-made challenges often exacerbate the hardships faced by farmers, making their lives miserable. Consequently, these challenges affect the well-being of future generations of those particular areas, perpetuating the cycle of suffering and deprivation. All these issues have a serious negative impact on agriculture in the border areas like Cooch Behar, making it difficult for farmers to make a living from their land. Under these peculiar circumstances, the local population adopt unconventional and ill-healthy economic options. Many of them take up unsafe migration to other states in search of a job. Some of them adopted even dangerous options like cross-border smuggling. SDG-8 emphasizes the importance of promoting inclusive and sustainable economic growth, along with decent work for all individuals. Regrettably, there have been challenges in ensuring hassle-free agricultural activities to the impoverished farmers in the border villages, where efforts of the state and union governments have fallen short. Significantly,the United Nations has special statute about ensuring Rights of Peasants and Other People

Working in Rural Areas. **Riya De and Arkadeep Goswami** in their paper "Cross-border Smuggling, Livelihood and the Question of Sustainable Development in the Indo-Bangladesh Border" tried to pinpoint the primary factors contributing to the current situation and to explore potential alternatives aimed at resolving or mitigating these issues.

The Santhal tribe, one of the largest indigenous communities in India, embodies a rich cultural heritage deeply intertwined with its socio-economic livelihood practices. Situated predominantly in the Bankura district of West Bengal, the Santhals have sustained their unique way of life amidst a rapidly changing sociocultural landscape. This study seeks to delve into the intricate fabric of Santhal livelihoods, examining the various sociocultural factors that shape their existence and exploring its implications on the SDGs. By shedding light on the lived experiences, traditions, and challenges faced by the Santhal community, this paper aims to contribute to a deeper understanding of indigenous cultures and informed strategies for sustainable development in alignment with the SDGs. **Sanjoy Karmakar** in his paper titled "Exploring the Sociocultural Livelihood of the Santhal Tribe and Its Implications for SDGs: A Study in Bankura District" captures the sociocultural livelihood of the Santhal tribe in the study area, offering a comprehensive examination of their unique way of life. Focused towards understanding the intricate interplay between tradition and adaptation, the paper explores the tribe's rituals, festivals, and performances, revealing a profound connection to nature and agricultural cycles. Furthermore, this paper contextualizes the sociocultural livelihood of the Santhal tribe within the framework of SDGs. By analysing the implications of their practices, particularly those related to poverty alleviation, gender equality, and environmental sustainability, it contributes to a broader understanding of how indigenous communities can play a vital role in achieving global sustainability objectives. The study brings out valuable insights for policymakers, development practitioners, and researchers, facilitating a more inclusive, and culturally sensitive approach towards sustainable development initiatives that align with the unique sociocultural context of tribal communities like the Santhals.

Microfinance has a long history, with Irish loan funds dating back to 1720 and later regulated by strong regulations, courtesy goes to Jonathan Swift. Credit cooperatives were established in Germany in the 1850s to serve those whom traditional banks were hesitant to serve. Various forms of microfinance, such as Susus in Ghana, Tandas in Mexico, Cheetu in Sri Lanka, Hui in China, and Chit Funds and Maroops in Manipur, have been providing credit to the underserved populations for generations. While these initiatives have helped meet the credit needs of the poor, there has been a focus on the purpose of the loan and repayment strategies. Microfinance has gone far beyond micro savings and microcredit, taking up micro leasing, micro insurance, micro pensions, etc. in order to examine the linkages of microfinance to the SDGs. **Dr Saibal Paul** in his paper entitled "Microfinance and Its Role in Achieving the Sustainable Development Goals with Reference to Indian Microfinance Sector" tried to assess the influence of microfinance on the lives of the borrowers. The data analysis of the impact of microfinance on a global scale, along with other sources, reviews the data set compiled by Sa-Dhan to identify the impact of the microfinance sector on the various parameters of the SDGs.

As we navigate through the complexities of sustainable development, it is essential to recognize the diverse perspectives and voices that shape our understanding manifested through different chapters, classified under four parts. This book incorporates insights from various disciplines, cultures, experiences, and regions by reflecting the multifaceted nature of sustainability. By embracing diversity and promoting inclusive dialogue, we can ensure that our approaches to the SDGs are equitable and just, leaving no one behind.

Part I

1

Tagore's Sriniketan Experiment

An Ideal Model for Achieving Sustainable Development Goals

Sujit Kumar Paul and *Sulagna Dutta*

The Sustainable Development Goals (SDGs) are a collection of seventeen worldwide accepted objectives formulated in 2015 by the United Nations General Assembly under the 2030 Agenda for Sustainable Development. These goals encompass a broad spectrum of interrelated issues starting from eradicating poverty and hunger to promote good health and well-being, ensuring quality education, promoting gender equality, availability of clean water and sanitation, ensuring affordable and clean energy, initiatives towards decent work and economic growth, promotion of industry innovation and infrastructure for reducing inequalities, ensuring sustainable cities and communities along with sustainable and responsible consumption and production ratio, taking climate action strategies for sustainable life below water and life on land, promoting peace, justice, and strong institutions through partnerships for the goals (NITI Aayog, 2020). They serve as a blueprint for addressing major global challenges and working towards a more sustainable and just future for everyone.

Eliminating poverty and hunger, and gender-based discriminations are central goals of SDGs, reflecting a global commitment to promote human dignity, equality, and social justice for all. By addressing the needs and challenges of these communities, the SDGs seek to establish a more balanced and inclusive world where people have the opportunity to excel.

Rabindranath Tagore's Sriniketan Experiment, launched in 1922 as a rural reconstruction project, holds significant relevance in contemporary discussions on sustainable development (Paul, 2015; Chattopadhyay, 2018). This study explores how Sriniketan serves as an exemplary model for achieving the SDGs, reflecting Tagore's humanist philosophy and commitment to social transformation. In many ways, Tagore's vision anticipated the principles underlying the SDGs, particularly the emphasis on "leaving no one behind" and "promoting inclusive development". By addressing the root causes of poverty and inequality in rural areas, the Sriniketan Experiment exemplified a localized yet comprehensive approach to sustainable development, echoing the ethos of the global SDGs framework (Joseph & Ghosh, 2002). Tagore's legacy continues to inspire initiatives aimed at building resilient and thriving communities worldwide.

Tagore's vision for rural reconstruction resonates strongly with the principles underlying the SDGs. Both emphasize holistic development approaches that prioritize not only economic progress but social inclusion, environmental stewardship, and cultural preservation as well. By examining the experiment's objectives, methodologies, and outcomes, this research aims to elucidate the ways in which Sriniketan addresses the multidimensional challenges of sustainable development, offering valuable lessons for global development efforts.

Tagore's Sriniketan Experiment

Rabindranath Tagore, a great figure of the Indian Renaissance, through his various poems, dramas, short stories, essays, music, artistry, etc. expressed his spiritual philosophies. He is not only the country's foremost poet but also a patriot, a philosopher, artist, educator, a human activist, and played so many other roles. He has been in the heart of India's cultural life for a great span. His work appeals to render knowledge for readers for all ages and backgrounds. He has such a broad spectrum of creativity that anyone can start with Tagore and find an entire world within (Basak, 1991).

Visva-Bharati, situated on the twin campus of Santiniketan and Sriniketan, carries the motto—"Where the world makes its home in a single nest". Connecting the global community was the major inception of Santiniketan. In other words, the ideal of total activity was focused on the attempt of making education relate to all facets of life. Sriniketan was intentionally made as a labouratory for testing these objectives, although the essence of it was always lying in the education-based approach. For instance, visiting the local villagers and getting familiar with their lifestyle had been a component of the curriculum for students and educators of Santiniketan. Tagore's belief was that the heart of India resides in villages and the true independence and a new era of social and economic justice could only be gained when the rural India will be revitalized and reached their full potential, and thus the principle of decentralization will be encapsulated.

Tagore's rural reconstruction mission was founded on the four principles—"self-interest", "self-respect", "self-reliant", and "joy in work". His vision was to construct the villages to be self-sufficient and to cultivate individual to be a "complete man" who were aware of the larger society through suitable education and foster cooperation and self-reliance (Das Gupta, 1983). Rabindranath Tagore was indeed the pioneer in the approach of rural reconstruction in India, and the institute he established at Sriniketan became a model for rural development in corners of the country (Paul, 2015). He perceived rural reconstruction not merely as a means for economic independence but also for cultural revival. He noted that people were undergoing a period of profound social and emotional disarray, narrow-mindedness, and orthodox belief, that undermined their sense of being humane. Additionally, he also recognized that people were enduring widespread cultural crises, poverty, ignorance, and diseases. Consequently, Tagore addressed the issues of stagnation and fighting for these systems of decay by initiating diverse social activities in rural India, designed to infuse life with validity, aesthetic beauty, and joy. He understood that improving the living standard of the rural communities will require addressing and solving the problems of reconstruction of the social and economic structure (Sen, 1991; Paul, 2015). He had a clear understanding of issues and conceptualized rural development comprehensively, that align with the Indian situation.

For the well-being and raising the living status of the deprived villages, Tagore launched the "Sriniketan Experiment" in Visva-Bharati, and which was subsequently recognized, and by the outside world as a distinguished institution. In words of Tagore, his programme aims

> "to bring back life in its completeness into the villages making them self-reliant and self-respectful, acquainted with the cultural tradition of their own country and competent to make an efficient use of modern resources for the improvement of their physical, intellectual and economic conditions".

A thorough overhaul of the socio-economic condition of the villages and a comprehensive scheme for addressing the issues related to agriculture, health and education, industry, and other developing and recreational work carried out by the effort of the villagers themselves, were the cornerstones of Tagore's rural revitalization programme. Thus, Sriniketan focused on enhancing traditional cultivation methods by helping farmers in adopting new and scientific farming technologies, hybrid seed varieties, improved fertilizer and pesticide; integrating the Indian traditional arts from India with foreign influences to nurture artefacts into our culture; advancing the health status with required preventive and curative care; upgrading village sanitation; enhance skills of rural artisans with modern tools and organize various credit and consumer cooperatives to ensure self-sufficiency (Sarkar, 1961). In other terms, the aim was to cultivate human resources, properly utilize the available resources and build sustainable rural institutions based on cooperative principles. For enhancement of rural India's living condition in a holistic way, Tagore thus believed that it is important to rebuild the deteriorating social and human elements of the villages by instilling the essence of self-reliance among people. Instead of attempting for improving the socio-economic and health aspects, or civic parameters separately with external development inputs, Tagore gave importance to the reconstruction of both the constructive and creative spirit of individual, strengthening the environment of joy and collective sensitization (Elmhirst, 1975).

The rural reconstruction programme envisioned by Rabindranath Tagore came into its effectiveness at the end of 1921 when Leonard Elmhirst arrived from England and joined it. Two teachers from Santiniketan—Kalimohan Ghosh and Gourgopal Ghosh, along with ten students started working with Elmhirst. The major focused area was Sriniketan and in 1922, the Institute of Rural Reconstruction was formally instituted within Tagore's broader educational principles at Visva-Bharati. In 1922, the Surul Samity was founded and had already initiated the Sriniketan project under the Surul Department of Agriculture. Initially, activities under Elmhirst focused on agricultural development in villages. However, Tagore aimed for holistic development of the village, integrating education, agriculture, health, and social living together. Thus, Sriniketan Experiment contribute to rural reconstruction work through the concept of an integrated approach (Joseph & Ghosh, 2002).

During the initial days, Sriniketan's activities were threefold. These included—(i) Research, experiments, and innovations; (ii) Training and capacity building; and (iii) Extension, outreach, and development. For conducting experiment and research related to agriculture, the Surul farm was established in 1922. In 1926, chemical fertilizers were first introduced. Nearby villagers observed the outcome very closely. Increasing the land productivity was the main goal of the Sriniketan initiative. Simultaneously, setting up health care system for basic medical care and eradication of diseases like malaria were equally crucial. In 1923, the Sriniketan dispensary was founded and in 1932, the cooperative health societies were established. Efforts were also made in sanitation project within the villages, cleaning of forests, application of kerosene oil to *dobas* and pits. All these efforts were extended beyond the boundaries of Sriniketan (Sen, 1991). These initiatives reached outside the territorial boundaries and brought it to the surrounding villages. As Sriniketan served as the hub for research, experimentation, training, and development for reconstruction. Villagers brought their problems and tested some of the experimental results in their fields. Additionally, the scout movement was launched and a *brati-balak samgathana* (children's scouts) was established in Mahidapur village as early as in 1922. The objective was to promote self-reliance within the village.

Education became the central component of the Sriniketan institute during its first decade. Education was served at a different level that includes the Brati Balak method too. There was also Sriniketan's extension service and its extension programme. Additionally, the Sriniketan officials offered and invited apprentices from villages, allowing them to spend one or more years in different departments of villages, focusing on village organizations, health and industries, and agriculture and industries, by offering them a stipend of twenty rupees (Sarkar, 1961).

The SDGs

The SDGs began with the initiative of sustainable development at the United Nations Conference in Rio de Janeiro in the year 2012. The conference aimed to create a set of universal goals addressing to meet the pressing environmental, economic, and political issues confronting the world. The set of goals was adopted in the year 2015 by the United Nations with a target for each goal to be achieved by 2030.

The SDGs replaced the millennium development goals

(MDGs), which was also a global effort started in the year 2000 (Raj, 2019). But the SDGs are distinct as they address challenges that impact everyone. The MDGs have set universal benchmark with an objective for combating severe poverty and hunger, preventing and curing fatal diseases, and extending universal primary education for all children, beside other issues (United Nations, 2011). The MDGs have advanced progress in several key focus areas such as poverty alleviation and income, access to clean water and sanitation facilities, reducing child mortality, enhance maternal health, etc. On the other hand, the SDGs encompass issues that affect all individuals, that brings out their importance. They validate the global pledge to eradicate poverty. They give assurance that no one is excluded. Essentially, they engage people in creating a more sustainable, secure, and prosperous world for all (UNDP, 2010).

India's commitment to the SDGs is crucial, given its significant population and its impact on global sustainability. The SDGs offer an all-encompassing and comprehensive framework for tackling various socio-economic, and environmental issues, and India has been proactively pursuing their realization (NITI Aayog, 2020).

At the national level, India has integrated the SDGs into its development agenda and regulations. The government has introduced various campaigns such as the National Action Plan for Climate Change, Swachh Bharat Mission (Clean India Mission), and Skill India Mission, among others, which align with multiple SDGs. These initiatives aim to address issues like poverty, health care, education, gender equality, clean energy, and environmental conservation. Moreover, India has also localized the SDGs, recognizing the importance of sub-national action in achieving these global goals. Many states have developed their own strategies and action plans to align with the SDGs, considering their unique socio-economic and environmental contexts. By integrating the SDGs into its policies and initiatives, India is playing a crucial role in advancing to a more resilient future for this planet and all its dwellers (Paul, 2021).

The seventeen Goals along with the developmental hurdles are described below:

- **Goal 1—No Poverty:** Target to eliminate poverty in all its kind and aspect by 2030. This goal acknowledges that poverty is a complex, multifaceted, and intricate concern that impact millions of people globally, depriving them from their basic and fundamental needs, opportunities, and rights.
- **Goal 2—Zero Hunger:** Target to achieve zero hunger by ensuring access to safe, nutritious, and adequate food for all people, particularly the most vulnerable populations. It's heartening to note the progress made in reducing hunger over the previous two decades, with the number of malnourished individuals nearly halving, largely due to factors such as economic growth and increased agricultural productivity.
- **Goal 3—Good Health and Well-being:** Target to guarantee health and enhance well-being for everyone at every age. This goal acknowledges that good health and well-being are crucial for enduring sustainable development and that improving health outcomes is central to achieving other development objectives. Several targets are outlined within Goal 3, including reducing rate of maternal mortality, eliminating newborn and infant mortality and morbidity, addressing communicable diseases such as malaria, Dengue, Typhoid, Tuberculosis, HIV/AIDS, etc., as well as non-communicable diseases like diabetes and cardiovascular diseases. Additionally, the goal emphasizes comprehensive health coverage, availability of essential medical services, and access to secure and reasonably priced medicines and immunization for everyone.
- **Goal 4—Quality Education:** This goal seeks to guarantee accessible and equitable quality education and encourage continuous and lifelong learning prospects for everyone. It emphasizes educational access, improving educational

quality, and promoting opportunities for skill development and vocational training.

- **Goal 5—Gender Equality:** This goal centred on attaining gender parity and empowering every woman and girl. It attends to various dimensions of gender discrimination, including ending inequalities and all types of abuse against women, ensuring equal chances for education and health care, and encouraging women's engagement and leadership over decision making roles.
- **Goal 6—Clean Water and Sanitation:** Targets securing the provision and sustainable oversight of water and sanitation for everyone. It emphasizes reach to safe and affordable drinking and consumable water, improved sanitation facilities, and suitable hygiene practices to prevent waterborne diseases and improve overall health and overall wellness.
- **Goal 7—Affordable and Clean Energy:** Strives to ensure availability of cost-effective, dependable and modern energy for everyone. It emphasizes on enhancing the proportion of renewable energy in the worldwide energy portfolio, boosting energy efficiency, and broadening access to clean energy system and technologies, particularly in developing nations.
- **Goal 8—Decent Work and Economic Growth:** This goal centres on advancing ongoing, inclusive, and sustainable economic expansion, achieving comprehensive and productive employment, and decent work for everyone. It focuses on issues such as job creation, labour rights, social protection, and reducing informal employment.
- **Goal 9—Industry, Innovation, and Infrastructure:** It strives to build infrastructure that are robust and encourage inclusive and sustainable growth of industrialization, and stimulate innovation. It emphasizes investment in infrastructure, technological progress, and enhancing connectivity, particularly in developing countries.

- **Goal 10—Reduced Inequalities:** This goal targets reducing disparities within and between nations. It handles various forms of discriminations, including income inequality, social inequality, and inequality of opportunity, and promotes policies that empower marginalized and vulnerable groups.
- **Goal 11—Sustainable Cities and Communities:** This goal seeks to build cities and human settlements that are inclusive, secure, robust, and sustainable. It addresses issues such as urbanization, slum growth, access to basic services, sustainable transportation, and environmental degradation in urban areas.
- **Goal 12—Responsible Consumption and Production:** Focuses on promoting sustainable and eco-friendly consumption and production practices. It gives importance to reduction of resource use, minimizing waste creation and implementing eco-friendly methods in manufacturing, distribution, and consumption.
- **Goal 13—Climate Action:** This target immediate action and measures to tackle climate change and its effects. It includes measures to lower greenhouse gas particularly carbon emissions, increase adaptability to climate related disasters, and foster climate adaptation and mitigation efforts at global, national, and local levels.
- **Goal 14—Life Below Water:** Emphasize on the protection and sustainable management of marine resources and marine environment. It addresses issues such as marine pollution, overfishing, habitat destruction, and ocean acidification, aiming to protect marine biodiversity and ecosystems.
- **Goal 15—Life on Land:** This objective targets to safeguard, rehabilitate, and sustainably manage land-based ecosystems, forests, and biodiversity in a sustainable manner. It tackles loss of forests by cutting down trees, desertification, degradation of land, and loss of biodiversity,

promoting preservation and sustainable use of land resources.

- **Goal 16—Peace, Justice, and Strong Institutions:** This goal emphasizes on fostering harmonious and inclusive communities, guaranteeing access to justice for everyone, and establishing efficient, participatory and transparent institutions at every level. It addresses issues such as violence, conflict, corruption, and human rights abuses.
- **Goal 17—Partnerships for the Goals:** This target emphasizes the value of worldwide partnerships in achieving the SDGs. It calls for enhanced international support, strengthening capacities, technology transfer, and partnership between governments, business communities, civil society and other involved parties.

Each of these goals is crucial for advancing sustainable development and addressing the complex challenges facing humanity and the planet. By working together and implementing coordinated actions across sectors and borders, significant progress can be made towards achieving these goals by 2030 and creating a more prosperous, equitable, and sustainable future for all.

Tagore's Sriniketan Experiment as an Ideal Model for Achieving SDGs

Tagore's Sriniketan Experiment was a pioneering effort in rural reconstruction and holistic development. Rooted in his deep concern for the plight of villagers, Tagore envisioned a comprehensive approach to uplift rural life, encompassing agriculture, education, health, and social well-being.

At its core, the Sriniketan Experiment aimed to restore vitality to villages, fostering self-reliance and self-respect among the inhabitants while preserving and promoting India's rich cultural heritage. Tagore believed that true independence for India could only be achieved when its villages thrived economically, intellectually, and culturally. The experiment unfolded in phases, with research and experimentation serving as the foundation (Paul, 2021).

Agricultural improvements were a focal point, with initiatives such as introducing modern farming techniques, hybrid seeds, and better fertilizers. This not only aimed at increasing productivity but also at empowering farmers with the latest knowledge and tools.

Health care played a crucial role, with efforts to establish dispensaries and cooperative health societies, addressing prevalent diseases like malaria, and promoting general medical care. Sanitation initiatives were also vital, including clearing jungles and implementing hygiene practices, extending beyond Sriniketan's boundaries to surrounding villages.

Education emerged as a cornerstone of the Sriniketan organization, embracing various levels and methods. The Brati Balak method, for instance, engaged children as scouts, fostering a sense of community feelings and self-reliance. Additionally, apprenticeships offered hands—on training in agriculture, industries, health, and sanitation, ensuring a well-rounded education that aligned with the needs of rural life. The Sriniketan Experiment exemplified a holistic approach to rural development, integrating economic, social, cultural, and educational dimensions. By empowering villagers to become agents of change in their communities, Tagore's vision transcended mere economic development, aiming to cultivate a sense of collective responsibility and pride in India's rural heritage (Chattopadhyay, 2018).

By analysing the experiment's holistic approach to community development, including education, health care, agriculture, and cultural revitalization, the study aims to underscore Sriniketan's relevance as a model for achieving sustainable development objectives; Tagore's emphasis on developing human resources aligns with SDG-4 (Quality Education), that seeks to guarantee accessible and equitable quality education and encourage continuous and lifelong learning prospects for everyone (Paul & Paul, 2004). By contributing to education and skills development, both Tagore and the SDGs recognize the importance of empowering individuals to contribute effectively to their communities and societies.

Similarly, Tagore's focus on utilizing existing resources and promoting sustainable rural organizations depending on cooperative values reflects several SDGs, including SDG-1 (No Poverty), SDG-2 (Zero Hunger), SDG-8 (Decent Work and Economic Growth), and SDG-11 (Sustainable Cities and Communities). These goals emphasize poverty alleviation, food security, economic empowerment, and sustainable urban and rural development, all of which are central to Tagore's approach. Moreover, Tagore's emphasis on cooperative principles echoes SDG-17 (Partnerships for the Goals), which highlights the importance of collabouration between governments, businesses, civil society, and communities to achieve the SDGs. By promoting cooperation and collective action, both Tagore and the SDGs recognize that addressing complex challenges requires inclusive and collabourative efforts.

In essence, Tagore's ideas for rural reconstruction embody various principles and goals of the SDGs that focuses on the interrelation between social, economic, and environmental aspect of development and the significance of inclusive and sustainable approaches.

The major interventions undertaken during Tagore's Sriniketan Experiment encompass a wide range of activities that align with various SDGs. Here's how each major initiative contributes to the SDGs.

I. Strengthening Village Development Societies and Mohila Samities

The following interventions undertaken in Tagore's Sriniketan Experiment aligns well with a number of SDGs as indicated below:

- Strengthening village development societies promotes community-based organizations and active participation of the community in local development. This fosters sustainable and resilient communities, contributing to SDG-11 (Sustainable Cities and Communities), that seeks to build cities and human settlements that are inclusive, secure, resilient, and sustainable (REC Annual Report, 2022-23).

- The formation of *mohila samities* (women's committees) addresses the social issues faced by women in rural communities. By empowering women and involving them in decision making processes, these initiatives contribute to SDG-5 (Gender Equality) that centred on attaining gender parity and empowering every woman and girl.
- By focusing on addressing the specific needs and challenges faced by women in rural areas, these interventions work towards reducing inequalities within communities. Providing support, awareness, and training programmes for women helps bridge the gender gap and promote inclusivity that contributes to SDG-10 (Reduced Inequalities).
- By empowering communities through participatory approaches and strengthening local institutions such as village development societies and *mohila samities*, these interventions contribute to SDG-16 (Peace, Justice, and Strong Institutions), promoting harmony, fairness, and robust institutions at the community level.

These initiatives demonstrate a commitment to promote gender equality, reducing inequalities, building sustainable communities, and fostering strong institutions, all of which are essential components of the SDGs.

II. Brati Balak Organization (Children Scout)

The Brati Balak Organization aligns with several SDGs as mentioned below:

- It aims to develop leadership skills, promote physical and mental exercises, and provide social services, all of which contribute to SDG-4 (Quality Education), holistic education for children. By organizing cultural programmes, excursions, and promoting individual interests, the initiative fosters a well-rounded educational experience (REC Annual Report, 2022-23).

- Through activities like physical exercises, *yoga*, and sports, it promotes physical well-being among children. With emphasis on mental exercises, cultural programmes, and nature observation, it contributes to mental well-being. Moreover, social service activities like community cleaning and awareness rallies promote community health and well-being. All these initiatives contribute to SDG-3 (Good Health and Well-being).
- By organizing programmes for both boys and girls groups, the initiative ensures SDG-5 (Gender Equality) that promotes the active participation of all in community development activities.
- Contributing to SDG-10 (Reduced Inequalities), the programme aims to address inequalities by providing opportunities for children from all backgrounds to participate in educational and developmental activities. Additionally, efforts to identify and support dropout children contribute towards achieving SDG-10 (reduced inequalities).
- By empowering children to take leadership roles and participate in community development, the initiative contributes to SDG-11(Sustainable Cities and Communities), building durable and resilient societies and communities. It fosters a sense of community ownership and involvement in local development processes.
- By promoting social cohesion, community service, and leadership skills among children, the programme contributes to SDG-16, fostering peaceful and inclusive societies. Moreover, the involvement of voluntary workers in supervising the programme strengthens local institutions and grassroots initiatives.

Overall, the Brati Balak Organization embodies principles of quality education, health and well-being, gender equality, reduced inequalities, sustainable communities, and inclusive institutions, all of which are integral to achieving the SDGs.

III. Rural Library Services

The rural library services initiative undertaken during Tagore's Sriniketan Experiment aligns with several SDGs as highlighted below:

- By providing access to books and periodicals, the rural library programme promotes literacy and lifelong learning opportunities. It helps to develop reading habits among villagers and supports the retention of acquired literacy skills, contributing to quality education for all. These activities align with SDG-4 (Quality Education).
- It aims to reduce inequalities by providing access to information and knowledge to all members of the community, regardless of their socio-economic status. Through the mobile library services and network of rural libraries, it ensures SDG-10 (Reduced Inequalities), that even remote and marginalized communities have access to educational resources (Paul & Paul, 2004).
- By establishing rural libraries as nodal centres for information, literacy, culture, and recreation, it contributes to SDG-11 (Sustainable Cities and Communities), building sustainable and resilient communities. The libraries serve as cultural communication and education centres, fostering community engagement and cohesion.
- Access to information on health, science, and technology through the rural libraries contribute to SDG-3 (Good Health and Well-being), improving community health and well-being. People can access information on preventive health measures, sanitation, and advancements in medical science, leading to better health outcomes.
- By providing access to information on modern and advanced science and technology, the rural library programme contributes to SDG-9 (Industry, Innovation, and Infrastructure) that promotes innovation and technological advancement in rural communities. It helps

bridge the digital divide by providing access to knowledge and information resources.

- By promoting literacy, education, and access to information, it contributes to SDG-16 (Peace, Justice, and Inclusive Institutions) making peaceful and inclusive societies. It empowers individuals with knowledge and critical thinking skills, fostering social cohesion and strengthening community institutions.

The rural library services initiative embodies principles of quality education, reduced inequalities, sustainable communities, good health and well-being, innovation, and strong institutions, all of which are essential for achieving the SDGs.

IV. Self-Help Groups (SHGs)

The SHGs initiated and supported during Tagore's Sriniketan Experiment embodies the SDGs as indicated below:

- By empowering rural women through SHGs, the initiative aims to alleviate poverty by enabling them to generate income, save money, and access credit facilities and embodies the SDG-1 (No Poverty). This helps to improve the economic status of the community members and contributes to eradicate poverty (Paul, 2015).
- The SHG movement focuses on women's empowerment, addressing gender disparities by providing them with opportunities for economic and social participation. This initiative aligns to SDG-5 (Gender Equality). It promotes gender equality by enhancing women's decision making power, leadership skills, and socio-economic status.
- Through the formation of SHGs, the initiative promotes entrepreneurship and self-employment opportunities, contributing to economic growth and creating decent work opportunities in rural areas. It encourages the development of sustainable livelihoods and income-generating activities

that aligns with SDG-8 (Decent Work and Economic Growth).

- By enabling rural women, particularly marginalized and disadvantaged groups, to access financial resources and participate in decision making processes, the SHG initiative helps reduce inequalities within communities and contributes to SDG-10 (Reduced Inequalities). It promotes social inclusion and empowers marginalized individuals to improve their socio-economic status.
- SHGs offer a forum for community members to converse and develop solutions to the shared challenges, fostering cooperation, social cohesion, and community resilience. By promoting participatory decision making and community leadership, it contributes to SDG-16 (Peace, Justice, and Inclusive Institutions), building strong and inclusive institutions at the grassroots level.

Overall, the SHG initiative aligns with the SDGs concerning to poverty eradication, gender equity and equality, economic growth, reduced inequalities, and building inclusive and resilient communities (Paul, 2021). It demonstrates the potential of community-driven approaches to empower marginalized groups and achieve sustainable development outcomes.

V. Health Extension

The health extension programme implemented at Tagore's Sriniketan Experiment aligns with the following SDGs:

- The basic goal of the health extension programme is to foster the welfare and prosperity of villagers by improving public health and providing affordable medical relief. By focusing on preventive measures, treatment of ailments, anti-malaria efforts, first aid training, and health education, the initiative contributes to SDG-3 (Good Health and Well-being), improving the overall health and well-being of the community members.

- Sensitizing villagers, especially women, regarding health issues is an important aspect of the programme. By ensuring that women are actively involved in health awareness camps and have access to health-care services, the initiative promotes SDG-5 (Gender Equality) gender equality in health-care access and decision making.
- By providing financial assistance for medicine purchases and organizing free medical check-up camps, the health extension programme aims to reduce inequalities in health-care access. It ensures that even marginalized and economically disadvantaged individuals have access to essential health-care services and treatments. This initiative aligns with SDG-10 (Reduced Inequalities).
- Collabouration with the block primary health centres and the establishment of the Surul Swastha Samity demonstrate the importance of partnerships for achieving SDGs. By working together with government health agencies and local health organizations, the initiative strengthens health-care delivery and promotes community-based health-care solutions align with SDG-17 (Partnerships for the Goals).

The health extension programme at Sriniketan embodies the principles of sustainable development by tackling health inequalities, encouraging preventive and promotive health-care initiatives, empowering communities, and fostering partnerships for improved health outcomes.

VI. Agricultural Extension

The agricultural extension programme implemented at Tagore's Sriniketan Experiment aligns with SDGs:

- By promoting agricultural activities and providing technical know-how to improve agricultural production, the programme contributes to SDG-1 (No Poverty). Access to improved agricultural practices can increase productivity and income, thereby lifting people out of poverty.

- The focus on agricultural extension services aims to refine food security and nutrition by boosting agricultural output and expanding income sources. By providing support for dairy and poultry farming, pisciculture, and piggery, the programme helps to ensure a more sustainable and diversified food supply for the community, that aligns with SDG-2 (Zero Hunger).
- By promoting agricultural activities and allied occupations, the programme creates opportunities for decent work and economic growth in rural areas. It encourages entrepreneurship, skill development, and income-generating activities related to agriculture, contributing to local economic development, that aligns with SDG-8 (Decent Work and Economic Growth).
- By adopting scientific farming methods and practices, it promotes sustainable agriculture and responsible production that contributes to SDG-12 (Responsible Consumption and Production). This includes the efficient use of resources such as soil, water, and pesticides, as well as the implementation of eco-friendly farming practices that reduces the negative and adverse effect on the environment.
- By introducing new experiments and methods of cultivation, the programme contributes to SDG-13 (Climate Action), climate resilience and adaptation in agriculture. This may include practices that enhance soil health, increase crop resilience to climate variability, and mitigate greenhouse gas emissions from agricultural activities.
- Collabouration with the Department of Agriculture and Rathindra Krishi Vigyan Kendra demonstrates the importance of partnerships for achieving sustainable agricultural development. By working with government agencies and agricultural research institutions, the programme enhances technical support, knowledge

sharing, and capacity building in rural communities that embodies SDG-17 (Partnerships for the Goals).

Overall, the agricultural extension programme at Sriniketan embodies the principles of sustainable agriculture and rural development by addressing poverty, hunger, economic growth, responsible consumption, climate resilience, and partnership-building for sustainable development.

VII. Development of Crafts

The initiative of developing crafts and cottage industries at Sriniketan contributes to the SDGs, as mentioned below:

- By providing training and employment opportunities in crafts and cottage industries to rural poor communities, the initiative contributes to SDG-1 (No Poverty). It helps to alleviate poverty by enabling individuals to generate income and improve their livelihoods.
- The initiative promotes SDG-8 (Decent Work and Economic Growth) through creation of decent work opportunities, particularly through training programmes aimed at developing skills in various crafts and cottage industries. By fostering entrepreneurship and supporting local artisans, it contributes to economic growth in rural areas.
- Supporting the development of cottage industries and craftsmanship, contributing to SDG-9 (Industry, Innovation, and Infrastructure), the growth of sustainable and eco-friendly industrial development and fostering advancement within traditional crafts.
- By promoting the revival of traditional crafts and providing artisans with design support to compete in the market, the initiative encourages sustainable production practices and the preservation of cultural heritage that is aligned to SDG-12 (Responsible Consumption and Production).

- Cottage industries often rely on traditional methods and materials, which can be more environmentally friendly than large-scale industrial production. By supporting these industries, the initiative indirectly promotes sustainable consumption and production patterns, contributing to realise SDG-13 (Climate Action).
- Through collabourations with local artisans, training programmes, and support from the production unit of the university, the initiative demonstrates and contributes to SDG-17 (Partnerships for the Goals), the significance of collabouration among diverse stakeholders in attaining sustainable development goals.

Overall, the development of crafts and cottage industries at Sriniketan aligns with multiple SDGs by addressing poverty, promoting economic growth, fostering innovation, encouraging sustainable consumption and production, and fostering partnerships for sustainable development (Paul, 2014b).

VIII. Other Activities

The initiatives described contribute to a number of SDGs as indicated below:

- The self-employment-oriented training programmes provide skills and knowledge necessary for individuals to create their own livelihoods, thus helping and contributing to SDG-1 (No Poverty), to alleviate poverty within the community.
- Awareness and sensitization programmes enhance the education and awareness levels of community members, promoting a better understanding of various issues and encouraging informed decision making through contributing to SDG-4 (Quality Education).
- By providing self-employment training and promoting sports and cultural activities, these initiatives contribute

to SDG-5 (Gender Equality) by women empowerment within the community, promoting gender equality and social inclusion.
- Self-employment training initiatives contribute to SDG-8 (Decent Work and Economic Growth) leading to the creation of fair work opportunities.
- By providing support for self-employment and promoting sports and cultural activities within the community, these initiatives aim to SDG-10 (Reduced Inequalities) by providing opportunities for all community members, regardless of background or socio-economic status.
- Supporting the development of village societies and promoting cultural activities helps build stronger, more resilient communities, contributing to realise SDG-11 (Sustainable Cities and Communities).
- Engaging community members in sports and cultural activities can promote social cohesion, peace, and justice within the community, fostering stronger institutions at the local level. This initiative aligns with SDG-16 (Peace, Justice, and Inclusive Institutions).

Overall, these initiatives contribute to the achievement of multiple SDGs by addressing poverty, promoting education and gender equality, creating decent work opportunities, reducing inequalities, building sustainable communities, and fostering peace and justice.

Conclusion

Thus, the aforementioned initiatives demonstrate how Tagore's Sriniketan Experiment encompassed a wide range of activities that align with the principles and objectives of the SDGs, focusing on the integration of economic, social, and environmental dimensions of development and the emphasis on inclusive and sustainable approaches.

This establishes Tagore's Sriniketan Experiment as an ideal model for achieving sustainable development, as articulated in the SDGs. Through its integrated approach to community development, Tagore's initiative of rural reconstruction through Sriniketan Experiment exemplifies the principles of equity, inclusion, and environmental stewardship that underpin sustainable development agendas. By documenting Sriniketan's transformative impact on rural livelihoods and well-being, this paper underscores the enduring relevance of Tagore's vision in addressing contemporary sustainability challenges. Ultimately, the study contributes to a more profound grasp of the potential of localized initiatives to catalyse positive transformation and progress toward global sustainability goals.

Thus, by demonstrating how Sriniketan Experiment embodies the principles of sustainability and social justice, the research highlights its enduring relevance in addressing contemporary global challenges. The study reiterates the importance of integrating localized approaches like Sriniketan Experiment along with specific strategies for achieving SDGs worldwide.

Keywords

Self-reliance, gender equality, reconstruction, poverty, sustainable development.

REFERENCES

Basak, K. (1991). *Rabindranath Tagore: A Humanist.* New Delhi: Classical Publishing Company.

Bhat, P. M. (2002). "Maternal mortality in India: An update." *Studies in Family Planning, 33*(3): 227-36.

Chattopadhyay, M. (2018). "Rabindranath Tagore's Model of Rural Reconstruction: A Review." *International Journal of Research and Analytical Reviews, 5*(4): 142-46.

Das Gupta, U. (1983). *Santiniketan and Sriniketan.* Calcutta: Visva-Bharati.

Deolalikar, A.B. (2004). "Attaining the Millennium Development Goals in India." *A Report Prepared for the World Bank.* Retrieved from www.worldbank.org.in

Deolalikar, A.B. (2005). *Attaining the Millennium Development Goals in India.* The World Bank, Oxford University Press.

Department of Lifelong Learning and Extension, Rural Extension Centre, Visva-Bharati, Sriniketan (2023). *Annual Report 2022-23.*

Elmhirst, L.K. (1975). *Poet and Plowman.* Calcutta: Visva-Bharati.

India, N.A.U. (2019). *Localising the SDGs: Early Lessons from India.*

Jhamb, B. & N. Sinha (2011). *Millennium Development Goals and Gender Budgeting: Where Does India Stand?* Centre for Legislative Research and Advocacy.

Joseph, S. & P.K. Ghosh (2002). *Sriniketan: From Experiment to Experience.* Department of Social Work, Visva-Bharati, Sriniketan.

Kejariwal, O.P. (2003, 2-8 August). "Rabindranath Tagore: A Towering Personality." *Employment News, 28*(18).

Measuring India's Progress on the Millennium Development Goals: A Citizens Report 2007. Retrieved from www.udyem.org

Ministry of Statistics and Programme Implementation, Government of India. (2005). *Millennium Development Goals India Country Report 2005.* New Delhi. Retrieved from http://www.mospi.nic.in

Ministry of Statistics and Programme Implementation, Government of India. (2010). *Millennium Development Goals States of India Report 2010 (Special Edition).* New Delhi.

NITI Aayog (2019). *Localizing SDGs: Early Lessons from India,* New Delhi.

NITI Aayog (2020). *Decade of Actions: Taking SDGs Global to Local,* New Delhi.

Paul, S.K. (2003). "Vision of Tagore and Grundtvig towards Education and Development." *Journal of World Education*, Publication of the Association for World Education: An International NGO with Consultative Status in the United Nations, *33*(2).

Paul, K. & S.K. Paul (2004). "Tagore's Philosophy of Education and Rural Reconstruction." *Journal of World Education*, Publication of the Association for World Education: An International NGO with Consultative Status in the United Nations, *34*(1).

Paul, S.K. (2014a). "Lifelong Learning for Enlightenment." *Indian Journal of Adult Education, 75*(3).

Paul, S.K. (2014b). "Tagore's Philosophy on Rural Reconstruction Experiment." *Korean-Indian Culture, 19.*

Paul, S.K. (2015). *Rural Development: Concept and Recent Approaches.* New Delhi: Concept Publishing Company Pvt. Limited.

Paul, S.K. (2021). "SDGs with Special Reference to Rural India." *Journal of World Education*, Publication of the Association for World Education: An International NGO with Consultative Status in the United Nations, *43*(1).

Rohit Raj, V.S. (2019). *NTA UGC Social Work.* New Delhi: Arihant.

Sarkar, S. (1961). *Tagore's Educational Philosophy and Experiment*, Visva-Bharati, Santiniketan.

Sen, S. (1991). *Rabindranath Tagore on Rural Reconstruction*. Calcutta: Visva-Bharati.

The World Bank. (2007). *Millennium Development Goals: Confronting the Challenges of Gender Equality and Fragile States*. Global Monitoring Report 2007. Retrieved from www.worldbank.org

UNDP. (n.d.). *Sustainable Development Goals*. Retrieved from https://www.undp.org/sustainable-development-goals

UNDP. (2010). *Beyond the Midpoint: Achieving the Millennium Development Goals*.

United Nations (n.d.). *Transforming Our World: The 2030 Agenda for Sustainable Development*. Retrieved from https://sdgs.un.org/2030agenda

United Nations (2011). *The Millennium Development Goals Report 2011*.

2

Fostering Growth and Well-being

Best Practices for SDGs, Leadership, Peace Education, Inner Development, and Lifelong Learning

Asmaa Sleem

In a world increasingly polarized, where opinions clash and divisions deepen, the youth emerge as catalysts for change, weaving threads of understanding through the fabric of controversy. This article explores the pivotal role and a few of the best practices of youth education for peace building, as part of peace education, sustainable development goals (SDGs) and inner development goals. Shedding light on the integral role of peace education and involvement of youth in peace building illuminates the pathways to achieve the SDG goals.

In the pursuit of a more equitable and prosperous world and within the framework of the 2030 agenda for sustainable development lies a profound acknowledgement of the deep relationship between peace, justice, and quality education. The 2030 agenda for sustainable development stands as a beacon, advocating for rigorous efforts across nations to address pressing global challenges. At its core lies a fundamental truth: peace and sustainable development are intrinsically intertwined.

The 2030 agenda's statement, "Without peace, there's no sustainable development, and without sustainable development, there's no peace", really hits home, showing how these things rely on each other. It's like a wake-up call, urging us to work together to tackle issues like violence, insecurity, and other problems that hold back progress. As we strive for a world that is fairer and more peaceful, it is super important to look at the best ways to make progress on goals like peace, justice, and make sure everyone gets a good education. Thus, it is imperative to explore the best practices and strategies that can push us towards realizing these interconnected aspirations.

Who Am I?

I am Asmaa Sleem, an Egyptian educator, content strategist, and trainer/facilitator specializing in peace building, conflict transformation, and inner development. Alongside my roles as a storyteller and lifelong learner, I am deeply committed to foster awareness and co-creation of knowledge, particularly through initiatives that promote togetherness and community well-being. Currently, I am privileged to contribute to the organizational team of the "Creative Leadership" conference at the Caux Forum, Initiatives of Change Switzerland, currently "Caux initiatives of change foundation", while also being an active member of the facilitators/trainers' pool within the same organization. Furthermore, I am the founder of Lifelong Learning Talks, yet a starting small initiative aimed at revitalizing community spaces for learning and promoting "individual, communal, and planetary" well-being through experiential learning, storytelling, music, and participatory approaches.

Drawing from my academic background in social sciences, peace building, trauma healing, and training methodologies, my focus lies in youth development and empowerment. I design and facilitate compassionate learning experiences, guiding young individuals and lifelong learners in defining their life purpose and supporting their mental health and well-being. My passion extends to raise awareness about peace building, inner development, authenticity, and creative leadership on both local and international platforms. Notably, I serve as the Vice-President of the Association for World Education Int (AWE), where I continue to contribute to initiatives promoting holistic education and global citizenship.

Bridging Divides from Inside Out: Why Peace and Leadership Education?

Peace and leadership education equips individuals with the knowledge, skills, and attitudes necessary to listen and connect with themselves, to understand who they really are, to lead their life, to develop from inside first and then to impact their surroundings, then to resolve conflicts peacefully, fostering social cohesion and resilience, which are vital components of several SDGs, including Goal 16 on peace, justice, and strong institutions, as well Goal 4 on quality education. Similarly, engaging youth in peace building initiatives not only empowers them as agents of change, but also cultivates inclusive societies, aligning with SDG targets aimed at reducing inequalities and promoting peaceful and inclusive societies.

In the realm of youth-led initiatives, peace building transcends traditional boundaries. Young individuals utilize various platforms, including community dialogues and online forums, to foster understanding, empathy, and collabouration. Through grassroots efforts, they challenge stereotypes and address underlying issues, promoting sustainable peace and leadership. Engaging conversations with youth, even elders and experts offer insights into navigating societal divides, while also examining the impact of digital communication on peace building efforts amidst the prevalence of misinformation.

Best Practices

(a) On Creative Leadership, Inner Development, Peace Building and Quality Education

In the context of promoting effective learning spaces for youth, the "Creative Leadership" stands out as a shining example of best practices for leadership, peace building and quality education. Through its programmes, youth from diverse backgrounds are provided with platforms and opportunities to engage in open dialogues, express their perspectives, and collabourate on peace building initiatives. By harnessing the power of social media, community forums, and interactive workshops, the "Creative Leadership Conference" fosters inclusive communication channels, allowing for the exchange of ideas and the bridging of divides. This grassroots approach not only empowers youth and youth at heart as agents of change but also cultivates a culture of understanding, empathy, and solidarity, laying the foundation for sustainable peace.

(b) Creative Leadership: Inspiring Authentic Transformation

Creative leadership,

> an initiative led by Caux Initiatives of Change Foundation, provides an inclusive platform where individuals from diverse backgrounds worldwide converge to reconceptualize leadership through a journey of personal and collective growth, using arts, story sharing, workshops, quiet reflective times and dialogue groups. Participants embark on a journey of personal and collective growth and our initiative caters to individuals of all ages who aspire to embody conscious leadership and inner development within their communities.
>
> The Creative Leadership vision is aligned with the vision of Initiatives of Change. Creative leadership aspires to foster a just, peaceful, and sustainable world rooted in global interdependence and responsibility. Specifically, it seeks to ignite regenerative change by nurturing authentic transformation at the individual level.

The inspiration of creative leadership comes from more than 250 changemakers in their 20s and 30s, of 98 nationalities, who were participants in the Caux Peace and Leadership Programme.

The creative leadership conferences and programmes are developed by a diverse team, flat-hierarchy team of twenty core volunteers from twelve countries. The core team works with more than inspiring fifty facilitators from twenty-seven different countries, all passionate to make an impact, starting with oneself.

Creative leadership has reached a community of more than 1,200 inspired changemakers from 120 countries worldwide since 2020 till current. Creative leadership has so far invited over sixty international speakers to share their stories, guiding sessions of moments of quiet reflection, art workshops, skill-sharing webinars, and human libraries.

(c) Lifelong Learning Talks: A Space for Learned Hopefulness

> The illiterate of the twenty-first century will not be those who cannot read and write, but those who cannot learn, unlearn and relearn.
>
> **—Alvin Toffler**

"Lifelong learning talks" is an initiative in Egypt that started in 2023 to renew an engaged experiential community learning spaces for learning opportunities that aim at "learning for oneself, for others and for the planet" through a diverse array of creative mediums.

Aligned with SDG-4 to "ensure inclusive and equitable quality education and promote lifelong learning opportunities for all", lifelong learning now contributes to a greater awareness of all the dimensions of sustainability. Individuals are empowered by lifelong learning to change behavioural patterns.

Lifelong learning talks "approach integrates talks, discussions, arts, music, storytelling, mindfulness" meditation through community events, workshops, and immersive team retreats to facilitate dynamic learning opportunities that transcend conventional boundaries.

At the core of our mission is the belief in the power of experiential learning to inspire personal growth and societal change. Through engaging in diverse forms of expression, individuals are invited to explore, reflect, and connect with themselves, others, and the planet on a deeper level. We recognize that creativity is a powerful catalyst for learning and innovation. By weaving arts, music, storytelling, and team retreats into our learning experiences, we aim to ignite curiosity, foster collabouration, and stimulate transformative insights. It is a journey of discovery and renewal, as we reimagine learning spaces and empower individuals to unleash their full potential for positive impact.

At lifelong learning talks, our flagship workshop is a captivating fusion of storytelling, artistic expression, and traditional Egyptian singing, creating an immersive experience known as "A Story and a Song حدوتة و غنواية". This workshop serves as a cornerstone of our initiative, providing a unique and enriching platform for individuals to explore, reflect, and connect on various themes that promote personal and communal well-being. Steeped in the rich tradition of oral storytelling and infused with the emotive melodies of oriental Egyptian singing, "A Story and a Song" offers participants a safe and inviting space to embark on a transformative journey. Each session is carefully curated to delve into themes that resonate with the human experience, such as resilience, identity, belonging, and purpose.

Through the art of storytelling, participants are transported to worlds both familiar and unknown, where characters and narratives come alive, stirring the imagination and evoking profound emotions. Complemented by the soul-stirring melodies of traditional Egyptian songs, the workshop creates a harmonious blend of auditory and visual stimuli, engaging all senses and deepening the experience.

More than just a workshop, "A Story and a Song" serves as a catalyst for self-discovery, healing, and connection. Participants are encouraged to share their own stories, experiences, and insights, fostering a sense of community and mutual support. Facilitated by skilled storytellers and musicians, each workshop is curated to create a nurturing and inclusive environment where individuals feel empowered to explore the depths of their being and forge meaningful connections with others. Through "A Story and a Song", lifelong learning talks aims to harness the power of storytelling, arts, and music to promote holistic well-being and cultivate a sense of belonging and interconnectedness among the participants. It is a transformative journey as we weave together the threads of storytelling, music, mindfulness, and community to nurture the mind, body, and soul.

Conclusion

The imperative for peace and leadership education, youth involvement in advancing SDGs and having safe enough participatory learning spaces is undeniable. As we navigate through a world marked by increasing complexities and challenges, the role of education in fostering peace, justice, and sustainable development cannot be overstated. Through initiatives like "creative leadership", "lifelong learning talks" and grassroots peace building efforts, young individuals are not only empowered as agents of change but are also instrumental in fostering inclusive societies and bridging divides. As we strive towards the vision outlined in the 2030 agenda for sustainable development, it is essential to recognize the interconnectedness of peace, justice, and lifelong learning/quality education.

The innovative and best practices from Egypt highlighted in this article serve as beacons of hope, demonstrating the transformative power of education and youth engagement in achieving SDGs. By harnessing the collective wisdom and commitment of individuals like those mentioned above, we can create a more equitable, peaceful, and sustainable world for current and future generations. In the journey towards realizing our shared aspirations for a better world, let us remain steadfast in our commitment to promote peace, justice, and quality education. By working together, embracing diversity, and nurturing empathy and solidarity, we can truly make a difference and leave a lasting legacy of peace and prosperity for generations to come.

Finally, by reflecting on the above insights shared in this article, I would like to invite you as my respective reader to consider the following questions: How can we further empower youth to take proactive roles in peace building and sustainable development? What innovative approaches can we adopt to create more inclusive and participatory safe enough learning environments? And finally, what actions can each of us take today to contribute to a more equitable, peaceful, and sustainable future?

Keywords

Creative leadership, peace education, lifelong learning, SDGs.

REFERENCES

For more details on creative leadership, please visit, https://www.iofc.ch/initiatives/creative-leadership

For more details on lifelong learning talks, please visit, https://www.facebook.com/profile.php?id=100093031943624&mibextid=ZbWKw

3

Sustainability: An Alternative Approach

Andre Bèteille's Thoughts on Developing Sustainable Sociology

Sreyasi Ray and *Ramanuj Ganguly*

Bèteille in answer to the question "What sociology is?", ends up by saying "What sociologists do?". Sociology in India, till date, remains not only a very loosely defined intellectual subject, but also many a time disapproved the status by the scholars and intellectuals who are concerned with methods and methodology of sociological enquiry. Sociology as a discipline was lagging behind many established mainstream disciplines and hence the sociologists required to strain themselves to move faster to keep pace with the rest. The earlier sociologists to Bèteille were trained to be Sanskritists, philosophers, and economists. They were seeking to arrive at an understanding of social reality.[1] Later, the first generation of Indian sociologists "were mostly self taught".[2]

To Bèteille, sociology is a "craft that needs patience and care".[3] It is based on "two fundamental pre-occupations: (a) rigorous search for interconnections among the different domains of society and (b) its systematic use of comparisons".[4] By method, Bèteille mainly concentrated on comparative method. To him, the study of "society through the systematic application of the comparative method is very different from the casual use of comparisons between societies to which we frequently take recourse in our everyday discussions"[5] and hence to him is different from common sense. Comparative method to Bèteille, meant certain form of detachment from the point of view of the investigator from his investigation. This certainly is not the criterion for any other methods like historical methods. The aim of comparative method to Bèteille, was to "treat subjective evaluations in an objective way".[6] Sociology being an empirical science, in actual practice, has both data and method which goes hand in hand. It is thus, impossible to be a professional sociologist without any knowledge of empirical research in recent times. The research and the techniques have grown enormously in variety and sophistication and have become far more advanced than those earlier used by classical sociologists leading to tremendous volatility of status of the subject particularly in India. To Bèteille, this ambiguous and uncertain situation of sociology arose because of the subject's endeavour to touch the everyday experience of the ordinary person so much so that it appeared to be too close to their common sense making the information volatile and replaceable. To him, sociology is definitely not common sense. It has some definite concepts, methods and data, which however loosely defined can never be close to common sense. Sociological knowledge to him has a universal appeal whereas common sense is more situational, local and ethnocentric.

Andre Bèteille, has been perfectly described by Dipankar Gupta as "an intellectual marathon runner", with a message to deliver. As a sociologist and a social anthropologist, he held interest in myriad of subjects of sociology like caste, class, institutions, university, nation, civil society, and more generally, politics. However, Bèteille, inspired by M.N. Srinivas, in his sociological discourse on inequality and stratification, along with many other topics, always posed concern on methods and methodology of sociological enquiry. In India, many times, sociologists need to depend on the data that others collect. However, to Bèteille, "sociology is much more than mere collection of facts". "It is the systematic study of facts, aiming at an interpretative understanding of their meanings and the explanation of their causes and consequences."[7] Thus, sociology as a subject not only has a rich theoretical side but also a scientific empirical side too. Indian sociologists, over the years, though have contributed to the empirical study of Indian society, but have moved in baby steps in creating indigenous concepts or methods to study human society in general. It is this lack of innovation on the methodological side that has led the Indian sociologists to develop a myopic view, restricting themselves only to their own society. This is against the basic principles of systematic comparative method. To Bèteille, the ignorance and neglect in development of indigenous methodology in sociology over the years came from the extravagant concern among Indian sociologists for matters of urgent practical importance for over all development and thereby delving mostly into current affairs.

The word sustainability is associated with environment and natural resources. Its simple meaning in dictionary still stands as the quality of being able to continue over time. In this paper, the word sustainability has been associated with "creation of intellectual capital", thereby leading to overall development of the knowledge of the subject. The concern with current affairs has proportionately led to the deterioration of concern in the fundamental features of the subject thereby reducing the sustenance and growth of the subject in itself. To Bèteille, "a sociologist does not construct a new society unlike an engineer who constructs a bridge; he only contributes in creating the awareness among the members which leads them to construct and create their own society".[8] Sociology contributes to the "critical understanding as against social engineering".[9] Hence the development of the subject itself, without only concentrating on solving the current social problems, should always be a fundamental objective of interest to the sociologists.

Objectives

The chapter tries to explore the broader perspective of the usage of the term sustainability as beyond the common usage in environment and natural resources. It also tries to consolidate the contributions of a famous Indian sociologist—Andre Bèteille in the field of sustainability of knowledge. As Bèteille, through his experience of academics and teaching, suggests to the present day sociologists to move beyond the given knowledge of the discipline and develop concepts that would make the study of their own society relevant ensuring growth and intellectual sustainability.The paper also analyses the advice of Bèteille to use systematic comparisons, not just the casual ones, to make sociology rise above the tag of sheer common sense and secure its position as an established discipline. Finally, the paper tries to enumerate the advice given by Bèteille to all the present-day sociologists to move beyond the motives of the sponsored agencies of the research and focus on the quality of the actual work and innovate own indigenous method and concepts to ensure development and sustainability of the discipline.

Literature Review

Sociology as a subject grew tremendously in the twentieth century not only in the West but also in India. Primarily with the social reconstruction and economic rebuilding as objectives, after Independence, growth of the subject took place heavily in India. Though the development of the subject did not happen in a synchronized and unified manner but over the years, intellectuals from all across have shown tremendous interest in the subject. "As an intellectual discipline, sociology has developed its own body of concepts, methods and data."[10] Methods used by sociologists were far more ambiguous and amorphous than natural sciences but they definitely transcended common sense.

Public awareness of sociology in India increased tremendously since Independence. Along with the increasing number of producers of the subject, there were equally large numbers of consumers too. In spite of its increasing mass appeal, there still remained doubtful in the ways sociological knowledge diffused within the minds of the people and impacted their thoughts about society. To Bèteille, it is true that every member of society has some generic understanding of society, family, community, and class, but this generic idea does not make him eligible to be a specialist in sociology. Hence, this proves how sociology differs from common sense. Indian sociologists throughout suffer from the problem of dependence of concepts, methods that have been created by others outside India, mainly the Westerners. In case of any collabourative work, it is the Indians who provide the facts, and external specialists provide them the tools for interpretation. This unique division of labour posed a serious concern for sociologists in India. The problem seemed not to stem from lack of talent but to Bèteille, it stemmed from the growing strong concern of Indian sociologists for matters of "urgent practical importance".[11] To Bèteille, this concern became stronger and more demanding over the years. Earlier it was only the government who wanted practical results, gradually it was government along with NGOs who asked for practical results too. It is beyond doubt that an interest in current affairs can stimulate sociological enquiry and investigation, and has already done so in all places and at all times. To Bèteille, "a long-term growth of an intellectual discipline becomes distorted and even jeopardized when it allows itself to be driven entirely by the interest in current affairs to the exclusion of all other interests".[12] Since most of the funding and impetus came from the government, and certain NGOs, research and writings of long-term theoretical importance in sociology were not prevented, but the funding mainly went to the studies that were application based and of direct practical interest.

As India began its sojourn of reconstruction and reconstitution of a new economy, a great deal of intellectual energy from all sources was spent to bring about a social change, after Independence. Though the impetus came mainly from the economists among the social scientists, it was sure that the effort of economic development would end in vain, unless a proper understanding of obstacles, causes and consequences in the social context were comprehended. It is in this endeavour that development in the field of sociology came into parlance. Separate research institutes began to be set up for providing intellectual advises for analysing change and recommending measures for developing, moving ahead, and carrying forward.

To Bèteille, due to the misconception of characterizing sociology with that of common sense, all concerned citizens and individuals thought of possessing the trait of understanding the sociological problems, but lest could they understand that there remains a great distinction between social and sociological problems. They felt and still now feel that whenever there comes If any sociologist is unable to recommend any solution, then he or she must be incompetent. However, history revealed that over the years and throughout all societies, sociologists have contributed indirectly, more so by providing critical understanding to the persons in building their own society than directly. The pre-occupation of sociologists with the "interpretation and analysis of enduring social institutions and long-term social processes is viewed with impatience by the lot who want sociologists to tell them how to set things right here and now".[13] Such study is considered as academic and not applicational, hence not useful. To Bèteille, a great many studies and reports have been published with regard to various social problems like "poverty, corruption, communal violence, child abuse, environmental topics".[14] These have definitely contributed to the understanding and knowledge of these problems in the Indian context but their objective of providing solution to these problems still remains doubtful. Though the solutions to the social problems still remain phantasmagoric, sociological problems have lost their attractiveness as regards to when and where they do not have any immediate bearing with the practical and social problems.

The other reason for the failure to create sustainability in sociology, according to Bèteille is the lack of usage of comparative method. To Bèteille, Indian sociologists lacked and still lack intellectual interest to study societies other than their own. Though the study of sociology has traversed a long path in India, the concentration remains in the Indian society and Indian sociology as a branch of general sociology rather than general sociology itself. Bèteille further attributed that sociology as rightly pointed out by Durkheim and Radcliffe Brown, by nature is a comparative science, and its concepts and methods have developed over the years through constant comparison and contrast of societies of different kinds. Studying one's own society rather than studying other societies have always been typified as "anthropology" and not "sociology". Bèteille further substantiated his views by saying that in teaching sociology, there remained a great discrepancy in the theoretical teaching and substantive teaching. Theoretically, the students may be made to jump over to sociologists from other countries like Max Weber, Emile Durkheim, Talcott Parsons, Robert K. Merton, Bronislaw Malinowski, but their practical implication, research projects, and their substantive courses were and still at present remain restricted to Indian society only.

To Bèteille, universities are expected to be repositories of long-term intellectual capital and it is expected that a discipline as an intellectual discipline can take shape without expecting too much of immediate practical returns to the institutions' intellectual investment. However, that never meant, that sociologists would refrain from listening to the demands of everyday life but they should have their own autonomy and freedom to make a choice on their topics of research depending on their capability and point of interest and thereby respond to the situations.

Research to Bèteille, should be intellectually motivated. Earlier times, the endeavour used to be driven by the long-term interest and lifetime commitment rather than the interest of the donors. However, with the passage of time, research became a part of time-bound project, results of which would be directly beneficial to the sponsors and accordingly suffice the objective of the specific research project on the basis of which it has been designed. Donors wanted concrete results and that to within the stipulated period of time. "They were oriented to matters of the moment and had very little interest in the pursuit of ideas for their own sake."[15]

The final reason for lack of sustainable sociology, to Bèteille had been the intervention of NGOs, making it look attractive, receiving foreign funds to meet their commitment to development and democracy, as an alternative profession to the best students of the universities. This clearly reduced the pool of resources in university research. Along with this, too much of bureaucratization, lack of autonomy and cumbersome rules made the research procedures extremely slow moving and difficult. Contemporary generation lacked the patience to hold on to the "slow boring of hard boards" style of Weberian thought. Their desire for a faster simple process forced them to move out of the intellectual research of universities to various projects-based research or NGOs.

Bèteille with his strong affinity for Weber, rightly quoted him by saying it that, ideas come to us when "they please" rather than "when it pleases us".[16] Bèteille suggested that if we are to achieve fruitful innovation, we can never ignore our predecessors, rather their works need to be carried forward. Sociologists need not be ashamed of the previous and dismiss these works. If these voluminous works are carried forward, then the subject would remain sustainable and retain its intellectual capital.

Case Studies Creating Sustainable Knowledge in Sociology

The first case study as cited by Bèteille was "Religion and Society among the Coorgs of South India" by M.N. Srinivas. This, to Bèteille, was a pure research contributing to the theoretical side of the subject, instead of rendering any direct help to the planners, policy makers and social activists. The above-mentioned research became a breakthrough in the sociological study of India and inspired many in the next generation. Srinivas, according to Bèteille, introduced major innovations in approach, method and concepts in the said research. His advocacy of the "field view" in the then contemporary world of "book view" had tremendous influence in the study of sociological institutions like caste, village and family both in India and abroad. Even more than fifty years down the line, the research carries the legacy of same relevance in terms of freshness and newness in the field of research in sociology. Bèteille pointed out that the research raised an important question of approach, namely, whether, in the sociological study of religion, the balance of advantage lay with the religious believer or the religious sceptic.[17] Srinivas in his study endeavoured to refrain himself from any sort of value judgement and made it quite clear that the sociological study of religion is not about the truth of religious belief or the effectiveness of religious practice but to arrive at a "critical understanding of it".[18] To Bèteille, the research never meant to prove the ultimate unity of Hinduism as a faith or doctrine, but to show empirically how the beliefs and the practices operated in the region under the social context and over the years the same beliefs and practices were refracted by the social structure. Conceptually, Bèteille said that Srinivas in his research ushered a new beginning in the study of Indian society. The research led Srinivas to introduce the concept of field view "Sanskritization". The terminologies introduced paved a new way of analysing systematically the "dynamics of continuity and change in India".[19] Later along with Sanskritization, as he moved on to the study of politics in sociology, Srinivas came up with the terminology of "dominant caste". This invention later on became a seminal point in the subject of sociology of politics.

The next example that Bèteille gave was the work on *Family and Kinship* by T.N. Madan (1965). The mentioned work again tried to be value free and refrained from any attachment. Methodologically the work showed, how being a member of the same community that was his subject of research, he maintained detachment that is so very essential to be followed by a scholar in a scientific study.

> The basic purpose of the study by Madan was to provide deeper understanding of the fundamental institutions of family, kinship and marriage rather than to advise policy makers on how to improve the operation of those institutions.[20]

Many years have passed after publication of such work, Indian sociology, is yet to see such work of great impact in the development of knowledge of the subject. The reason for lack of such work to Bèteille has been one and only because of excess attention of sociologists to the social problems, viewing the subject close to common sense and the effort of sociologists to come up with practical solutions to the social problems, rendering help and assistance to the policy makers and planners or sufficing the objectives of the sponsors.

Methodology

The methodology followed in this chapter is a qualitative historical method. Bèteille's writings published in various journals and books have been analysed to find out his ideas and views on the present topic.

Limitations

This chapter happens to be a part of idea and thought that Bèteille holds regarding the methodology that sociology as a discipline follows and should follow to ensure its development and sustainability. It also tries to analyse various flaws the discipline in its developmental journey entails leading to contradiction in teaching sociology and practising sociology. Bèteille was ever eager to make the discipline popular and sustainable. Comparing and analysing the discourses of other sociologists could have been complementary to the study, but they said endeavour needs much time and resources. Mapping of Bèteille's thought on methodology to his other topics of his trajectories like inequality, stratification, "positive discrimination" and "affirmative action" in terms of reservation policy in India, his thoughts on university would have provided a better insight of the implementation of his ideas of methodology that the discipline should follow keeping an eye to development of the discipline that would ensure sustainability.

Conclusion

Considering the kind of substantial advancement that Indian sociology has had over the years, it would be a dishonour to the discipline to only concentrate on the current affairs and provide practical solution to the immediate social problems, without developing much to the theoretical side of the subject. The policymakers and the intellectuals should keep in mind that sociology is a descriptive and not a prescriptive social science.Hence providing direct solutions or recommending policies or building policies would always be difficult. Bèteille himself went on to form several political opinions on matters that he has specialized as a sociologist, but in doing so, he has always maintained a safe distance from his subject of research.

Bèteille being always grounded but ever optimistic spoke in favour of the capability that Indian sociologists possess. Bèteille neither enthusiast or euphoric, has never been a fatalist too. He, from his very nature posed a warning not to justify the happenings that are taking place in sociology at present. To him, Indian sociologists over the years and particularly after Independence have touched almost every social institution and process which has been to a certain extent of practical use by planners, policymakers, and concerned citizens. But the kind of talent and resources that is available in the discipline, certainly pose an expectation of more comparative works, broader perspectives, and innovation of new concepts and methodologies that are beneficial for the development of discipline and its sustainability. To quote Bèteille,

> one would have expected a few more Indian sociologists to take their eyes off the ground to attend in a more sustained and continuous manner to issues of more general interest to the discipline as a whole.

In doing so, replacing the existing discourses created by our predecessors is unnecessary rather an effort needs to be given to greater consolidation by carrying forward the old ones along with the discovery of the new. This would refurbish the discipline making it a breakthrough in future in its endeavour of knowledge development and sustainability. To Bèteille, sociologists need to have the entrepreneurial capability of taking risks. Unless one takes the risk of moving ahead of the practical outcomes of the research, one cannot innovate new concepts and methodologies that would help to create the sustainability and intellectual capital of the subject. To Bèteille, researches of the funded projects are mainly all about specific formats and their main objectives. Researches that play safe are done mainly for the attraction of funds by the sociologists. Though these have at times led to the innovation of concepts and methodologies, but their outcomes seemed to be less tangible and hence not beneficial for the future generation sociologists. As an advice, Bèteille suggested concoction of academics with research as there would not be much improvement without the help of each of the two, and one would always stimulate the other. Building intellectual capital to Bèteille is important not only because the knowledge can be used at present, but also in the future creating sustainability of the subject.

Innovation matters, thus innovations that are sustainable matters all the more. To Bèteille, the important advice that the current sociologists and intellectuals active in the profession should keep in mind is that "they should be little less mindful of what funding agencies think of their work and a little more mindful of what their students think of it". Sociological research would tend to remain incomplete, if too much attention is provided to deadlines and the objectives of the funding agencies. Government, policy makers, universities, NGOs, and funding agencies shall motivate researchers to work on topics of their interest and aid them in developing diverse concepts and methodologies, thereby adding to the sustainability of the subject. As a method, there should be more concentration on the comparative approach as that would bring about a perfect analogy among the societies by putting all of them on the same plane. It is through this continuous endeavour that sociology can ensure sustainability and create intellectual capital. Bèteille suggested that we need more prolific original researches as done by our predecessors like Srinivas and Madan and also carry on from where they left their journey. Bèteille's concern for creating sustainable innovations in the field of sociology would definitely make Indian sociologists less dependent on the occidental concepts that were created for the study of societies of their own, implementing which made our studies non-contextual and irrelevant thereby affecting the sustainability of the subject.

Keywords

Theory, current affairs, sustainability, intellectual capital, Andre Bèteille.

NOTES

1. A. Bèteille (September 1973). "The Teaching of Sociology in India", *Sociological Bulletin, 22*(2): 218.
2. *Ibid.*, p. 216.
3. A. Bèteille (September 1996). "Sociology and Common Sense", *Economic & Political Weekly, 31*(35/37): 2363.
4. *Ibid.*
5. A. Bèteille (May-August 2006). "Sociology and Current Affairs", *Sociological Bulletin, 55*(2): 202.
6. A. Bèteille (September 1998). "The Comparative Method and the Standpoint of the Investigator", *Sociological Bulletin, 47*(2): 149.
7. A. Bèteille (May-August 2006). "Sociology and Current Affairs", *Sociological Bulletin, 55*(2): 203.
8. *Ibid.*, p. 207.
9. *Ibid.*
10. *Ibid.*, p. 202.
11. *Ibid.*, p. 205.
12. *Ibid.*
13. *Ibid.*, p. 207.
14. *Ibid.*
15. *Ibid.*, p. 211.
16. *Ibid.*
17. *Ibid.*, p. 208.
18. *Ibid.*

19. *Ibid.*
20. *Ibid.*, p. 209.

REFERENCES

Bèteille, A. (2000). *Antinomies of Society.* New Delhi: Oxford University Press.

Bèteille, A. (2000). *Chronicles of Our Time.* New Delhi: Penguin Books, India.

Bèteille, A. (1996). "Sociology and Common Sense." *Economic & Political Weekly, 31*(35/37): 2361-65.

Bèteille, A. (2006). "Sociology and Current Affairs." *Sociological Bulletin, 55(2)*: 201-14.

Bèteille, A. (1973). "The Teaching of Sociology in India." *Sociological Bulletin, 22(2)*: 216-33.

Bèteille, A. (1998). "The Comparative Method and the Standpoint of the Investigator." *Sociological Bulletin, 47(2)*: 137-54.

Bèteille, A. (2009). *Sociology Essays on Approach & Method* (2nd edn.). New Delhi: Oxford India Paperbacks.

Bèteille, A. (2010). *Universities at the Cross Roads.* New Delhi: Oxford University Press.

4

Role of Women Leaders at the Local Level to Achieve the Sustainable Development Goals

K. Gireesan

Women account for about half of the population, but their economic, social, and environmental contributions go unrealized to a great extent. The invisibility of women's contributions to the economy, polity and society has always been an important topic for research. Women's invisible and invaluable contributions to the economy through unpaid care work, parenting and domestic responsibilities have been a matter of serious deliberations across the world.

During the last one decade, there has been a growing effort around the world to recognize and value unpaid work, as the countries increasingly understand its significant contributions. In the year 2016, the United Nations integrated this focus into the Sustainable Development Goals (SDGs). SDG-5 emphasizes "gender equality and empower all women and girls" as it is not only a fundamental right, but a necessary prerequisite for a peaceful, prosperous and sustainable world. SDG Target 5.4 seeks to recognize and value unpaid care and domestic work through the provision of public services, infrastructure and social protection policies, and the promotion of shared responsibility within the household and the family as nationally appropriate.

Scope, significance and practices of leadership roles for women in decision making at all levels have been another important area for research studies and discussions. SDG Target 5.5 aims to "ensure women's full and effective participation and equal opportunities for leadership at all levels of decision making in political, economic and public life". It needs no emphasis that women's active participation and assuming leadership is crucial to gender equality, promotion of inclusive institutions and political empowerment.

The role of women in sustainable development is multi-dimensional. Their voices, comments and suggestions are quite significant as most often, they are the first responders in their families. In addition, they have unique ideas and perspectives to drive changes for protection, preservation, and conservation of resources at different levels. The impact of women in key sustainability areas such as food security, water conservation, and renewable energy, are quite invaluable; they are more closely related to climate change than what it appears to be.

In this paper, an attempt has been made to achieve the SDGs with a thrust on the role of women leaders at the local level by analysing the economic, social, and environmental dimensions in governance and development.

Economic Dimensions

Women constitute half of the human capital across the world. Better involvement and participation of the female population could enhance economic growth, improve societal well-being, and ensure sustainable development. Sustainable economic growth depends on more and more women joining the labour force and optimum utilization of their capabilities and skills. However, it is noted that they are one of the most underrated, underutilized, and undervalued resources.

In a study measuring the monetary value of unpaid household work within the Indian context, it is reported that

> in 2022-23, women spent an average of 4.6 hours on domestic chores, which is more than double the 2.2 hours spent by men. Using replacement cost and gross opportunity cost approaches, the estimated value of unpaid household work in India ranged from 26 per cent to 36 per cent of GDP in 2022-23. (Sahoo, Sarkar, and Kumar, 2024)

The study points towards the need for policy reforms acknowledging the economic contributions of unpaid household activities, seeking more equitable recognition of women's labour in the economy of the country.

It is reported that "the rate of female participation in the labour force is significantly lower than that of men in all countries" (OECD, 2008). Does it mean that the involvement and participation of women in growth and development is lower than that of men? Definitely not. Then, what are the reasons behind the low work participation rate for women in India? Probably, one of the reasons could be the engagement of several women in part-time engagements due to personal commitments and domestic engagements. This naturally lowers their economic contributions. Even when women work for the same duration as men, the gender wage gaps have been practised in many domains. And, women remain underrepresented in engineering and technology studies, resulting in their less share in the overall technical workforce. "Greater female participation in computer science, engineering and technology-oriented jobs would spur innovation and economic advances" (OECD, 2007).

Despite all advancements, a large segment of women is engaged in "female-dominated" sectors such as education and health, which are "comparatively underpaid" than science, technology and management. And, "the wage gaps are highest in management positions where the educational background and work experience of women and men are very similar" (OECD, 2008).

More importantly, women's work at home is undervalued even though they perform the bulk of the household functions, like household work, child care, parental care, etc. In addition,

> women are disadvantaged in the workplace by time poverty (juggling the needs of home and work), intermittency (taking time off to care for children or elderly parents), and lack of mobility (needing a job closer to home and family). (OECD, 2008)

One could find several examples where women preferred a job closer to home and family and even avoided career prospects for "family". Provision of gender-friendly practices such as improved access to child care facilities at the workplace, paid parental leave, flexible work arrangements, etc. could bring lot of positive changes.

More importantly, in the national income calculations, the daily housework done by a homemaker (housewife or house husband) has not been counted as an economic activity. It is known that a homemaker (housewife or a house-husband) doing household work is not included in national income as the service cannot be estimated in monetary terms. At present, only those economic activity is included in national income which can be measured and estimated in terms of money.

It is suggested that the criteria for calculation of national income needs to be revisited. But then, how? Can we not do the costing of the domestic/household work that includes cooking, cleaning utencils, washing clothes, sanitizing rooms, baby sitting, care for the elderly, etc.? By raising this question, the intention is not to fix the monetary value for the love, care, and concern to the family members, but it is more to do with the attitude towards the domestic/household work carried out by the home maker (housewife or house husband).

While assessing the monetary value of unpaid work like household activities, it is important to cost their impacts as well. It is noted that

> doing unpaid care and domestic work could perpetuate gender inequality and economic disempowerment. It could also affect women's health, education, and employment opportunities while increasing their vulnerability to violence. (Hernando, 2022)

It is reported that "the failure to value women's work is a significant barrier to reducing poverty and fostering economic growth" (OECD, 2008).

Drawing inputs from the estimates by the International Labour Organization (ILO), it is known that

> the value of unpaid care and domestic work accounts for as much as 9 per cent of global GDP. Of that, women's unpaid work comes in at around 6.6 per cent of GDP, and men's at 2.4 per cent of GDP (Hernando, 2022).

It shows that men's contribution towards the domestic/household work and unpaid care is less than half of their female counterpart.

Collection of gender-based disaggregated data and taking up "work-time-motion studies" could determine the monetary value of domestic works. It will enable to bring about change in mindsets, address gender stereotyping, and encourage the boys and men to share the domestic responsibilities. The researchers of gender and sustainable development shall take up this matter seriously, with more empirical studies to justify the inferences that may result in policy changes.

Social Dimensions

Raising the literacy and educational standards of women is one of the most effective investments for increasing female productivity and their well-being. Reducing the educational gender gap in favour of women shall be given a special focus. At the same time, there is a significant difference in the subjects that young men and women study in higher education. Disciplines in arts, education, health, humanities, and social sciences are still preferred by women. However, in the domains of computer science, engineering, mathematics, manufacturing, etc., dominance of men is still high. A huge disparity exists in the diverse disciplinary domains of higher education which cannot be ignored when we need to address "gender and sustainable development".

In this context, it is significant to note that UNESCO is the United Nations' specialized agency for education. It provides "global and regional leadership in education, strengthens national education systems and responds to contemporary global challenges through education with a special focus on gender equality". UNESCO's document on education for sustainable development (ESD) brings out a

> cross-disciplinary and systemic approach that links gender equality to specific gendered challenges related to each of the SDGs. ESD for 2030 actively promotes gender equality and creates conditions to empower women. (UNESCO, 2020)

Professionalization of occupation depends on unbiased job evaluation, better wages, job security, and better career prospects. In many ways, gender discrimination starts while assessing the knowledge and skills needed for certain jobs. "Male-dominated" professions tend to be rated as more complex and of higher value than several "female-dominant" ones. At the same time, it is noted that

> most of the labour-intensive operations in agriculture such as seed preparation, planting the saplings, weeding, harvesting, etc. are generally carried out by women. However, the machine-intensive activities such as land preparation, tilling, application of

> fertilizers and pesticides, etc. are taken up by male members. (Gireesan, 2020)

And, there is a serious wage disparity exists among men and women labourers in the agricultural sector. This needs to be relooked, redefined, and restructured on top priority, which will have multiple ramifications in the society. In the present times, there is no job which could be considered as the sole property of male or female. For example, nursing which was once considered as a female occupation, is not any more treated so. The scope and opportunities for a "male nurse' in the developed countries is very high. It is high time to reassess the qualification and skills needed for different types of jobs on a gender-neutral scale.

Gender perspectives are very important in health sector, due to biological and social factors of men and women. It is imperative to adopt a gender perspective, by not only considering the physical differences between men and women, but also the social and cultural factors. It is reported that

> women by virtue of their sex are vulnerable to many threats to their health and, as it happens, to their lives. Some of these threats may be sporadic or situational. But most of them are deeply rooted in the persistent social structures that reproduce and perpetuate stratified societies in which systematic inequities and discrimination against women are tolerated. In addition, pregnancy, childbirth, and puerperium put women through significant physiological, physical, and emotional changes with their consequent health risks. (Safaei, 2009)

In this context, health research and programmes cannot be gender-blind as there are biological, social, and environmental factors. During the formulation/revision of health care policy, a special focus shall be made for gender-specific diseases and reproduction needs.

Despite achievement of equal citizenship status, women in India remain vastly underrepresented in governance forums. Though the provision of equal citizenship status and measures for affirmative action is available, with the exception of local governments (where there was a mandatory provision of reservation ensured by Article 243 by the 73rd and 74th Constitutional Amendment Acts), there is a poor representation of women in the decision making forms such as state legislatures and national parliament. The recent exercise of passing the bill for reservation for women in the state legislatures and national parliament becomes significant in this context. Though the legislative exercise can be considered as historic and progressive, the conditions laid down for its operationalization (such as the completion of national census that has been pending, delimitation of constituencies, listing of reserved constituencies, etc.) will take a few more years to come into effect.

There are several examples to prove that when women participate in governance, there is a greater chance that policies will reflect more closely the needs of all citizens, especially that benefit children, adolescent girls, young women, elderly, differently abled, etc. Studies have showed that women leaders tend to give more thrust on the basic sectors such as education, drinking water, hygiene and sanitation, public health, social security, labour rights, social welfare, etc. that are essential to have a better Human Development Index.

Enhanced participation of women in political processes is an important prerequisite for the empowerment of women in governance. Targeted capacity building programmes, that are need-based and demand-driven, shall be organized more with its thrust on women leaders. In addition, timely mentoring, professional guidance, and networks also help women in performing their new roles in political life.

Environmental Dimensions

Gender is an important factor to be analysed while considering actions to adapt and mitigate climate change. Owing to the cultural aspects, economic factors, and social roles, women tend to be affected more harshly by the vagaries of climate change. Women are more vulnerable in the present ecosystem with low access to finance, technology, and information to adapt to climate change impacts. Climate change that affects crop yields invariably impact the livelihoods and food security of women as they are generally considered responsible for food production and family nutrition. In addition, collection of water and cooking fuel, that are traditionally considered as "women's responsibilities", becomes more difficult, when affected by environmental changes.

Climate change could also result in severe shortage of resources and unreliable job markets, causing migration of male members or the whole family. Such a scenario further increases their engagement in agricultural activities and household functions of women. In all types of disasters, be it natural or human-made, women and children are more vulnerable. For example, the information available in the public domain from the ongoing war between Israel and Hamas, most of the casualties were women and children. Looking through the details of casualties of natural disasters in the past in our country, the data seems to show similar trends. For example, Bhuj-Kutch earthquake, Latur earthquake, Uttarakhand floods, Odisha super cyclone, Tsunami, etc. including the recent disasters in Wayanad, Kerala.

Many technological changes may not be gender-neutral and may adversely affect women or bypass their roles. As homemakers, women shall be more productively engaged in the application of renewable and sustainable energy for cooking and other domestic purposes. Women shall be engaged more actively, towards finding better solutions to mitigate adverse effects of climate change.

Role of Women Leaders at the Local Level

In this section, certain suggestions are put forward which could be considered by the leadership, especially by the women leaders at the local level, towards achieving the SDGs.

- Take initiatives for the formulation and functioning of "child-friendly *anganawadis*" (child care centres) in their area of jurisdiction. *Anganawadis*, being the most basic unit for a healthy and productive nation, shall be made more child-friendly by taking strategic initiatives by the leadership.
- Organize orientation sessions on menstrual hygiene management (MHM) for adolescent girls and young women. Generating requisite awareness of MHM could contribute towards women empowerment in multiple ways. It will enable the adolescent girls and young women to break the barriers of silence, shame and secrecy. It will help to demystify the myths, misconceptions and wrong perceptions about this physical phenomenon.

  Effective interventions in MHM can immensely contribute towards the psychosomatic well-being of adolescent girls and young women, leading to the overall development of the nation. It has the capability to transform their physiological pain into a psychological gain. (Sharma and Gireesan, 2022).

  It could boost the confidence of adolescent girls and young women significantly and enhance their productivity.
- Rejuvenation of participatory structures at the local level, be it youth club, *mahila mandal*, self-help groups (SHGs), parent teacher association (PTA), etc. shall be made on priority (Gireesan, 2012). This will help to ensure "participation in development" by the key stakeholders.
- Encourage more women to participate actively in the *grama sabha*, a constitutional forum of decentralized governance. The women leaders could take initiatives to organize *bala sabha*, *yuvajana sabha*, *mahila sabha*, *vayojana sabha*, *divyanga sabha*, etc. prior to the formal meeting of *grama sabha* to seek specific inputs from diverse demographic segments of the society. Collection of inputs and ensuring

participation of these demographic segments will result in rejuvenation of *grama sabha* as a participatory structure at the local level leading to "planning from below" more effectively.

- Motivate the school management, teachers, parents, and students to start a "model agricultural farm" in the school in their locality. This suggestion is equally or more important in the schools in urban settings. This will create awareness among the future citizens about the importance of agriculture, value of labour, importance of cooperation, significance of team work, etc.
- Initiation of organic farming practices for vegetables, horticulture, etc. and ensuring adequate technological support, financial support, marketing support, etc. to individuals and groups engaged in organic farming. This will result in making significant contributions towards achieving "food safety" and "food sovereignty".
- Water budgeting at the local level can be made which could lead to water audit, water literacy, changes in cropping pattern, etc. to address the vagaries of climate change.
- Works taken up under MGNREGA could be analysed and reviewed by the women leaders from the perspectives of "inclusive governance" and "sustainable development".
- Non-conventional energy is an important area of intervention by the women leaders. They might practise and promote solar cookers, solar panels, electric vehicles, etc. more aggressively than other leaders, for multiple reasons. It will also result in lowering the domestic expenses, does not create any pollution, and reduce the "carbon footprint". It is expected that women leaders will be more keen for the formulation of "carbon neutral panchayats" which is multidimensional and multi-functional.
- Generally, a large part of funds used to be spent for creation of infrastructure facilities. It is expected that before taking measures for any new construction of public for public

services, an assessment of the existing infrastructure facilities shall be made. Conduct of a resource mapping about the facilities (including non-performing assets) will enable to ensure optimum utilization of existing infrastructure. The same building/facility could be used by multiple stakeholders, by judicious application of time-sharing technique. A survey of non-performing assets in the locality also shall be taken up in the larger interests of sustainable development. While going ahead for new constructions, preference shall be given to the creation of multi-purpose buildings that could provide diverse services from the same infrastructure. Such multi-purpose buildings will be very much beneficial in disaster situations as well. At the same time, necessary measures shall be made to address the operational issues of such structures, as they may be under the administrative control of different government departments/agencies. But with the effective intervention of local leadership, these issues could be addressed efficiently and optimum utilization of existing infrastructure and other resources could be made. It is expected that women leaders have a natural talent and skill to optimally utilize the resources, that has been endorsed by many researchers.

Endnotes

Review of a recent study report highlighted the need

> to refine methodologies for research in this direction, promote equitable recognition and redistribution of care responsibilities, and ultimately enhance women's labour force participaton. (Varghese, 2024)

It is significant to realize the "undervalued" contributions of women towards economic, social, and environmental dimensions in governance and development. Identifying, analysing, and practising different practical and strategic functions with a gender perspective could contribute significantly towards addressing the existing gender gaps and achieving the SDGs at a faster pace.

It is imperative that policy formulation in multiple domains shall be made for meeting the needs of future generations with due thrust and weightage on diverse demographic segments keeping in view the principles of "equity" and "empowerment". For making that happen, what is needed is recognition of the abilities of women leaders, acceptance of their views, and respect for their contributions. The author believes that women leaders, by their natural talents, multi-tasking ability, and compassion, could contribute more vigorously to achieve the SDGs earlier than anticipated.

Keywords

Climate change, environment, gender, governance, leadership, SDGS, women, education for sustainable development.

REFERENCES

Gireesan, K. (2012). "Participatory Structures at the Local Level and Interventions by the Youth". *The Grassroots Governance Journal, X*(1): 114-25.

Gireesan, K. (2020). "Youth in Agriculture: Opportunities, Challenges and the Way Forward in the Post-COVID-19 Scenario". *IAHRW International Journal of Social Sciences Review, 8*(7-9): 321-29.

Hernando, R.C. (2022). *Policy Brief No. 43: Unpaid Care and Domestic Work: Counting the Costs.* Singapore: Asia Pacific Economic Cooperation (APEC) Policy Support Unit.

OECD. (2007). *Science, Technology and Industry Scoreboard 2007: Innovation and Performance in the Global Economy.* Paris: Organisation for Economic Cooperation and Development.

OECD. (2008). *Gender and Sustainable Development: Maximising the Economic, Social and Environmental Role of Women.* Paris: Organisation for Economic Cooperation and Development.

Safaei, J. (2009). "Democracy and Women's Health". *Mens Sana Monogr, 7*(1): 20-36. doi: 10.4103/0973-1229.42101

Sahoo, S., K.K. Sarkar, and A. Kumar (2024). "Valuation of unpaid Household Activities in India". *Economic and Political Weekly, 59*(39): September, 28.

Sharma, S. and K. Gireesan (2022). "Interventions in Menstrual Hygiene Management: Perceptions and Reflections from Adolescent Girls and Young Women". In: A Radhakrishnan Nair (ed). *Essays on Women Empowerment,* Chennai: Notionpress.com, 109-28.

UNESCO. (2020). *Education for Sustainable Development: A Roadmap.* Paris: United Nations Educational, Scientific and Cultural Organisation. https://doi.org/10.54675/YFRE1448

Varghese, R.R. (2024). "Recognising the Economic Value of Unpaid Work in India". *The Hindu,* Mohali Edition, October, 31.

Part II

5

Trauma Responsive Equitable Education

A Model for Communities Seeking to Bring the UN's Sustainable Development Goals to Life

Mark Tappan, Jakob Erle, and *Alan Furth*

Sarah, is a fifth grade student receiving special services in a rural elementary school. Because she struggles in her regular classroom she spends most of her time working one-on-one with the special education teacher. As a result, she has few opportunities to engage both academically and socially with her classmates, her peers know little about her, and she doesn't have many friends. She also doesn't know her teacher very well, and her teacher doesn't know her. Days at school are hard and lonely.

Sarah's school is participating in the Trauma Responsive Equitable Education (TREE) project (Brown, Biddle, & Tappan, 2022b). As part of the "Somedays" initiative, all of the students in the school were asked about something special they would like to do in school. Sarah, who has a passion for baking, said that she wanted to bake with her whole class.

As her teacher explained,

> We watched a children's bake-off on YouTube, and then they baked. For [her] just, it's huge. Just to be part of a

> group. I mean, she struggles to be part of a group, and she doesn't have a group outside of school. For her, it would have been pretty understandable to have picked a Someday that was just centred on herself, but she did one that included everybody. (p. 28)

And, as a result, Sarah herself began to feel more included and more connected to both her classmates and her teacher.

Valerie, Sarah's classmate, wanted to teach kindergarteners in her school to make artificial snow. It was a great success. In reflecting on her Someday experience, she says:

> What I like about Somedays is that you can trust that yours will come true. Let's say you don't really like a teacher and you don't really trust them, and then they make your Someday come true—and it's like, I can sort of trust these people. (p. 34)

In this essay, we describe in some detail the (TREE) project, an innovative and empowering programme that centres student voice and equity, and foregrounds issues and ideas that are on the minds of students, including early elementary school students, to make school life attractive and relevant for them. We then assert that a local initiative such as TREE, with its impacts and approach, is strengthened and compounded when it is connected to, and informed by, the UN sustainable development goals (SDGs). The TREE project contributes to the achievement of the national obligations of the SDGs, especially in education. In addition, the integrated agenda of the SDGs gives the scope for learning and reflection for educators, students, and the families and communities they are a part of, to understand their work in the context of the world they live in. The SDGs also provides a framework for dialogue on why learning environments, as exemplified by TREE, are needed to cope with and even help shape our hyper-complex world.

The TREE Project: Putting Voice and Equity at the Centre of Trauma-informed Schooling

TREE Project grew out of a multi-year community-led process to address challenges facing rural communities. The process began in 2013, when Cobscook Institute (Cobscook), a non-profit organization with a mission to create educational opportunities that strengthen personal, community, and global well-being. The project brought together a diverse array of stakeholders (tribal and non-tribal members of our communities, PreK-12 educators and administrators, social service providers, other non-profit organizations, and college/university researchers) in rural Washington County, Maine, in the north-east corner of the United States, to envision a coordinated response to childhood adversity, trauma, and other stresses facing many local families. They came together to keep their kids from dying literally and spiritually.

Washington County, the most rural county in Maine, faces the highest rates of poverty in the state. Substance use disorder and mental health access are also among residents' chief concerns. The entire international region is within the ancestral lands of the Passamaquoddy Nation whose people now reside in one of the two Passamaquoddy reservations in the central and northern part of the county. The southern part of the county is home to a growing Latinx population, initially drawn to the area through migrant work related to blueberry harvesting. As a result, the stakeholders gathered by Cobscook recognized that a multi-faceted approach would be required to meet the complex needs of their diverse, rural community. They identified schools, as one of the few robust social institutions present in communities across the county, as a leverage point and potential asset in addressing these challenges.

Growing concern about the impact of toxic stress on the lives of children and youth has given rise, in recent years, to a number of significant theoretical and empirical efforts to understand the neurobiological, physical, psychological, and social effects of traumatic experiences, and how best to respond to and support children, youth, and the families and communities they are a part of who suffer from such experiences (Cantor *et al.*, 2018; Chronholm *et al.*, 2015; Franke, 2014). When children and youth feel physically and emotionally safe, and engaged in supportive and authentic relationships with adults and peers, for example, they are more resilient and better able to cope with the impact of trauma (National Scientific Council on the Developing Child, 2004). Healthy, relationship-rich family and school environments not only buffer the impact of toxic stress, but support children and youth in developing the skills, competencies, and mindsets necessary for success in school and in life that may have been negatively impacted by early experiences of trauma (Souers & Hall, 2016). For children living in physically and emotionally unsafe environments (Gabarino, 1995), such relationship-rich environments include adults who enable a "transgenerational capacity for long-term sustainable critical hope" (Duncan-Andrade, 2009: 182) by engaging with youth in the struggle to challenge social injustice and, in this way, offer them a measure of control over those environments (Debold, *et al.*, 1999; Ginwright, 2015).

In 2015, Cobscook hired a project director for TREE and the research-practice partnership (RPP) between Colby College, the University of Maine, and Cobscook Institute's TREE division was formed. Informed by recent scholarship, and the work of other practitioners around the country (in particular, the work of Pam Cantor [2016] and Turnaround for Children) the RPP's task was to give shape to the vision that had emerged out of the two years of cross-sector conversations of the stakeholders. The RPP team embarked on a series of county-wide community listening sessions to more broadly inform the design of a model.

The TREE RPP's work proceeded from several strengths-based assumptions as indicated below:

1. Rural communities can be powerful allies in creating healthy ecologies for youth, and communities already engage in many practices that support positive youth development.

2. Teachers are knowledgeable professionals doing their best within a context of fiscal constraints and accountability policies designed for larger school systems; skill development should build on personal experiences and challenge kindly.
3. Service delivery should focus on amplifying community and school assets while identifying ways to overcome challenges fostered by distance, poverty and associated economic marginalization, and structural or historical racism.
4. Highly skilled individuals with strong community relationships and the ability to bridge between communities, families, and educators exist in every rural community. These individuals possess unique, localized expertise that can be augmented and leveraged to bolster the sustenance of healthy developmental ecologies for youth.

The work of the TREE RPP team evolved over several phases:

1. eliciting school-based stakeholders visions on the resources and services they need to address childhood adversity, trauma, and poverty within their work;
2. a six-month design process that included a national best practice search, review of literature, analysis of the community listening data, and ultimately a collabouratively designed model of practice;
3. a half-year pilot programme that included regular developmental evaluation; and
4. a fully implemented multi-year model of trauma-responsive and equitable educational practice.

TREE in Practice

The TREE pilot project was conducted in two under-resourced rural Maine elementary schools during 2017-21. TREE's goal was to address the predictable and recurring barriers to healthy youth development and learning that exist in schools and communities facing high levels of adversity, stress, and trauma by providing relationship-rich ecologies that support the development of the whole child. TREE's whole-child, student-empowered, and equity-centred approach ensures that all students and families have access to the same resources and opportunities, children have a voice in their own healing, and teachers and administrators have the training, coaching, and support necessary to address adversity, stress, and trauma (Brown, Biddle, & Tappan, 2022b).

TREE's work was guided by four key understandings:

1. Chronic adversity, stress, and trauma are not just individual mental health issues for which families are solely responsible. These are also the result of systemic conditions and structural inequities that disproportionately affect certain populations and geographic areas.
2. Student success and community vitality in regions impacted by serious and entrenched challenges are best restored through thoughtful, informed, and committed action on the part of all members of a community in partnership with students, teachers, and families.
3. Trauma-responsive and equitable practices centre student voice and empowerment. Children and youth engaged in genuine relationships with adults and considered partners in their own healing are more resilient and better able to cope with the impacts of trauma.
4. A genuinely trauma-responsive climate is best achieved through engaging youth as full and active participants in school and community transformation. Relationship-rich environments include adults who enable hope by offering children and youth power and control, engaging with them in the struggle to challenge hurt and injustice, and helping them to identify conditions and experiences within which they can and will thrive (Brown, Biddle, & Tappan, 2022b).

TREE's trauma-responsive approach to educational practice begins with a commitment to equity, to providing fair and just access to resources and opportunities that enable students to learn, grow, succeed, and thrive, in school and beyond. Focusing on equity means asking "Who isn't thriving?", "What historic or current policies—in school and out of school—contribute to inequities?", and "What will it take for that to change?". It also means providing specific, targeted supports to those with access to fewer opportunities and resources. Consequently, this entailed establishing a school-based food pantry and a coat and boot closet (Maine is cold and snowy through much of the school year!), and expanding in-school mental health services. As such, equity and its corollary, increased voice and empowerment, require a redistribution of access and opportunity, rather than a mitigation or an add-on.

Student-Empowered Social-Emotional Learning

Most importantly, TREE project was grounded in the understanding that developing and sustaining authentic relationships with children is the best way to establish a trauma-responsive school culture. To do so, however, requires time, energy, and will power. Adults must genuinely listen to students, trust them as experts in their own experience, and engage them as full and active partners in their learning, and, ultimately, in school and community transformation. Therefore, if promoting agency, control, and empowerment is critical to addressing and mitigating adversity, stress, and trauma, educators must create opportunities for student voice, engagement, and meaningful participation (Biddle, Brown, & Tappan, 2022a, 2022b).

The TREE team worked with teachers and school staff to develop a common understanding of the role that voice and empowerment play in trauma-responsive schooling. This led to a set of school-wide practices designed to engage children around meaningful aspects of their lives, to provide opportunities to share what they love and want from school, and to encourage them to speak about and explore what feels difficult or unfair. We describe two of these practices, below: "Somedays" and "microadventures" (Brown, Biddle, & Tappan, 2022a, 2022b).

Somedays

TREE started with a low-effort, high-impact activity called "Somedays" (Preble & Gordon, 2011). Every student and teacher in the TREE partner schools completed this sentence: "Someday in school, I would like to ________." The responses were collected and the TREE team worked with teachers and staff to make sure that each and every student's "Someday wish" came true.

The Someday wishes were, by and large, modest and achievable. One student, a fourth grader, wanted to have recess with her second-grade cousin whose lunch schedule was different from hers. A third grader wanted everyone in his class to start the new quarter with a 100 already in the grade book, so they could all feel successful for one day. Another student wanted to have his mother read a book in Spanish while he translated for the rest of the class. Teachers were able to join in too: one asked for a compliment day where people left nice notes for one another; another teacher wished to leave school a bit early one day to be able to meet her son at the bus stop (Biddle, Tappan, & Brown, 2022).

As Someday wishes began to come true, enthusiasm rippled through the school. Whether their requests were simple or ambitious, students became mini rock stars on their Someday, each one at the centre of something fun and unique. Offering an opportunity to voice their desires enabled every child and adult to share a little bit more of themselves, what they liked, what they valued, what they were good at. With their voices heard, children, some for the very first time, experienced a sense of their own power to impact the school.

Somedays also had a wider impact. Teachers' views of children changed, relationships deepened, and families reappraised the social boundaries (often experienced as barriers) between home and school. "What I like about Somedays", a fifth-grade girl said, "is that you can trust that yours will come true. Let's say you don't really like a teacher and you don't really trust them, and then they make your Someday come true—and it's like, I can sort of trust these people". A fourth-grade boy loved Somedays, "because they put everybody in a happy mood if they just had a rough day". A mother of three children said, "Our school has always been a homey place. Now it feels more . . . it's more electrified". (Brown, Biddle, & Tappan, 2022b)

Microadventures

When the TREE team asked students what they would change about their school to make it better, again and again, they heard versions of the same answer: more outdoor time together, more recess, more movement. In response, the team brainstormed ways to incorporate more physical activity and outdoor time into the school day. In the vernacular of the outdoor education field, "microadventures" are small, low-cost, and easy-to-run expeditions. Ultimately, the TREE team worked with students and teachers, and joined with a local outdoor school to adapt this idea and build it into the curriculum (Brown & Flaumenhaft, 2019; Brown, Biddle, & Tappan, 2022a, 2022b).

Student-initiated Somedays often led to microadventures that highlighted children's interests, skills, and abilities. As a parent of a third-grade boy explained:

> He has trouble at school just staying focused on basic things and he gets very frustrated. And like he just shuts down. . . . He liked the [microadventure] day that they built the shelters. He said that was awesome. The teachers are like, "We just can't get over how this kid can be such a leader outside of the classroom, whereas in the classroom he's quiet and reserved, and not sure of himself." But he's an outdoor boy. Yeah . . . I feel like sometimes he's untapped on the potential that he has.

It's the way microadventures ensure equitable access to non-material resources that moved the principal of one of our partner schools to tears. Initiating and taking part in outdoor learning, she says, "makes students feel wanted and whole, an involved part of something bigger than themselves. It is building the happiness of students who come to school with something to look forward to". She links happiness to the capacity for every student

> to access their learning lives at school, and be the kind of students or people they want to be. Kids are learning more about themselves. That's a trust. They are learning to trust that they are going to be taken care of and that they can take care of themselves even better. (Brown, Biddle, & Tappan, 2022b)

One of the unique successes of the TREE project was thus a focus on "student-empowered social-emotional learning" (SESEL). SESEL extends social-emotional learning (SEL) to include opportunities for elementary school students to develop social and emotional competencies and skills by initiating personally meaningful educational experiences, working on curriculum development, and improving the social climate in genuine partnership with both peers and adults. Both Somedays and microadventures, via team-building and collective problem-solving, became a consistent and effective way to enable and promote SESEL (Brown, Biddle, & Tappan, 2022a, 2022b).

Opportunities for students to share their thoughts and feelings, to voice their interests, desires, and concerns, and to speak for themselves led to several important outcomes over the three-year span of the TREE pilot project—chronic absenteeism decreased, standardized test scores increased, and school climate improved. Students reported at much higher rates that they felt listened to by the adults around them, that they felt safe, and that they mattered (Brown, Biddle, & Tappan, 2022b). TREE brought about positive changes within the pilot schools and the communities they are a part of that we had only hoped for decades of entrenched and chronic failure. It offers a roadmap for building towards enduring improvements from within our communities.

TREE and the UN's SDGs

Although the TREE project was not initially conceived with the

SDGs in mind, it harbours the immense potential to contribute to these global goals significantly. By aligning the project with the SDGs, we can amplify TREE's impact and pave the way for a more sustainable future in communities around the earth.

The seventeen SDGs constitute a comprehensive framework that tackles the most urgent issues of our era. As an educational initiative, the TREE project aligns with SDG-4, "Quality Education". It also intersects with sub-targets, such as 4.5, "Eliminate all discrimination in education", and 4.3, 4.4, and 4.6, which focus on equal access to vocational and higher education, workplace skills, and literacy and numeracy. By directly empowering students, the TREE project not only aids in student and school academic success, but also contributes to the broader goals of the SDGs.

The SDGs are an interconnected body of issues that have been extensively researched and documented worldwide. The Commission of the European Union, through its Joint Research Center (JRC), plays a crucial role in this, providing independent, evidence-based knowledge to support policy development. The JRC's research, available as an online tool at https://knowsdgs.jrc.ec.europa.eu/interlinkages/targets, demonstrates how the SDG targets are interconnected. It further enhances the credibility of the TREE project's alignment with the SDGs.

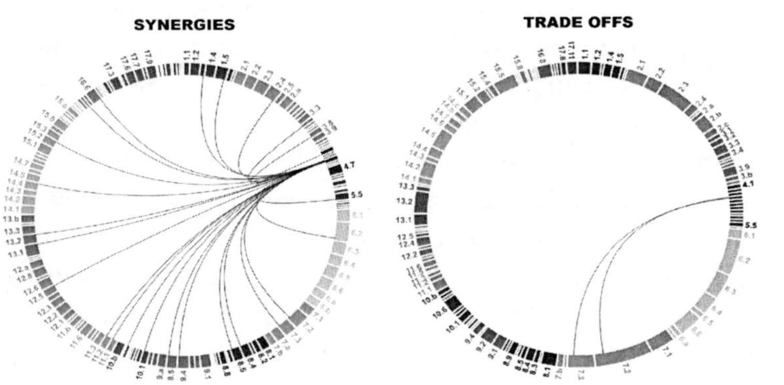

Fig. 5.1: SDG Target 4.4 Interlinkages

Here, you see the graphic representation that shows the synergies and trade-offs related to SDG target 4.4, which relates to "youth and adults who have relevant skills, including technical and vocational, for employment, decent jobs, and entrepreneurship". There is research showing two issues of trade-offs when the issues related to target 4.4 are improved and both of them relate to SDG-7, "Affordable and Clean Energy". The research shows that fulfilment of target 4.4 leads to more consumption of electricity, and when that happens through more use of non-renewable energy, then it becomes more difficult to live up to the commitments in SDG-7. Otherwise, the JRC points to twenty-seven targets where the fulfilment of target 4.4 leads to synergies and improvement—from Goal 1, targets 1.3 and 1.5 that relate to social protection systems as well as resilience concerning disasters to Goal 16, targets 16.4 and 16.6 that relate to diminishing illegal arms trade, organized crime and effective, accountable and transparent institutions.

The TREE project expands the concept of social-emotional learning (SEL) by introducing the student's empowerment in this—therefore, self-empowered SEL or SESEL (Brown, Biddle, & Tappan, 2022a, 2022b). This reinforces the recognition of the uniqueness of each student, which is much needed in our modern hyper-complex society, where mass-produced products, including cultural products, dominate daily lives and objectify people. The introduction of the SDGs can contribute with further dimensions to the learning process and the student's life and empowerment.

By understanding our efforts within the framework of the SDGs, we open ourselves and our communities to a discussion of our world and society, including the relations between nature and human culture. This opens to a renewed reflection on the rationale of schooling, discussions among the students about the reasons for going to school, and an understanding of and appreciation for the broad range of subjects present in the school. It supports conditions within which the relevance of schools can be mutually appreciated and our respective expectations and responsibilities can be embraced.

Additionally, the SDGs encourage individual and collective thought processes around the challenges present within the community and invite perspectives, creative thinking, and collective action for future innovation and development.

Our Contribution to this Collection: A Conclusion and a Beginning

The SDGs were adopted in 2015 by the United Nations, unanimously, by all 193 member countries. This happened after three years of negotiation that also involved NGOs, transnational companies, and representatives of the world religions. They are a comprehensive agenda for positive change that has legitimacy coming from the support of the entire world.

A gift of being actively linked with the UN is the opportunity to understand one's homeplace or circumstance within the context of the great diversity of "homeplaces" and circumstances around the planet. TREE project emerged in an extremely rural (13 people per square mile) and poor region. Poverty and rurality, with its associated isolation and unyielding stress and trauma, conspire creating entrenched conditions that seem insurmountable. The conditions alone cause tensions and behaviours that too often expand the problems, and the toll mounts in personal, social, and ecological compromise. The successes researched, documented, and realized by the TREE RPP, and as experienced within its partner schools and communities, could have been all but swallowed by COVID-19 which crested just as the project was drawing to a conclusion. Trauma and chaos engulfed every level of society including within our rural communities. As we all re-emerge from COVID-19 into a changed landscape, we are grateful to the visionary global thinkers who have invited articles like this one that bring forth the stories from around the world of community initiatives like TREE. This invitation helps us connect our efforts and the real and measurable gains we have made to the globally-adopted SDGs, and, through that overarching commitment, to connect with you in your community. We honour our gains by sharing with one another.

And so, a new chapter begins for us, and, we hope, for you. Here in Washington County Maine, in North America, Cobscook Institute, in partnership with the Rural Vitality Lab, has embarked on building upon the successes and lessons learned with the initial TREE effort. We invite your inquiry and partnership in adapting this effective model to be of service to you in your community. And, we look forward to learning from and with you about your visionary responses that also contribute to addressing those essential SDGs that have been adopted by all of our nations. Together we can set the roots of these initiatives in our home communities and grow within and through them into the health and well-being we have envisioned for ourselves and one another.

Keywords

Education, innovation, trauma-responsive, equitable, student-empowered, local initiative, local/global, SDGS, learning environments, community.

REFERENCES

Biddle, C., L.M. Brown & M. Tappan (2022). "Letting Student Voice Lead the Way." *Educational Leadership, 79*(9).

Biddle, C., M. Tappan & L.M. Brown (2022, April). "Schools Should Make Students' Wishes come true. Here's How." *Education Week.*

Brown, L.M., C. Biddle, & M. Tappan (2022a). "Student-led SEL." *Educational Leadership, 80*(3).

Brown, L.M., C. Biddle, & M. Tappan (2022b). *Trauma-responsive Schooling: Centering Student Voice and Healing.* Cambridge, MA: Harvard Education Press.

Brown, L.M. & J. Flaumenhaft (2019). "Student-empowered Curricular Change as Trauma Informed Practice." *Phi Delta Kappan, 100*(6): 13-19.

Cantor, P. (2016, November 22). *The Science of Adversity.* [Video File: Turnaround for Children]. Retrieved from https://www.youtube.com/watch?v=SNZvMZkzg28

Cantor, P., D. Osher, J. Berg, L. Steyer & T. Rose (2018). "Malleability, Plasticity, and Individuality: How Children Learn and Develop in Context." *Journal of Applied Developmental Science,* doi: 10.1080/10888691.2017.1398649

Chronholm, P., C. Forke, R. Wade, M. Bair-Merritt, M. Davis, M. Harkins-Schwarz, L. Pachter & J. Fein (2015). "Adverse Childhood Experiences: Expanding the Concept of Adversity." *American Journal of Preventive Medicine, 49*(3): 354-61.

Debold, E., L.M. Brown, S. Weseen & G.K. Brookins (1999). "Cultivating Hardiness Zones for Adolescent Girls: A Reconceptualization of Resilience in Relationships with Caring Adults." In N. Johnson, M. Roberts, & J. Worell (Eds.), *Beyond Appearances: A New Look at Adolescent Girls.* Washington, DC: American Psychological Association.

Duncan-Andrade, J. (2009). "Note to Educators: Hope Required when Growing Roses in Concrete." *Harvard Education Review. 79*(2): 181-94.

Erle, J. (2020). *Sustainable Development Goals: Dialogue Game for Learning and Action,* IAED, Copenhagen.

Franke, H. (2014). "Toxic Stress: Effects, Prevention, and Treatment." *Children* (Basel) *1*: 390-402.

Garbarino, J. (1995). *Raising Children in a Socially Toxic Environment.* San Francisco: Jossey-Bass.

Ginwright, S.A. (2015). *Hope and Healing in Urban Education: How Urban Activists and Teachers are Reclaiming Matters of the Heart.* New York: Routledge.

National Scientific Council on the Developing Child (2004). *Young Children Develop in An Environment of Relationships:* Working paper No. 1. Retrieved from www.developingchild.harvard.edu.

Preble, W. & R. Gordon (2011). *Transforming School Climate and Learning: Beyond Bullying and Compliance.* Thousand Oaks, CA: Corwin.

Souers, K. & P. Hall (2016). *Fostering Resilient Learners: Strategies for Creating a Trauma-Sensitive Classroom.* ACSD.

https://knowsdgs.jrc.ec.europa.eu/interlinkages

https://sdgs.un.org/goals

https://sustainable.iaed.info/fmi/webd/sdg_reports

6

LAKAS High School in the Philippines

Advancing Indigenous People's Education Toward Sustainable Development

May Rendon-Cinco

Advancing indigenous people's education contributes greatly to break the historic discrimination, marginalization, and inequalities experienced by indigenous people. Providing them context-based basic literacy and leadership formation, equal opportunity to quality and culture-sensitive formal education and alternative learning systems, recognizing, and respecting their indigenous knowledge systems and practices are fundamentals to enhance their full potentials and uplift their self-esteem.

As the education system discriminates and marginalize the indigenous people, advancing indigenous people's education is a pathway to empower them. This was shown in the experience of the Aeta, the indigenous people around Mt. Pinatubo in the Philippines. Through the collective effort of their elders and leaders of their organization called LAKAS, they were able to negotiate with the government's Department of Education to build their own school which they named LAKAS High School (LHS). LHS becomes an institution of mainstreaming the Aeta knowledge systems and practices in the basic formal education and at the same time, sustaining other forms and modes of learning to enrich their life and environment (principally their ancestral domain) that meet the development of the Aeta at present without compromising the needs of the future generation of their tribe.

Indigenous People, Aeta, and LAKAS

Out of 109,035,343 (about 110 million) Filipinos,[1] an estimated 14-17 million are indigenous people in the Philippines. They belong to 110 ethno-linguistic groups and have retained much of their traditional, pre-colonial culture, social institutions and livelihood practices.[2] Generally, they live in geographically isolated areas with lack of access to basic social services and few opportunities for mainstream economic activities, education, and political participation. Commercially valuable natural resources such as minerals, forests and rivers can be found primarily in their areas, making them continuously vulnerable to mining, development aggression, and land grabbing that displaced them and worst loss of their ancestral domain.[3]

Among these indigenous peoples are the Aeta who are considered to be the First People in the Philippines.[4] In 2015, the Aeta numbered 57,707 and lived mostly around near Mount Pinatubo in Zambales Province in the central part of Luzon Island of the Philippines.[5] This is where LAKAS was founded and organized on 1 March 1982. LAKAS stands for *Lubos na Alyansa ng mga Katutubong Ayta sa Sambales* (literally translated as United Alliance of Aeta in Zambales) is an organization of Aeta children, youth, men, and women in Bihawo, Botolan, Zambales to preserve their culture, protect and develop their ancestral domain, and uphold their rights.

Historical Discrimination and Marginalization

Like any other indigenous people, Aeta has been subject to discrimination and marginalization for long years. Lowlanders (*unat* or people with straight hair) labelled and treated them as uncivilized, primitive, pagans, lazy, dirty, stupid, ugly because of dark skin and kinky hair, with tails like monkey, and many more because of their physical characteristics and colour. Lowlanders deceived them in pricing their farm produce since they do not know how to read, write, count and compute.

Aeta children and youth experienced bullying in school and most of them cannot bear it and suffer mental stress, hence, they were forced to quit formal schooling. This was substantiated in 2023 Youth Action Research conducted by LAKAS Kabataan in partnership with E-Net Philippines and ASPBAE entitled "Combating Racism and Identity-based Discrimination in Education", which concluded that,

> The verbal bullying of Ayta students frequently involves making offensive comments about their race as Aytas, as well as making fun of their curly hair and dark skin. They experienced symptoms of trauma because of the hurtful words, which results in stress, anxiety, low self-esteem, and long-term negative effects that affect them, such as dropping out of school and being reluctant to wear their traditional clothing.[6]

The school plays a role as institution of discrimination. Who are the teachers? Who are mostly the students? What is the content of the curriculum and learning materials? What is the methodology and language of teaching and assessment of learning? Majority of the teachers and students are non-Aeta. Curriculum, learning materials, methodology, and language of teaching and assessment of learning are uncontextualized to the condition and needs of Aeta. Access and equity to public education is a concern to achieve education for all. In 2016, only 2.4 million out of 5 million indigenous children were enrolled in Kindergarten to Grade 11.[7] Distance between home and school is another challenge in accessing education since the indigenous people lived in geographically isolated and disadvantaged areas.

Learning Journey of LAKAS

Education can be both the cause of and the potential cure for the loss of indigenous knowledge (UNESCO, 2009).[8] LAKAS chose the path of education as potential cure to the loss of indigenous knowledge. If education discriminates and marginalize the Aeta, education is also a means to empowerment them and achieve genuine development that is sustainable. The learning journey of LAKAS evolves from elders' generation to the present generation.

In partnership with the Franciscan Missionaries of Mary (FMM), a Basic Literacy Programme was launched upon the organization of LAKAS in 1982. They adopted the Paulo Freire learning philosophy, particularly the problem posting vs banking system as used in most formal education system. Current issue in the community is the subject to teach writing, reading, and counting using available indigenous materials around the learning environment. The community is the entire school.

The programme started teaching the forty-five elders and heads of families to read, write, and count using indigenous materials and community context.[9] Sessions were held where the learners are like in the *gasak* (rice fields), houses, under the trees, anywhere. They relate the teaching to everyday life activities and experiences like farming rice and root crops, backyard vegetable planting, cooking, etc. The programme lasted until 2014 when everyone in the community were able to read, write, and count. The immediate effect to the elders and heads of family is to free themselves from unfair trade practices in the low land and gained more reasonable income for their families. Learners claimed their self-confidence, self-esteem, and self-identity were strengthened that they can face and talk to different types of people and even people in authority.

From being learners, some of them became basic literacy teachers, the likes of the late Ben Jugatan and Carling Domulot who became also the chieftains of the tribe. Women like the late Josie Jugatan and still active Arel Domulot became teachers, too. Josie served also as Barangay (village) Health Worker (BHW). After years of experience in conducting basic literacy programme, they have manualized it and used it in giving training to other tribes in various parts of the country. Subsequently, their children turned out to be basic literacy teachers when the elders were busy with organizational matters.

Out of this experience, they valued education and continuing learning. LAKAS as an organization saved money from farming income and donations as scholarship fund to finance college education for at least one child of every family in their community who is willing to graduate and serve the community for a certain number of years. Others who dropped out of school because of discrimination had enrolled and finished elementary and secondary levels of basic education through the alternative learning system (ALS), a non-formal education programme of the Department of Education (DepEd) that deals with accreditation and equivalency (A&E). This is parallel to the formal education system in terms of providing basic education. Learners undergone functional literacy test to establish their level of knowledge and skills were provided with level-based learning materials, were required to attend learning sessions and to comply with individual or group learning activities and projects for ten months. After which, they are assessed to determine if they are ready to take an A&E examination given by DepEd during a particular period of the school year and if they are ready, they will be provided with review sessions. If they passed the A & E, they will receive certification from DepEd as graduates of basic education, whether elementary or secondary, based on their enrollment.

Alternative Learning System (ALS): The LAKAS Way

LAKAS was a service provider of ALS programme of the DepEd. As a service provider, their ALS project is recognized by DepEd and received financial support of P100,000 (about USD 1,700) for a ten-month implementation. Despite the minimal financial support LAKAS had obtained from government agency, they continued to serve as many learners as they could. But prior to this in 2003, LAKAS in partnership with Education for Life Foundation (ELF) and support from Ford Foundation had initiated a community-based ALS programme. ELF helped LAKAS to install the ALS programme, trained community facilitators, provided modules to learners, facilitation guide, and transportation support to facilitators, conducted facilitators' consultation and monitoring and evaluation to gauge the learning development of the learners. When funds are available, *lakbay-aral* (educational trips) were carried out.

They included *kuwentong buhay* (guided life story sharing) to bring about confidence and camaraderie among the learners as well as to determine the context why they stopped schooling and identify ways how they can help each other in studying. They developed additional modules that were not in DepEd modules but they needed it to give a boost to their roots and identity, protect the environment and ancestral domain, preserve indigenous lifestyle, promote self-determination, and uphold their rights. Elders and youth of LAKAS worked hand-in-hand as developers and writers to come up with modules on Indigenous People Rights Act (IPRA), customs and traditions, medical and healing practices, rituals, indigenous songs, dances, and musical instruments. These modules have been essential part of discussion during group learning sessions.

LAKAS produced more A&E passers that impressed the DepEd Division of Zambales. This can be attributed to the commitment of Aeta leaders and parents to tutor the learners anytime and anywhere, rapport of the learning facilitator with the learners because they belong in the same community, use of mother tongue in explaining the modules, and use of examples based on the community setting.

LAKAS and Folkschool (*Paaralang Bayan. Paaralang Buhay*)

In 1995, LAKAS and ELF partnered in the six-week residential All Aeta General Leadership Course (GLC), a leadership formation programme of ELF in its Philippine-Danish Folkschool project. This project aims to empower grassroots leaders in grassroots communities like the community of Aeta through continuing training and education using the learning philosophy of *mula sa buhay, tungo sa buhay* (from life, for life). Among the core modules in GLC were culture, Filipino psychology, presentation of self and idea (communication in public), negotiation, gender, conflict management, politics, economics, leadership, and empowerment. This formation consists of theoretical and practical applications in every module.

The Philippine-Danish Folkschool project is a product of the influences of Danish tradition of *folkeoplysning* and Philippines popular education. Ove Korsgaard wrote,

> The Nordic tradition of *folkeoplysning* (Denmark, Norway) or *folkbildning* (Sweden) is a form of adult education—"people's enlightenment"—linked to the emergence of democracy. Differing social, political, and cultural emphases attached to "folk"/"people" in various European languages have implications for the role of *folkeoplysning* in the development of a European democracy and a European citizenry. The term "people's enlightenment" (*folkeoplysning*) has been defined as different ways to create empowered citizens, to provide enlightenment on the people's culture, and to educate the under enlightened and marginalized.[10]

The tradition of popular education emerged evidently during the time of authoritarian rule in Philippine society to conscientize the deprived and oppressed people to fight for their rights to effect democratization from below. After the dictatorship regime was toppled down by people power revolution in 1986, popular education had focused to train leaders on how to engage with government that opened a democratic space for people participation. Context-Content-Method (CCM) framework guides the popular educators in providing trainings especially among the grassroots sectors—farmers, fisherfolks, urban poor settlers, among others. Based on the context of the learners, the content and method of specific module were developed and formulated that include its application at home, in the organization, and community where the learners belong.

LAKAS and ELF conducted more GLCs for other Aeta heads of the family, women, and youth and introduced the Distance Learning Programme (DLP) to first batches of GLCs as continuing education programme. DLP courses were about leadership and entrepreneurship, participatory local governance, and advocacy work. Experiences in DLP implementation helped Aeta in administering the ALS programme because both systems involved module development, and facilitation of individual learning and group sessions. To sustain the conduct of GLC, DLP and community-based ALS in the context of leadership formation, ELF did trainers' training and since then LAKAS continued this leadership formation programme.

ELF through its partnership with LO Vinterskolen 2004 and 2007 student exchange programme on democracy and cultural development, sent a number of Aeta leaders to LO Skolen in Denmark to share their folkschool initiatives and experience the *folkehojskole* life to gain more lessons on democratization, leadership and empowerment.

Synergy of Formal Basic Education and Leadership Formation Programme

Graduates of GLC formed an organization *Paaralang Bayan ng mga Ayta sa Zambales* (PBAZ) in which LAKAS has a great role and participation. They continue to conduct leadership and value formation trainings that emphasized the Aeta way of life in the multi-purpose hall inside the LAKAS community. Besides attending formal basic education children and youth were taught about the importance of culture, identity, and self-determination to keep their race/tribe. What were being taught were practised in the community like the wearing of traditional *bahag* (g-string) for boys and men, and *baheling* (dress) for girls and women, indigenous singing and dancing, *pag-aanito* (healing rituals), *dororo* (praying to ask the blessings of the sacred Apo Namalyari, the deity on Mt. Pinatubo), speaking and writing the Sambal language, traditional farming, among others.

When Mt. Pinatubo erupted on 15 June 1991, and *lahar* buried the community several times they were displaced in the ancestral land and moved twelve times to different evacuation centres holding on to each other together. When the authority told them to evacuate 5 km away, they will evacuate 10 km away to be safer. For a couple of years, they lived in resettlement area, held rituals, cultivated the land no matter how barren it was.

In 2010, they reclaimed their ancestral domain and restarted sustainable agriculture and livelihood projects. From a dead land because of *lahar*, they made it to a productive land again. To reclaim their ancestral domain, they wrote their family tree, customs traditions, medical and healing practices, rituals, traditional songs, dances and musical instruments, food, indigenous trees, plants, and animals, and made a transect map. Having basic literacy training and background in formal basic education, ALS, and leadership formation they did the documentation required by the National Commission on Indigenous People (NCIP) to reclaim their ancestral domain.

Practicum in the Communication and Negotiation modules helped them to claim projects from local government unit and local government agency like construction of concrete bridge from town centre to their village, nursery and greenhouse for their seedlings, farming facilities and warehouse to boost and protect their food production, and establishment of ram pump for the source of water.

Family Literacy and Intergenerational Learning

According to the UN Department of Economic and Social Affairs (DESA, 2016) many of the targets of the SDGs benefit from explicit and implicit family policies and programmes.[11] The families of Domulot and Jugatan had showcased the role of shared responsibility in promoting and advancing indigenous people education as a human right. Literacy as social skills for everyday life is a means of empowerment. Generating skills and knowledge from life experiences contribute to the dignity of the Aeta, provides greater participation in the community governance and labour market, and expand opportunities in life. The value of having education for sustainability and development was transferred to the next generation. The children of Domulot had become area coordinator for technical and vocational education and training, day care worker, and teacher in LHS. Likewise, the children of Jugatan were agriculturists who helped in the sustainable farming of LAKAS, teachers in LHS, and paralegal workers that provide training on legal matters how to protect their rights as indigenous people.

The Birth of LAKAS High School: Fulfilment of a Dream

LAKAS leaders and elders led by the late Carlito "Carling" Domulot negotiated with the DepEd and local government of Zambales to establish its High School within the LAKAS community. LHS was established in June 2013. Through DepEd Order No. 71 s. 2003, LHS was approved as a newly established school in the Division of Zambales with Government Permit No. 043 series of 2013. Due to the perseverance of elders and leaders, LAKAS track record in implementing Basic Literacy and ALS programmes, and presence of Aeta graduates with bachelor's in education, their persistent dream of having a high school of their own was fulfilled.

LHS Curriculum adopted the Junior and Senior High School curriculum of DepEd (K-12) and the Indigenous Knowledge Systems and Practices (IKSP) that include Indigenous People's Rights, Sustainable Agriculture, Aeta Customs & Traditions, Aeta Dances, Music and Sports, Survival Skills, and observation and celebration of the National Indigenous People's Day. While there were structures and classrooms, the entire LAKAS community is the school and the natural resources around are their learning materials bearing in mind that the learning system they established and maintained is within the context of sustainable development of their ancestral domain and culture.

LHS Administration and Faculty are composed of LAKAS leaders, Aeta teachers, and DepEd teachers with ten Junior High teachers, three Senior High teachers, and two IKSP Facilitators.[12] Leaders of LAKAS do voluntary teaching on Aeta rights, sustainable agriculture, and customs and traditions. LHS serves not only the Aeta in the community but also non-Aeta children and youth in the nearby communities.

Enrollment of LHS increased throughout the school years as indicated below:[13]

School Year	Male	Female	Total
2013-14	13	15	28
2014-15	21	24	45
2015-16	48	39	87
2016-17	57	65	122
2017-18	83	96	179
2018-19	93	115	208
2019-20	93	133	226

LHS continued to operate during pandemic COVID-19 observing proper health protocols, utilizing herbal, and indigenous medicines, sustaining organic farming, and home visits to learners. From the sharing of leaders, there has been no report of COVID-19 incidents inside the LAKAS community.

They developed manuals on orthography to keep the Sambal language alive in proper norms of spelling, hyphenation, capitalization, word breaks, emphasis, and punctuation. They also documented and manualized their indigenous seeds to protect and preserve it which was entitled, *Pamatobo-an nin Katotoban Kayo*.

Continuing Advocacy of LAKAS

Indigenous elders and local facilitators who are tapped as resource persons in the integration of indigenous learning into the high school must also be part of the education budget as a recognition of their significant role. Maintenance and Other Operating Expenses for the high school should be allocated with higher funds.

The DepEd must ensure that the development of teachers in the IP education programme is continuing in formal education and alternative learning systems. The DepEd must ensure that indigenous people education is integral to sustaining natural systems and ecosystem and thus sustainable agriculture and environment-resilient activities like reforestation are being taught and practised in the high school. The conduct of research and documentation of the IKSPs must be done as part of learning materials, knowledge management, and references for indigenous people education advocacy.

Indigenous People Education and Sustainable Development

The LAKAS learning journey and the establishment and sustaining the LAKAS High School enhance rootedness and identity, protect and care for ancestral domain, nurture and cultivate indigenous way of life, enhance the well-being of the individual and community, and uphold self-determination are evident contributions to attain the SDGs particularly the SDG-4 (Ensure inclusive and equitable quality education and promote lifelong learning opportunities for all) and most of its targets which include free primary and secondary education, increase the number of people with relevant skills for financial success, eliminate all discrimination in education, and build and upgrade inclusive and safe schools.

To quote UNESCO statement during the transition period from Millennium Development Goals (MDGs) to SDGs, it states: "Sustainable development begins with education".[14]

Conclusion

The development of LAKAS education initiatives has gone a long way—from providing basic literacy to establishing a high school of their own—and can be achieved through negotiation and progressive engagement with government as the duty bearer. The Aeta of LAKAS has showcased comprehensive, contextualized, and culture-sensitive education and learning systems and practices. Sustaining these systems and practices, and continuing their advocacies to advance indigenous people education is a practice of making the SDGs specifically on education a reality on the ground that is grassroots initiated in collabouration with the government.

Keywords

Indigenous people, LAKAS, alternative learning system, folk school, people's enlightenment.

NOTES

1. *2020 Census of Population and Housing*, Philippine Statistic Authority (PSA), https://psa.gov.ph/statistics/population-and-housing/node/164786
2. *Fast Facts: Indigenous Peoples in the Philippines*, United Nations Development Programme (UNDP), 24 July 2013, https://www.undp.org/philippines/publications/fast-facts-indigenous-peoples-philippines
3. *The Indigenous World 2022: Philippines, IWGIA*, https://www.iwgia.org/en/philippines/4656-iw-2022-philippines.html
4. *Early History of the Philippines*, https://factsanddetails.com/southeast-asia/Philippines/sub5_6a/entry-3832.html
5. *Minority Population Analysis: The Aeta of the Philippines, 2020*, Olivier Serrat, https://www.researchgate.net/publication/344467822_Minority_Population_Analysis_The_Aeta_of_the_Philippines
6. *2023 Lubos na Alyansa ng mga Katutubong Ayta sa Sambales (LAKAS) Youth-led Action Research*, https://enetphil.org.ph/?p=2242
7. *Senator Loren Legarda Privilege Speech on Indigenous Children*, 18 October 2016, Senate Session Hall, http://legacy.senate.gov.ph/press_release/2016/1018_legarda2.asp
8. *Indigenous Knowledge and Implications for Sustainable Development*, https://unesdoc.unesco.org/ark:/48223/pf0000245623
9. *Story of Change: The Power of Being the Narrator,* Education Out Loud, https://educationoutloud.org/story-change-power-being-narrator
10. *A European Demos?: The Nordic Adult Education Tradition—Folkeoplysning: Faces a Challenge,* Comparative Education, v36 n1 p 7-16, February 2002, Korsgaard, Ove, https://eric.ed.gov/?id=EJ639820
11. *2016 International Day of Families*, United Nations Department of Economic and Social Affairs, Family, https://www.un.org/development/desa/family/international-day-of-families/2016idf.html

12. *Establishing LAKAS High School: Baseline Data Presentation*, Research Forum on Inclusive Education, 3 December 2019, Carol Saribay, IPEd Focal Person, LAKAS High School, https://pidswebs.pids.gov.ph/CDN/EVENTS/saribay_ppt_lakas_hs_ie_research_forum_carol_saribay_presenter_2.pdf
13. *Ibid.*
14. *UNESCO: Sustainable Development Begins with Education*, EFA GMR, https://en.unesco.org/gem-report/sites/default/files/UNGA_PR_en.pdf

7

Accessibility and Affordability of Mental Health Services in India

Heenakshi Bhansali, Shamim Mohammad, and *Devashree Desai*

The Sustainable Development Goals (SDGs) are global blueprints that, by 2030, aim to achieve peace and prosperity for both people and the environment. To reduce poverty and all forms of deprivation, the countries that are industrialized and developing, are urgently urged to unite in an international collabouration guided by the seventeen SDGs. This will entail coordinated measures to combat climate change, protect our forests and oceans, improve health and education, lessen inequality, and promote economic growth.[1]

According to the WHO, health is defined as "a state of complete physical, mental, and social well-being and not merely the absence of disease or infirmity". This definition is a broad one, covering socio-economic and psychological determinants of health as well apart from biogenic factors as is the case with the biogenic model of health.[2]

The agenda of the SDGs aims at inclusion and health equity. It is characterized as the absence of health disparities that can be reasonably prevented. The socio-economic determinants such as availability and affordability of food, nutrition, education, income, water, sanitation, decent work, health care, employment, built and natural environment need to be assessed and monitored regularly to bring about health equities.[3]

The WHO defines mental health as "a state of mental well-being known as mental health makes it possible for people to manage life's stressors, reach their full potential, learn and work effectively, and contribute back to their communities". Mental wellness is more than absence of mental illness. Each person has a unique experience, and it ranges in difficulty and distress throughout a complex continuum. Mental health challenges encompass a wide range of mental states and diseases, including psychosocial disabilities and mental disorders, that are linked to substantial suffering, impaired functioning, or a risk of self-harm. The mental health agenda under the SDGs are shown in the Table 7.1 below.

Table 7.1: Mental Health Related SDGs Data and Gaps Globally

SDG	Indicator Topic	Country Data Available	Disaggregation	Source Estimates
3.4.2	Suicide Mortality Rate	Fair	Poor	WHO
3.5.1	Treatment Substance Abuse Disorder	Poor	Poor	UNODC/ WHO
3.5.2	Harmful Use of Alcohol	Fair	Poor	WHO
16.1	Homicide	Fair	Fair	WHO

Mental health problems and their connections with that of developmental goals have been acknowledged worldwide; Depression is a major contributor to disability and suicide related mortalities are all time high. People with mental conditions face severe discrimination, stigma, and human rights violations. Quality health care access and good treatment remains extremely low.[4] Mental health and substance abuse find their place under the

SDG-3, Goal 3.4 too which states "to cut down mortalities by 1/3rd owing to non-communicable diseases through prevention, promotion, and mental health well-being". The SDGs strongly advocate for addressing mental health issues through multi-pronged strategies with utmost urgency.[5] In order to ensure access to mental health care, there is a need to incorporate mental health services with mainstream medical care. This will lead to easy access to services, enhanced chances of recovery and better social integration of the people living with mental illnesses.[6]

There is a high degree of co-morbidities between mental health conditions such as anxiety or depression with that of the non-communicable diseases (NCDs) such as cardiovascular diseases (CVDs), diabetes, cancer, substance abuse, etc. The children and adolescents are affected with mental disorders at disproportionately high level, the situation gets complicated due to lack of knowledge, stigma, and discrimination. These mental health conditions are treatable, many in primary care by doctors (psychiatrists), clinical psychologists, psychiatric social workers, health workers, and community mental health nurses, etc. WHO (2018) reported that the governments across the globe spend less than 2 per cent of their health care expenditure on mental health, despite the fact that the mental health morbidity is very high, around 1 billion people suffer from mental health disorders or diseases. The mental health treatment is beyond reach across the globe. The COVID-19 pandemic has exacerbated the crisis further.[7]

The access to treatment remains extremely low and diagnosis rates remain dismal even in high income categories (HICs). Even 50 per cent of people suffering from depression do not get access to treatment. The importance, magnitude of the problem, and access to treatment for mental health remains unaddressed despite the fact that its importance is reflected in several policy documents of the WHO and the UN such as Mental Health Action Plan of the WHO and UN's SDGs. These documents also emphasize the importance of the integration of mental health care services into primary health care with a view to make these services accessible and affordable to the public at large.

Accessibility of Mental Health Services

WHO (2001) reported that one out of four families are likely to have at least one member with a mental or behavioural disorder. These families suffer the negative impact and discrimination due to myths, stigma, and poor awareness about mental illness. The majority of them remain untreated because of lack of treatment accessibility and shortage of specialized professionals.[8]

In 1982, the Government of India launched the National Mental Health Programme (NMHP), which was followed in 1996 by the District Mental Health Programme (DMHP), with a vision to promote mental health, destigmatization, desegregation, and prevention of mental illnesses.[9]

Urban vs. Rural Disparities

Urban and rural disparities in mental health services in India have been a significant concern due to various socio-economic factors affecting access and utilization of mental health care. There exists a significant gap in the accessibility of mental health services. Urban centres generally have more mental health facilities including clinics and hospitals, trained professionals, and resources compared to rural regions. However, even in urban areas, accessibility can be limited due to factors such as infrastructure challenges, high costs, stigma, lack of awareness, and, socio-economic disparities. National Mental Health Survey of India (2015-16) has shown that urban areas generally have better access to mental health facilities in comparison to rural areas.[10]

Rural areas face numerous challenges, including lack of infrastructure, a low number of trained professionals, and lesser awareness about mental health issues. Additionally, rural population often struggle with limited transportation options, making it difficult to access services available in urban centres.

While the majority of psychiatrists, psychologists, and counsellors work in urban areas, rural residents often lack access to these professionals. The availability of mental health services is still lower in rural than in urban areas, even if mental health problems are more common there. This is due to various barriers such as geographical distance, cost, and lack of culturally appropriate services.[11]

In order to fill these gaps, a thorough strategy is needed, involving policy interventions, increased investment in mental health infrastructure in rural areas, destigmatization campaigns, and innovative strategies to improve access to and utilization of mental health services among rural populations in India.

Barriers to Accessibility

Access to mental health services in India faces numerous barriers, leading to significant disparities in availability and utilization. These barriers can include financial constraints particularly among low-income populations, lack of transportation, lengthy appointment wait times along with problems in accessing the health-care system. Stigma surrounding mental illness remains prevalent, leading many to avoid seeking treatment due to fear of discrimination. Another factor in the underutilization of resources is not enough knowledge of mental health problems and the services that are accessible.[12] These barriers, rooted in socio-economic, cultural, and systemic factors, present challenges at various levels, hindering individuals from seeking and receiving appropriate mental health care.

National Mental Health Survey of India (2015-16) highlights a severe shortage of mental health professionals, especially in rural areas. A significant limited supply of mental health specialists exists in India, particularly in rural regions, according to the National Mental Health Survey of India (2015-16). India has a psychiatrist-population ratio well below the recommended norms set by the World Health Organization (WHO). This shortage results in limited access to specialized care, particularly in remote and rural regions, where the majority of the population resides.[13]

Stigma

Seeking help remains significantly hindered by the stigma associated with mental illness. In both urban and rural areas, individuals may be self-conscious about choosing to seek mental health treatment due to fear of judgement or discrimination from their communities. Studies indicate pervasive stigma and discrimination associated with mental illnesses in Indian society. According to the *Indian Journal of Psychiatry*, stigma continues to be a major obstacle to actions that involve seeking help. Fear of social ostracism and discrimination discourages individuals from acknowledging their mental health issues and seeking professional assistance. This stigma is often more pronounced in rural areas due to traditional beliefs and lack of awareness.

Lack of Awareness

Surveys reveal low levels of mental health literacy among the general population in India. Many individuals lack awareness about common mental health conditions, available treatments, and the importance of seeking timely help. Many people, particularly in rural locations, might not be aware of the mental health services that are accessible to them may not be conscious of the available mental health resources or might not be able to identify the symptoms and indicators of mental illness. This lack of awareness may hinder people from getting support until their symptoms become severe. Limited awareness contributes to delays in seeking treatment, as well as reliance on alternative healing practices or self-medication, which may not be effective or safe.

Infrastructure Challenges

Rural areas often face infrastructure challenges that can impact the delivery of mental health services. These challenges may include limited internet access, shortage of health-care facilities, and lack of mental health professionals willing to work in rural areas. Limited government investment results in insufficient infrastructure, workforce shortages, and inadequate support for community-based mental health programmes, impeding efforts to improve accessibility and quality of care.[14]

Addressing these disparities and barriers to accessibility has to take a holistic strategy, increasing funds for mental health care among other things in under-served areas, improving infrastructure in rural areas to support the delivery of mental health services, implementing telehealth initiatives to reach rural population, raising awareness and reducing stigma through education and community outreach programmes. Furthermore, providing mental health experts with the necessary training and incentives to work in remote locations can assist guarantee that residents of these communities have access to the care they require. In order to overcome these obstacles, a multifaceted strategy including community involvement, government actions, capacity-building initiatives, and public awareness campaigns. India can advance towards a more inclusive and equitable mental health-care system in rural areas by tackling these issues.

Affordability of Mental Health Services: Socio-economic Disparities

The concept of "socio-economic status" refers to the absolute or relative levels of wealth that are associated with a person, organization, or country. These include financial assets, authority, and position. It is a multifaceted idea that takes into account a lot of factors, such as income, education, and employment status. In India, poverty and socio-economic inequality are major contributors to the onset and progression of mental health illnesses.[15] Socio-economic factors affect people's capacity to control their stress, engage in healthy activities, and pay for housing and medical care. For example, earning money through employment enables one to cover costs for housing, food, health care, child care, education, and other essentials. Living in a stressful environment, having unstable finances, and having little opportunity for professional growth all raise psychological distress and the likelihood of mental health issues.[16] There is a decreased likelihood of high-quality health care being available in lower-income regions. The NMHS survey 2016, found that there is a higher prevalence of one or more mental problems in those from lower income classes.[17]

Financial Accessibility

As to the findings of a 2016 study carried out by the National Institute of Mental Health and Neurosciences, insufficient infrastructure and capacity prevent over 80 per cent of Indians from obtaining therapy. A WHO study indicates that, in India, there are approximately 0.29 psychiatrists and 0.07 psychologists per 1,00,000 people, while the median for low and middle-income nations is 0.3–0.5 and for high-income countries is 9-11 per 1,00,000 people. Furthermore, India has a mere 1.43 hospital beds available per 1,00,000 people for mental health patients, while the median for low-income countries is seven, and for high-income countries it is fifty.[18] A study by Ahmed in the year 2022 shows that the budget for the national mental health programme has been reduced for the past few years. The national economy may eventually suffer long-term consequences if mental health illnesses become more common as a result of this substantial financial shortage.

Public vs. Private Mental Health Services

In view of its multiple diversity, India has specific difficulties in providing its 1.3 billion people with access to cost-effective health care. Under the framework of government efforts aimed at promoting mental health, it is critical to address the needs of those who are struggling with mental health issues in addition to protecting and improving the mental health of everyone. There are significant differences in the accessibility and quality of mental health services in India, in addition to lack of mental health professionals, especially in rural areas. These issues raise serious concerns about access to mental health care.[19] Lack of information, inadequate infrastructure, and poor integration into primary health care systems all hinder access to quality care.

Every citizen has the inherent right to get high-quality health care, yet India's health-care system is still insufficient and disjointed. Both public and private health-care systems, each with unique advantages and disadvantages, make up the nation's health-care infrastructure. India offers free or extremely inexpensive public health care that focuses on primary care. Urban locations are home to the majority of the costly, for-profit private health-care system. Majority of health-care costs are covered by private providers, who provide specialized services. But, there is a lack of transparency and regulation. Public-private partnerships can help to promote collabourations between the public and private sectors in order to improve the delivery of mental health-care services. These kinds of collabourations can improve the distribution of resources, the development of skills, and the creation of novel mental health strategies.

Insurance Coverage and Mental Health

Many physical health insurances are present in today's world because of increasing physical health complications, but on the other hand, there is hardly any talk about increasing mental illnesses and the need for policies for people with disability and mental health illness. According to a study by WHO, over 90 million Indians suffer from some kind of mental disorder. After the pandemic, a strike increase in demand for online consultation from doctors was observed, which has led as a reminder of the urgent need to pay attention to the mental health sector in India.

According to the Mental Healthcare Act, 2017 which was implemented in 2018, the insurance company providing health insurance plans must treat policyholders with mental illnesses in the same manner that it treats those with physical illnesses or injuries. The law now ensures that any individual regardless of their socio-economic status, area of living will have the freedom to select the mental health-care facility. There are some eligibility criteria that a person must have to receive mental health insurance. The criteria are age, pre-existing mental health conditions, medical history, premium payment and insurer's policy guidelines.

Some of the common disorders covered under mental health insurance are: Major Depressive Disorder, Generalized Anxiety Disorder, Bipolar Disorder, Schizophrenia, OCD, PTSD,

Substance use Disorders, Panic Disorder, Eating Disorder (Bulimia Nervosa, Anorexia Nervosa), Personality Disorders, Social Anxiety Disorder, Attention Deficit/Hyperactivity Disorder, Autism Spectrum Disorders, Sleep Disorders and many more.

Aditya Birla Health Insurance is one of the health insurances which covers mental illnesses. Alzheimer's and Parkinson's disease are among the mental health conditions covered by HDFC Ergo's critical illness plan-Platinum. Another insurance policy is the Niramaya Health Insurance Scheme for Disabled Persons.[20]

It was observed that even though many insurance policies are made for mental health illness but very limited insurance coverage is present. Most of the individuals are not eligible for the insurance as they do not meet the eligibility criteria which the policy maker has very smartly made. Many clients are not even aware of the insurance policy which can help them with the treatment and hospital bills. The sad reality is that a majority of the population suffering from mental illnesses is from rural population and often from a lower socio-economic status which makes it really important for them to have an insurance policy but unfortunately, they either are not made aware of them or are not eligible for the policy.

Historical Development in Mental Health Policies in India

Legislations, policies, and programmes on mental health in the Indian subcontinent has a history of more than one and half century. The entire history is marked with serious abuse of human rights of people with mental health disorders and conditions which still continues unabatedly even today. Post-Independence, India started adding General Hospital Psychiatric Units (GHPUs) in existing hospitals rather than building more mental hospitals and as a policy encouraging outpatient's care. Exception to this rule, new mental hospitals at Jaipur, Delhi, Kottayam, and Bengal were established. The national health policy envisaging "Health for all by 2020" led to evolution of national mental health programmes in 1982 which paved the path for the Model District Level Mental Health Programme.[21]

India came up with its National Mental Health Policy (MHP) very recently, i.e. in 2014. Significant changes occurred in the early twenty-first century that have affected India's mental health industry, including the UN Convention on the Rights of Persons with Disabilities (CRPD) and the Movement for Global Mental Health (GMH).[22]

Mental Health Laws

In British India, a series of mental health laws were enacted to control the treatment and control of people with mental illnesses, the details of which are as under:

- The Lunacy (Supreme Courts) Act, 1858
- The Lunacy (District Courts) Act, 1858
- The Indian Lunatic Asylum Act, 1858 (with amendments passed in 1886 and 1889)
- The Military Lunatic Acts, 1877

Under the Lunacy Act 1858, the Indian Lunatic Asylum Act 1858, and the Military Lunatic Act of 1877, patients had limited possibility of recovery or release and were held in subpar living conditions for an extended length of time. Protecting the population from individuals regarded harmful to society, such as PMI, was the main goal of the Indian Lunacy Act (ILA) Act. Then the Mental Health Act of 1987 was passed, defining mental illness in a way that prioritized care and treatment above detention. It outlined hospital admission processes and placed a strong emphasis on guardianship, patient property management, and human rights protection. However, the negative side of this law such as curtailment of liberty, no review by any judicial body, Rehab and treatment following hospital discharge were not discussed, and caretakers and family faced financial, social, and emotional challenges due to a lack of treatment facilities. Due to these concerns, the Mental Health Care Bill (MHCB) 2013 was eventually created by amending the Mental Health Act of 1987.[23]

The MHCB, 2013 has several features like decriminalizing suicides, nominated representatives, a rights-based approach for the PMI. The bill also prohibits branding "non-conformists" as cases of mental illnesses. It also incorporates the rights of people with mental illness and aims to harmonize with the Convention of the Rights of People with Disabilities. The Act has several demerits too. It continues to look at mental illnesses from medicalized points of view and ignores the socio-economic determinants of mental health. The law is also silent on predisposing factors leading to substantial disorders of thinking, mood, perception that grossly impairs judgement and behaviour. The bill does talk about mental health promotion and prevention, and community-based approaches but fails to lay down a mechanism for its implementation.[24]

Way Forward

The existing policies, laws, and programmes on mental health in India have made considerable progress in the last few decades. However, India still has a long way to go in order to make mental health services accessible to all Indians. For achieving universal coverage, India needs to address several roadblocks such as inadequacy of quality mental health professionals, funding, monitoring system, etc. Followings are the recommended ways to make mental services to reach too common Indian.

Expanding Coverage and Dimensions of NMHP

Not all the districts are covered under the NMHP and there is a need to cover the uncovered districts under the programme. In addition to the pharmacological approach, the programme must also consider the psycho-social aspects of mental illnesses. There should be enhanced participation of the community in the designing, development and implementation of this programme. The capacities of the managerial staff, transparency, and unobstructed flow of funds will make a great difference.

Strengthening Implementing Apparatus

Undefined and fragmented roles and responsibilities and poor coordination at all levels leads to poor performance. The MHCB, 2017 envisages the constitution of agencies like CMHA at central level and SMHA at state level. Though there is a provision of Nodal Officer for the purpose, lack of leadership in several places has led to poor implementation of the NMHP. Bridging these gaps and a defined unambiguous leadership will produce better results.

Smooth Funding and Spending

It is expected that the MHA, 2017 will cost around 94,073 crore to implement. However, the expenditure for the FY 2018 and FY 2019 was 5 crore each, extreme underutilization. Additionally, funding is split between centre and state 80:20 and in special category state 90:10, this also becomes a cause of concern due to competing priorities.[25]

Increasing Human Resources in Mental Health

Several government reports indicate the huge shortfalls of the trained manpower in the area 0.29 psychiatrist per 100,000 populations during 2017. For bridging the gap by training the existing medical staff on mental health lacked in terms of duration, specialist support and focused on the biomedical model and ignored psychosocial determinants of mental health. There is a need to train high quality practitioners in health care such as psychiatrist, psychiatric social workers, psychiatric nurses, and clinical psychologists and absorb them in well-defined roles with a clear encouraging career path.

Public-Private Partnership

Most governmental facilities face resource constraints therefore, there is a need to attract investment from the private investors in developing and running mental health facilities at primary, secondary and tertiary levels. The civil society organizations (NGOs) should be encouraged to take part in the implementation of the DMHP such as community mobilization, running primary level mental health facilities, monitoring and evaluation of the programme, capacity building, development of IEC material, community radio and research on mental health issues.

Community Engagement and Awareness: Role of Communities in Mental Health

In India, communities serve as foundational elements in promoting mental health and well-being amidst diverse sociocultural contexts. With a population exceeding 1.4 billion and significant variations in the availability of mental health care, communities serve as crucial hubs for support, awareness, and advocacy. They provide the social fabric within which individuals interact, seek support, and find belonging. The role of communities in mental health extends beyond mere geographical proximity; family structures, neighbourhood networks, and community organizations provide essential avenues for individuals to encompass shared values, cultural norms, and collective efforts to nurture mental well-being.[26]

Traditional practices, such as family-centric care and community healing rituals, coexist with modern interventions, reflecting the rich tapestry of India's cultural landscape in addressing mental health needs. By fostering community-based interventions, promoting awareness campaigns, and leveraging indigenous knowledge systems, India's diverse communities contribute significantly to the promotion of mental well-being and resilience.[27]

Awareness Campaigns and Psychoeducation

Awareness campaigns and psychoeducation play crucial roles in addressing mental health challenges in India, a nation where people's ability to get help is frequently hampered by stigma and ignorance. These public awareness efforts seek to lower stigma associated with mental health conditions and increase accessibility to mental health care.[28] Here's an overview of awareness campaigns and psychoeducation efforts in India.

National Mental Health Programme (NMHP)

The NMHP, launched by the Government of India, includes awareness campaigns as one of its key components. These campaigns aim to spread awareness about mental health issues and reduce stigma associated with them.[29]

The Live, Love, Laugh Foundation

This organization, which was started by Bollywood actress Deepika Padukone, aims to raise awareness, lessen stigma, and offer support for mental health concerns in India. The foundation conducts various campaigns and initiatives to promote mental well-being and educate the public about mental health concerns.[30]

Psychoeducation Programmes

Various organizations and mental health professionals conduct psychoeducation programmes across India. These programmes offer useful information on mental health conditions, coping skills, and relevant services. To address a varied audience, psychoeducation programmes can be delivered in schools, businesses, communities, and health-care settings. When it comes to teaching patients and their families about mental health disorders, treatment options, and available resources, health-care professionals are essential. Collabourations between mental health organizations and health-care practitioners help to integrate psychoeducation into clinical practice. Many organizations leverage online platforms and social media to disseminate information about mental health and offer psychoeducation resources. Websites, blogs, and social media accounts provide educational content, self-help resources, and links to professional services.[31]

Technological Innovations and Telemental Health

During the last four years, after COVID-19, many technological innovations and tele-mental health services have started. The Government of India launched applications like ABHA card and tele-MANAS. Online therapy sessions have become really popular these days, and many people prefer online counselling than in-person counselling. There have been many new innovations like chatbots, online communities where everyone come together and shares their worries, which gives them some relief. Also, an application (SMART Mental Health programme) was developed where screening, referral and management of disorders was done. It helped to reduce the time in understanding the problem and was quite useful in particularly rural areas.[32]

The Ayushman Bharat Digital Mission (ABDM) of the Government of India includes the ABHA card, an initiative designed to help citizens create a centralized database containing all of their health-related information.[33] A person can be uniquely identified by their 14-digit ABHA number, which is also used to authenticate them and, with their consent, link their health information to those of various health-care providers.[34]

Tele-MANAS was an initiative by the ministry of health and family welfare in the year 2022. It provides 24/7 mental health services in regional languages in all Indian states. By dialing a short code or toll-free number, the public can reach the tele-MANAS helpline. First, a qualified counsellor will assist the caller via the automated call back service. Depending on the degree of care needed, the counsellor will either send the caller to an expert or offer the necessary care within their means.[35]

Impact on Accessibility and Affordability

During the COVID-19 pandemic, tele mental health services became popular. A lot of people realized the importance of mental health and started being more open and comfortable in taking therapy. Majority of the population suffering from mental illness in India are from rural population which do not have much idea about how to use technology and often fail to make the best out of the services provided by the government for their betterment.

A study which was conducted during times of COVID-19 suggested that more than half of their sample preferred tele-mental health services than in-person services. The convenience, freedom from having to travel for services, comfort and security of receiving care at home, and increased open communication were among the reasons given by those who preferred telehealth. Additionally, it was observed that for treating a range of mental health conditions, telemedicine mental health treatments are just as successful as in-person therapy.[36]

Challenges and Opportunities

As any new technique is introduced, it faces both opportunities and challenges. Some of the challenges which tele-mental health is facing in India are shortage of professionals, uneven access to technology in rural as well as urban areas, technical glitches which may hamper the counselling session in between, confidentiality cannot be maintained in all cases and the major challenge is that as India is a culturally diverse country which makes it very difficult to integrate a technological system which can cater to this diversity.

Tele-mental health has led to people with mental illness, especially in the rural areas, to have access to online therapies and counselling, it has also helped in reducing stigma around mental health particularly in the past decade, it is cost-effective which is really needed in people with low economic status, and it is available for 24×7. It has a multi-disciplinary approach and in tele-mental health many different professionals have come together which has enhanced the reach and quality of mental health services in India.

Future Prospects

Many interesting and helpful innovations were made. Even though people now have more alternatives for intervention, thanks to these innovations, there is still a lot of uncertainty. Since there is little oversight in the app sector, there is no assurance that the app is supported by research.[37] Although there are some tech-based interventions available today, over time technology will play a major role in developing more useful devices in detection, diagnosing and treating mental health illness.

Case Studies: Successful Models

While talking about countries who have successfully maintained mental health problems of their citizens, Canada has a prominent position. Canada has been actively addressing mental health through various policies and initiatives. A significant force in promoting mental health policies is the Canadian Mental Health Association (CMHA). They carry out studies and offer suggestions for enhancing mental health support and services. The Canadian government focuses on promotion, recovery, diversity and shared responsibility.[38] They have many initiatives like the 9-8-8 crisis line which ensures individuals that they will receive care after the call. CMHA also emphasizes the need for community-based investments and also gives major focus on the fact that mental health can be influenced by factors like biology, environment, the situation they are in, etc.[39]

Sweden is another country which has good mental health services. The country adopt multiple strategies to promote well-being and prevent mental illness. In 2016, the Swedish government unveiled a national mental health policy that prioritized mental health illness prevention and awareness, service accessibility, and a strong emphasis on vulnerable population, including meeting their particular requirements.[40] Regular national public health surveys, such as "Health on Equal Terms", gives valuable insights to the mental health trends.[41]

Lessons Learned

India is a growing nation that is taking efforts to make improvements in the facilities which are required for good physical as well as mental health. It has increased the budget for mental health facilities from the last budget, which shows a good progress which India is making. But still as a country with a population of 1.3 billion, needs to make a lot of efforts to make it better.[32] Some of the strategies which can be learned from other countries with comparatively good mental health facilities are that India should focus more on increasing infrastructure, mental health professionals and mainly increase the awareness about mental illness. In India the awareness about LGBTQ+ community is still not at its best and this community have a lot of mental health issues that include acceptance by the society. A comprehensive survey could bring out the trends in the mental illness in the population, which will be helpful for the professionals to understand the problem which people are facing and make necessary changes to the treatment plans.

Replicability and Scalability

India can learn a lot of new techniques from other countries about how to develop and enhance the services in the mental health sector. We can try to make wise use of the budget allotted to mental health in the year 2024 by analysing where more funding is required. For example, in India, a lot of people of low economic status still face mental health problems. For them, we shall make primary health-care facilities more approachable. India can encourage collabourations across the public, NGOs, and private sectors to establish an inclusive ecosystem for mental health. India should align their strategy with SDG-3, emphasizing the need of health care for all, inexpensive essential medications, and access to excellent mental health services.[42]

Telemedicine and other digital platforms can extend mental health services to a wide range of population. To increase the scalability, we can train some enthusiastic non-specialists who want to contribute in this field to provide basic mental health support, and they can deliver interventions on the grassroot level.[42] Large scale awareness campaigns will help in reducing stigma and may encourage help-seeking behaviour. There can be a lot of challenges which India may face while doing this like data collection and monitoring which requires reliable data for evidence-based decision making, several changes in policy and regulatory framework, there is a constraint in resources available.[43] India is currently the fastest-developing nation with an expanding economy, therefore the likelihood that it will adopt the latest strategies is very strong.

Conclusion

Mental health services in India have garnered increasing attention in recent years due to growing recognition of their importance. However, challenges persist in ensuring accessibility and affordability for all segments of society. Addressing the accessibility and affordability of mental health services in India requires a multi-disciplinary strategy encompassing policy reform, technological innovation, and community engagement. By implementing these recommendations and fostering collabouration between government, health-care providers, technology developers, civil society organizations, and communities, India can take significant steps to ensure that all of its residents have access to a more comprehensive and fair mental health system.

As India grapples with the challenges of ensuring accessible and affordable mental health services for all, concerted efforts and strategic initiatives are imperative. This call-to-action outlines actionable strategies for moving forward and effecting positive change in the mental health landscape of the nation.

Expand the reach of mental health services by integrating them into primary health-care centres across the country. Provide training and capacity-building programmes for primary health-care workers to enhance their ability to identify and address mental health issues. Provide complete care through channels of referral from primary health-care institutions to specialized mental health services.

Explore innovative financing models, such as social impact bonds and health insurance schemes, to make mental health services more affordable for marginalized populations. Advocate for the inclusion of mental health coverage in universal health-care schemes and insurance policies to reduce out-of-pocket expenses for individuals seeking treatment.

Policy Recommendations

Increase budgetary allocation for mental health services to ensure adequate resources for infrastructure, personnel, and community outreach programmes. Integrate mental health services into primary health-care systems to reach rural and underserved areas effectively. Implement and enforce the Mental Healthcare Act, 2017, which mandates mental health-care services to be provided at affordable rates and prohibits discrimination against people with mental illnesses.

Establish community mental health centres with trained professionals such as psychologists, counsellors, and social workers to provide counselling, therapy, and support services. Train community health workers and volunteers to identify signs of mental illness and provide basic support and referrals. Encourage businesses to introduce employee assistance courses, stress management courses, and counselling services as part of their workplace mental health initiatives. Implement community-based interventions that focus on awareness-raising, early detection, and stigma reduction. This can involve partnerships with community organizations, schools, and local leaders to promote mental health literacy and support. Conduct public awareness campaigns and destigmatization efforts at the grassroots level to promote acceptance and understanding of mental health issues.[44]

Encourage collabourations between governmental, non-profit, and commercial entities in order to expand mental health services and increase affordability through subsidized programmes or sliding-scale fees. This can involve leveraging resources and expertise from multiple sectors to develop and implement effective mental health programmes. Encourage corporate social responsibility initiatives focusing on mental health, such as funding treatment programmes, sponsoring awareness campaigns, or providing free counseling services.

Keywords

Mental health, accessibility, affordability, successful models.

NOTES

1. UN. (2023). Department of Economic and Social Affairs Sustainable Development. https://www.lib.ncsu.edu/citationbuilder/#/website/apa7
2. WHO (2022). *Mental health.* World Health Organization. Retrieved on 22 March 2023, from https://www.who.int/health-topics/mental-health#tab=tab_1
3. Michael Marmot and Ruth Bell (January 2018). "The Sustainable Development Goals and Health Equity." *Epidemiology, 29*(1): 5-7, DOI: 10.1097/EDE.0000000000000773
4. WHO (2018). *Mental Health in Primary Care: Illusion or Inclusion?*
5. R. Dybdahl & L. Lien (2017). "Take a Look at the Recent Articles". *Mental Health is An Integral Part of the Sustainable Development Goals.* Retrieved on 22 March 2023, from https://www.oatext.com/mental-health-is-an-integral-part-of-the-sustainable-development-goals.php
6. M. Funk & E. Faydi (2008). "Integrating Mental Health into Primary Health Care." *Mental Health Family Medicine, 5*(1): 5-8. Retrieved from https://www.ncbi.nlm.nih.gov/pmc/articles/PMC2777555/
7. J.M. Barroso (22 February 2023). "Statement on G-20 Meeting for Reform for Resilience Commission." *Americas Hub Reform for Resilience.* Retrieved on 30 March 2023, from https://www.hsph.harvard.edu/r4r/2022/11/14/g20meeting-statement/
8. World Health Organization (WHO): https://www.who.int/
9. https://nhm.gov.in/index1.php?lang=1&level=2&sublinkid=1043&lid=359
10. *National Mental Health Survey of India, 2015-16.*
11. A. Singh & S.K. Mattoo (2017). "Recruitment, Retention, and Training in Psychiatry in India: A Critical Appraisal." *Indian Journal of Psychiatry, 59*(1): 23-30.
12. G. Gururaj, M. Varghese, V. Benegal, G.N. Rao, K. Pathak and L.K. Singh (2016). *National Mental Health Survey of India.*
13. *National Mental Health Survey of India* (2016). National Institute of Mental Health and Neuro Sciences, NIMHANS Publication No. 129.
14. V. Patel, S. Saxena, C. Lund, G. Thornicroft, F. Baingana, P. Bolton and J. Eaton (2018). "The Lancet Commission on Global Mental Health and Sustainable Development." *The Lancet, 392*(10157): 1553-1598.
15. CDC (1 September 2023). *Socio-economic Factors.* Retrieved from Division for Heart Disease and Stroke Prevention: https://www.cdc.gov/dhdsp/health_equity/socio-economic.htm

16. M.M. Vanee R. Meghrajani (2023). "A Comprehensive Analysis of Mental Health Problems in India and the Role of Mental Asylums." *Cureus.*
17. National Institute of Mental Health and Neurosciences (NIMHANS), https://nimhans.ac.in/
18. C. Sehgal (3 November 2021). *How India can Make Mental Health Care Affordable and Accessible to All.* Retrieved from Deloitte: https://www2.deloitte.com/in/en/pages/about-deloitte/articles/How-India-can-make-mental-health care-affordable-and-accessible-to-all.html
19. Niva (24 July 2023). *Public vs Private Health Care in India.* Retrieved from Niva Bupa: https://www.nivabupa.com/health-insurance-articles/public-vs-private-health care-in-india.html
20. *Mental Illness Coverage in Mental Insurance* (2024). Retrieved from PolicyX: https://www.policyx.com/health-insurance/articles/mental-illness-covered-in-a-health-insurance/
21. S.H. Nizamie, and N. Goyal (2010). "History of Psychiatry in India". *Indian J Psychiatry. 52*(Suppl 1): S7-S12. doi: 10.4103/0019-5545.69195. PMID: 21836719; PMCID: PMC3146221.
22. K. Ranade, A. Kapoor & T.N. Fernandes (2022). "Mental Health Law, Policy & Programme in India: A Fragmented Narrative of Change, Contradictions and Possibilities." *SSM Mental Health*, 2. https://www.sciencedirect.com/science/article/pii/S2666560322001141
23. L. Choudhary & D. Sikha (2013). *Indian Journal of Psychiatry. Indian Legal System and Mental Health, 55*(2): 177-81. https://www.ncbi.nlm.nih.gov/pmc/articles/PMC3705679/
24. K. Badola & R. Bhargava (December 2016). "The Mental Healthcare Bill Fails to Humanise How Mental Illness is Approached." *The Wire.* https://thewire.in/law/mental-health-bill
25. T. Ahmed, N. Dumka, E. Hannah, V. Chauhan, A. Kotwal "Understanding India's Response to Mental Health Care: A Systematic Review of the Literature and Overview of the National Mental Health Programme". *JoGHNP*. Published online, 10 June 2022: e2022010. doi:10.52872/001c.36128
26. *Indian Journal of Psychiatry*: https://www.indianjpsychiatry.org/
27. *Indian Psychiatric Society*: https://www.indianpsychiatricsociety.org/
28. *YourDOST*: https://www.yourdost.com/
29. V. Patel, M. Maj, A.J. Flisher, M.J. De Silva, M. Koschorke, M. Prince, & WPA Zonal and Member Society Representatives (2010). Reducing the Treatment Gap for Mental Disorders: A WPA Survey. *World Psychiatry, 9*(3): 169-76.

30. *The Live, Love, Laugh Foundation*, https://www.thelivelovelaughfoundation.org/
31. *Journal of Mental Health and Human Behaviour*: https://www.jmhhb.org/
32. S. Senger (1 February 2022). *How the Tele Mental Health Programme Will Help Eradicate Its Stigma in India*. Retrieved from India Times: https://www.indiatimes.com/news/india/tele-mental-health-programme-launched-importance-560847.html
33. *Create Ayushman Bharat Health Account* (February 2024). Retrieved from eka.care: https://www.eka.care/ayushman-bharat/create-abha-abdm-ndhm-health-id
34. eka.care (February 2024). Retrieved from Create Ayushman Bharat Health Account: https://www.eka.care/ayushman-bharat/create-abha-abdm-ndhm-health-id
35. *Tele MANAS* (2024). Retrieved from find a helpline: https://findahelpline.com/organizations/tele-manas
36. M.H. Anne Honey (2023). "Preferences for Telehealth: A Qualitative Study with People Accessing a New Mental Health Service." *Digit Health*.
37. The Future of Mental Health. (2024). Retrieved from Brains Way: https://www.brainsway.com/knowledge-centre/the-future-of-mental-health
38. C.M. Association (2024). *Changing Directions, Changing Lives: The Mental Health Strategy for Canada (Summary)*. Retrieved from Physician Welness Hub: https://www.cma.ca/physician-wellness-hub
39. Association, C.M. (7 February 2024). *Mental Health at the Pandemic's End: Youth still Reporting Higher Rates of Mental Health Problems*. Retrieved from policy and research: https://cmha.ca/what-we-do/policy-research/
40. N. DeLuca (27 June 2023). *Strengthening Mental Health Initiatives in Sweden*. Retrieved from the Borgen Project: https://borgenproject.org/mental-health-initiatives-in-sweden/
41. *Mental Health* (10 February 2022). Retrieved from the Public Health Agency of Sweden: https://www.folkhalsomyndigheten.se/the-public-health-agency-of-sweden/living-conditions-and-lifestyle/mental-health/
42. S.S. Pranab Mahapatra (2023). "Mental Health in India: Evolving Strategies, Initiatives, and Prospects." *The Lancet Regional Health-Sotheast Asia*.

43. S. Karthikeyan (6 July 2022). "Towards a Stronger Mental Health Strategy." Retrieved from *The Hindu*: https://www.thehindu.com/opinion/op-ed/towards-a-stronger-mental-health-strategy/article34755470.ece
44. R. Shidhaye & M. Kermode (2013). "Stigma and Discrimination as a Barrier to Mental Health Service Utilization in India." *International Health*, *5*(1): 6-8.

8

Enhancing Agency of Young Women and Girls for Improved Sexual and Reproductive Health

Moumita Sarkar, Titas Ghosh, and *Vinoj Manning*

The UN SDGs set a bold agenda to achieve equity and well-being for all by 2030. Navigating the landscape of sexual and reproductive health (SRH) poses significant hurdles for young people and adolescents, affecting their ability to achieve optimal well-being and productivity. Key impediments emphasize a lack of foundational understanding of SRH, restricted access to essential services, unfavourable and often hostile attitudes from health care providers, and the burden of social stigma and discrimination. There is a pressing need to address the challenges that hinder individuals from achieving universal access to sexual and reproductive health and rights (SRHR). A report by Niti Aayog, that measures India's progress on SDGs, shows some progress but significant regional disparities persist, and several areas including addressing the barriers to agency of young people need improvement.

Effective interventions play a crucial role in achieving the SDGs. Here are some key models that have worked in promoting SRHR of young people.

Comprehensive Sexuality Education (CSE)

CSE is a structured approach to teaching young people about all aspects of sexuality, including physical, emotional, social, and cognitive factors. Its goal is to equip them with the knowledge and skills to make informed decisions about their sexual health and relationships. By promoting safe sexual behaviours and increasing contraceptive use, CSE aims to reduce unintended pregnancies and sexually transmitted infections among young people.

A review of international studies showed that CSE interventions increased knowledge about HIV/AIDS, improved attitudes towards condom use, and reduced unsafe sexual behaviours in youth. Netherlands has a strong Comprehensive Sexuality Education (CSE) programme with government support. As an outcome, it has one of the lowest adolescent birth rates worldwide (less than 5 births per 1,000 women aged 15-19). High rates of contraceptive use and low STI rates among young people. A UNFPA report reviewing the CSE programmes in 2015 remarked that

> Evaluation findings indicate that children who participated in *Relaties and Seksualiteit* (Relationships and Sexuality) had more knowledge about sexuality, relationships and sexual abuse, and increased appreciation of the school and teachers as sources of information. Although these students reported an increase in assertiveness, there was no change in communication skills (levels were already high), self-confidence, or empathy (low at the start). The majority of students had increased positive attitudes towards sexual diversity, though this was not the case for students from cultural minorities. The overall conclusion: CSE has positive effects on 10- to 12-year-old children.

A Progressive Legal Framework

Decriminalizing abortion also ensures access to safe abortion services and reduced maternal mortality rate. Uruguay has one of the lowest adolescent birth rates in all Latin America. In 2013, when the abortion law (VTP or Voluntary Termination of Pregnancy) had just come into effect in Uruguay, the adolescent birth rate was 61 out of every 1,000 women. In 2020, that stood at 32.6 as opposed to 102.6 in Nicaragua[6] where abortion is completely illegal.

Community-Based Interventions

Collabourating with local NGOs, communities, parents, and youth leaders is vital in fostering positive attitudes around SRHR. Community-led programmes that promote gender equality, challenge harmful social norms, and increase access to health-care services have significant positive impacts. In Delhi, The YP Foundation's youth-led audits to assess the accessibility of youth-friendly health services, the quality of care received and their continued engagement with the communities with the objective of strengthening the same is a great example to note here.

Youth-Friendly Health Services (YFHS)

YFHS caters to the unique SRH needs and rights of young people and adolescents. They create a welcoming and confidential environment where young people can seek information, counselling, and health-care services without fear of stigma or judgement. By offering SRH care alongside other services relevant to young people, such as mental health counselling or vocational training, programmes increase young people's utilization of SRH services, resulting in better knowledge outcomes, improved contraceptive use, and fewer unintended pregnancies. A notable service/programme under this could be peer-education programmes where young people train and educate their peers on issues related to SRHR much like Ipas Development Foundation's (IDF) work in West Bengal and Jharkhand to increase awareness on several SRH-related issues under the project "Enhancing Agency of Young Women and Girls for Improved Sexual & Reproductive Health".

In Sweden, youth-friendly health clinics integrated into the overall health system provides easy access to SRH information, services, counselling, and various contraceptive options. According to a study conducted in 2020 to assess the youth-friendliness of the youth-friendly clinics in Sweden highlights that girls and young women attend these clinics more frequently than boys and young men. Although most young people (primarily, cisgendered heterosexual youth) responded positively to questions around accessibility, availability and acceptability, people with diverse sexualities and gender identities continue to face increased barriers to accessing these services.

Contextualizing the Indian Landscape

Sexual and reproductive health rights are essential for everyone, including young people, and are vital for attaining comprehensive health care that encompasses more than just preventing diseases—it also includes overall wellness, including physical, mental, emotional, and social aspects. According to the UN,

> Rights to reproductive and sexual health include the right to life, liberty, and security of the person; the right to health care and information; and the right to non-discrimination in the allocation of resources to health services and in their availability and accessibility.

One of the key challenges in achieving sexual and reproductive health rights is lack of women's autonomy and agency. Independent decision making by women regarding their own health was as low as 10 per cent according to the National Family Health Survey (NFHS-5). Marriage under 18 years age reported at 23.3 per cent for women aged 20-24. Teenage pregnancy rate stands at 9.3 per cent with an alarming adolescent fertility rate of 43 per cent. With nearly eight women dying each day due to complications related to unsafe abortion, unsafe abortion is the third leading cause of maternal mortality (State of the World Population Report 2022, UNFPA).

In recent years, India has made substantial progress in recognizing sexual and reproductive health as human rights, even though historically the government prioritized population control measures over enhancing agency and access to comprehensive sexual and reproductive health education and services.

Menstrual health has been a major public health issue in India and globally, with significant unmet needs among adolescents and young people. The Indian government initiated several programmes to address this, including the Menstrual Hygiene Scheme in 2011 and the incorporation of menstrual hygiene management into the Swachh Bharat Mission in 2014. Despite these efforts, a comprehensive national policy was lacking. In November 2023, the Indian government announced the development of a National Menstrual Hygiene Policy, which adopts a life cycle approach to support individuals from menarche to menopause. This policy aims to enhance menstrual health and hygiene and aligns with the SDGs.

The Medical Termination of Pregnancy (MTP) Amendment Act passed in 2021, updating the longstanding abortion law, is another initiative of the government to improve access to safe abortion. Key amendments include extending the gestational limit to twenty-four weeks for specific circumstances and removing the requirement to state marital status for abortion access, abortion after twenty-four weeks with approval of medical boards for congenital anomalies, thus better addressing the needs of young unmarried women while enhancing privacy and confidentiality. Although the MTP Act remains provider-centric with significant state oversight, recent amendments indicate a trend toward liberalizing abortion access.

The SRHR landscape in India is dynamic, influenced both by progressive legislations, policies and persistent challenges. While advancements in abortion access and menstrual health policies are positive steps, the complex interplay of laws and the need for an inclusive and rights-based service delivery highlights the need to establish a central agency. Within this context, it also becomes important for us to learn to adapt to local contexts while ensuring universal access to SRHR services remains crucial for empowering young people.

IDF's Project Overview

The project adopted a comprehensive strategy, incorporating interventions at both community and public health-facility levels to enhance the SRH knowledge and decision making abilities of young women; ensuring youth-friendly SRH services in public health facilities while bolstering connections between communities and the services provided. A pivotal emphasis was placed on cultivating a supportive environment for young women's SRH, by engaging with the key community influencers, including partners, family elders, and community gatekeepers. A vital component of our approach involved the creation and mentoring of youth leaders and community champions—individuals from the communities who underwent training and mentorship, subsequently spearheading the programme and evolving into enduring resources within their local communities.

The intervention yielded notable advancements in the availability of SRH information and services, as well as in the awareness and realization of SRH rights among young individuals, thus the contribution directly aligns with the SDG targets of access to sexual and reproductive health services and information (SDG-3.7), as well as universal access to sexual and reproductive health and rights (SDG-5.6).

Key Strategy

Improving Knowledge and Agency and Access to SRH Services

To drive sustainable community improvements, the project empowered women as youth leaders, involving them in all stages from needs assessment to outreach planning. These leaders were mentored to connect with girls and young women in their communities and schools, providing age-appropriate SRH information and engaging with their partners and families to support girls' and young women's SRH needs. To address COVID-19 limitations, the project introduced the AI-powered chatbot Disha Didi for additional SRH information and tele-counselling, while youth leaders supported young women in accessing health services.

Creating Sustainable Social Capital

Establishing social capital involved creation of a cadre of community champions known as Yuva Sathis to serve as catalysts for change. The Yuva Sathis were empowered through range of capacity building workshops on leadership, communication, and life skills. Yuva Sathis created peer support groups, led community dialogues on SRH Rights of young people, negative social practices affecting SRH and fostered collabourative actions by their peers that contribute to positive transformation in their community.

Fostering a Sustainable Youth-friendly Environment

Creating an enabling environment supportive of young women's SRH was one of the key focus areas. Community influencers including local government representatives, community leaders and family members were sensitized on the SRH needs and rights of the young people to address restrictive gender and social norms, and garner support for young people's SRH. To engage the influencers in addressing SRH barriers, Yuva Sathis played a pivotal role in initiating dialogues on the identified barriers in interface meetings with the influencers, specifically with the local government representatives.

Strengthening Availability of Youth-friendly SRH Services

Strengthening youth-friendly health services involved making public health facilities more accessible and responsive to young people's SRH needs. The project, in partnership with state health departments, focused on building the capacity of the public health system and decentralizing SRH services to lower-level facilities. It included sensitization workshops for service providers to address gaps in knowledge, stigma, and attitudes, while also expanding the provider base and streamlining supply chain processes to ensure adequate resources and supplies.

Leveraging Ayushman Bharat—a flagship scheme of the Government of India, SRH services were decentralized to Ayushman Arogya Mandirs closer to communities. This involved ensuring availability of trained providers, supplies and equipment and age specific documentation of SRH services at the health and wellness centres. The capacity of community health workers was enhanced to offer counselling, referrals, and contraceptive services to young women.

Synergy with National Adolescent Health Programme

Launched in 2014, the Rashtriya Kishor Swasthy Karyakram (RKSK) is India's national adolescent health programme aimed at improving communication, workforce development, and performance monitoring. Despite its focus on sexual and reproductive health, implementation has been inadequate, with restricted messages on menstrual hygiene and sexual health. IDF's project prioritized SRH within RKSK, advocating for allocation of adequate state funding and capacity building of RKSK workforce, enhancing counsellor skills, and addressing supply gaps to improve on-ground services and documentation.

Coverage

40,000 Adolescents & Young Women

22,800 Family Members including Male Partners

800 Community Influencers

2200 Community Health Intermediaries

30 Public Health Facilities

Evaluation of the Intervention

The outcomes of the intervention were assessed through a cross-sectional baseline and endline assessment in Jharkhand, as well as a qualitative study in West Bengal.

Objective of the Evaluation

The programme intervention aimed at increasing individual knowledge and agency and creating enabling environment and referral linkages at the community level and ensuring youth-responsive services by strengthening public sector health facilities. The purpose of the evaluation was to:

- Explore the association between intervention exposure and transition in desired behaviour including, service utilization, menstrual hygiene, seeking information on SRH, and SRH knowledge.
- Understand the utilization of SRH services and experience of accessing services.
- Assess the improvement in young women's self-efficacy and agency with regard to SRH decisions and service access.

Methodology

In West Bengal, cross-sectional qualitative study was conducted among adolescents, young women and other stakeholders:

- In-depth interviews with adolescent girls and young women and health-care providers from public health facilities.

- Interactive workshop with adolescent girls and young women from intervention and non-intervention areas to explore the experiential aspects of programming that may have had a significant impact on target beneficiaries.
- Client Exit Interviews to understand the quality of SRH care received.

In Jharkhand, pre-post-quasi-experimental research methodology was used assess the outcomes. Cross-sectional baseline study was conducted in intervention and comparison blocks prior to intervention in March 2019 and post-intervention in March 2021 (endline). Participants were selected from the intervention and comparison blocks using two-stage stratified random sampling.

Findings

The qualitative study in West Bengal revealed the multifaceted impact of the intervention on the target respondents. Community outreach meetings led by youth leaders were effective in destigmatizing and normalizing conversations on sexual and reproductive health, thus increasing the comfort level of intervention participants in addressing SRH issues compared to those not involved in the intervention. Through in-depth explanations, demonstrations, and two-way discussions, the intervention group developed a comprehensive understanding of SRH issues relevant to their lives, in contrast to the non-intervention group. Participants in the intervention reported increased self-confidence in identifying and making decisions about SRH, translating their knowledge into practice in their own lives, and sharing their experiences with peers and family members. Significant improvements in knowledge and practices across all SRH parameters were observed, with a marked intensity. Youth leaders were instrumental in creating pathways for accessing services and navigating SRH issues.

Findings from client exit interviews and communication monitoring also substantiated the qualitative evaluation findings in West Bengal. Correct knowledge on SRH among adolescent and young women increased from 49 per cent at baseline to

55 per cent at endline. Similarly, self-efficacy to access SRH services improved substantially from 14 per cent at baseline to 92 per cent at endline. Few barriers also emerged highlighting the need for future intervention, such as, greater sensitization and familiarization of health service providers and counsellors, family counselling/sensitization specifically for mother and mother-in-law, greater involvement of the duty bearers to initiate actions on social norms and gaps in services.

In Jharkhand, the cross-sectional community assessment revealed significant improvements across various sexual and reproductive health components, including knowledge, attitudes, practices, and stigma reduction.

Exposure to SRH information increased significantly from 56 per cent at baseline to 82 per cent at endline, and the composite SRH knowledge score improved from 5.0 at baseline to 7.9 at endline, both changes being statistically significant. This is further evidenced by changes in behaviours and practices: contraceptive prevalence rate increased significantly from 41 per cent at baseline to 67 per cent at endline, and the use of modern contraceptive methods rose by three percentage points, from 29 per cent to 32 per cent, between the two survey periods. In the comparison area, exposure to information on SRH issues decreased, while the intervention model effectively reached young women with a comprehensive range of SRH-related information in the intervention area.

The findings highlighted a shift in young women's attitudes towards hygienic practices during menstruation. The use of sanitary napkins significantly increased from 62 per cent to 69 per cent in the intervention area.

The targeted intervention model effectively enhanced comprehensive knowledge of SRH issues and led to significant behavioural changes, such as increased utilization of services. For example, the use of health services for menstruation-related problems rose markedly from 9 per cent at baseline to 25 per cent at endline, with notable improvements also observed in uptake of services related to ANC, delivery, menstrual problems, and white discharge/RTI.

A notable reduction in stigma among young women in the intervention area was documented, with the mean stigma score decreasing significantly from 25 at baseline to 23 at endline.

Social support from partners and families significantly aided young married women in meeting their SRH needs. In the intervention area, support from partners and families for married women increased substantially from 32 per cent at baseline to 62 per cent at endline.

The overall agency score in the intervention area remained unchanged between the two assessment rounds (32.8 out of 52), indicating a need for further work to enhance young women's agency and improve their SRH rights. In contrast, the agency score in the comparison area decreased significantly, falling from 29.8 at baseline to 28.9 at endline.

The gender transformative approach was evident, as a significant increase in interspousal communication on SRH issues was observed from pre- to post-intervention. Notably, men's attitudes toward young women's needs and access to SRH services improved significantly in the intervention area, rising from 29 per cent at baseline to 53 per cent at endline. In contrast, the variation in attitudes in the comparison area was not significant.

Learnings

(a) Power of Community-based Youth Leaders and Amplified Voices

The approach focused on recognizing and guiding emerging leaders among the youth in intervention communities, collabouratively developing strategies and messages, and ensuring accurate, tailored information is shared within the community. Additionally, during crises such as the COVID-19 pandemic, young women in the community leaned on these peer leaders for information and support.

Harnessing the collective power of youth and amplifying their voices has demonstrated significant effectiveness in challenging adverse social norms and overcoming barriers related to sexual and reproductive health and rights. This approach has facilitated increased participation of young people in public forums and sparked constructive dialogues on SRH issues with the duty bearers.

(b) Engagement With Family Members and Community Influencers is Essential to Enable SRH Access for Young Women

Sensitizing key decision-makers and gaining their support for young women's access to sexual and reproductive health is critical. Engaging the family members and the influencers created supportive environment for adolescents and young women, enabling them to exercise agency and effectively utilize the newly acquired information. Joint meetings of adolescents/young women and family members/male partners proved effective in promoting interspousal/inter-generational communication. Interface meetings of the young women with duty bearers led to active involvement of the duty bearers (local government representatives and traditional leaders) in addressing negative social norms impacting their SRH issues.

(c) Responsive to the Changing Context on the Ground

Given the changing on-ground realities (especially in the context of the pandemic) including the advent of technology in rural areas, outreach strategies were continuously adapted to meet the emerging needs. Starting with traditional in-person group meetings, various innovations—notably Disha Didi, IDF AI chatbot was introduced to adapt to the context and maintain target audience engagement.

(d) Improving Access to Rights is Challenging and is a Gradual Process

While family elders, male partners, and community influencers show a willingness to support sexual and reproductive health for the betterment of women's well-being, explicitly framing these as rights has encountered more resistance. Persistent community engagement effort is required to gradually shape their perspectives and foster increased acceptance of women's rights over time.

(e) Continuous Advocacy and Engagement Needed for Health System Strengthening

In public health facilities, the frequent occurrence of transfers, trainings, among service providers and counsellors is a common challenge in the public health system. The absence of service providers or their unfavourable attitudes directly impacts service delivery at facilities, for adolescents and young women. To ensure uninterrupted services and sustain provider engagement, continuous advocacy with the health system is essential. Orientation and reorientation of providers and support staff are crucial components to address gaps in technical skills, knowledge, and biases for SRH issues of young people.

Conclusion

The project successfully advanced SRH outcomes for adolescent girls and young women through a multifaceted approach, even amid the disruptions caused by the COVID-19 pandemic. By implementing interventions at both community and public health facility levels, the project significantly enhanced SRH knowledge and decision making among young women. Key strategies included capacity building of community youth to serve as SRH ambassadors and peer educators, leveraging technology such as the AI-powered chatbot Disha Didi to deliver reliable SRH information, and strengthening youth-friendly SRH services within the public health facilities.

The integration of community influencers and family engagement played a crucial role in fostering supportive environments and challenging restrictive social norms. Notable improvements were observed in SRH knowledge, service utilization, and reduction in stigma, aligning with SDGs related to SRH services and rights.

The project's success underscores the importance of continued efforts to engage both young people and communities, adapt to changing contexts, and advocate for ongoing health system strengthening. These outcomes provide a strong foundation for future interventions aimed at sustaining and expanding improvements in sexual and reproductive health by incorporating a more targeted strategy to strengthen the agency of young people.

Keywords

Adolescent girls, young women, sexual and reproductive health, community health, public health, youth-friendly health services.

REFERENCES

Antón, J.I. (2016). "Evolution of Adolescent Fertility after Decriminalization of Abortion in Montevideo, Uruguay." *International Journal of Gynecology & Obstetrics*, *134*(S1): S24-S27. https://doi.org/10.1016/j.ijgo.2016.06.002

Fang, J., S. Tang, and X. Tan *et al.* (2020). "Achieving SDG Related Sexual and Reproductive Health Targets in China: What are Appropriate Indicators and How we Interpret Them?" *Reproductive Health*, *17*(84): 1-13. https://doi.org/10.1186/s12978-020-00924-9

Ministry of Health and Family Welfare (n.d.). Draft Menstrual Hygiene Policy. Retrieved from https://main.mohfw.gov.in/sites/default/files/Draft%20Menstrual%20Hygiene%20Policy%202023%20-For%20Comments.pdf

NITI Aayog (3 June 2021). NITI Aayog Releases SDG India Index and Dashboard 2020-21 [Press release]. Press Information Bureau. https://pib.gov.in/PressReleaseIframePage.aspx?PRID=1723952

Rutgers (2022). *Sexuality Education in the Netherlands* [PDF]. Sexuality-education-in-the-Netherlands-2022-Digitaal_LowRes (1).pdf

Statista (2020). Adolescent Birth Rate in Latin America by Country. Retrieved from https://www.statista.com/statistics/945546/latin-america-number-births-adolescent-women-country/

The YP Foundation (2019). *Audit Report and Study Design: The Access Project.* Retrieved from https://theypfoundation.org/resources/audit-report/

United Nations Population Fund (2015). The Evaluation of Comprehensive Sexuality Education Programmes [PDF]. UNFPAEvaluationWEB4.pdf

Waenerlund, A.K., M. San Sebastian, A.K. Hurtig, & Byström, P. (2020). "Assessing the Youth-friendliness of Youth Clinics in Northern Sweden: A Survey Analysing the Perspective of the Youth." *BMC Health Services Research*, *20*(1): 346. https://doi.org/10.1186/s12913-020-05188-4

9

Eradication of Hunger and Malnutrition

Practices and Approaches in Malnutrition Reduction in India

Ganesh Mane and *Shamim Mohammad*

After commencement of Millennium Development Goals (MDGs) in 2015, the UN member states adopted the ambitious and specific set of the Sustainable Development Goals (SDGs) in which urgency of call for action is highlighted for progress through partnership of the member countries. In this chapter, SDGs were developed as a result of work of member countries and UN including UN Department of Economic and Social Affairs for several years; they are the set of seventeen goals, 169 targets to be achieved by the year 2030.[1] The progress of MDGs was observed in some of the areas by member countries, but still many goals remained unaccomplished and they were taken into account in the SDGs 2030 agenda. This was done with a major aim to benefit all and having the theme of "Leaving no one Behind".[2] As per the World Commission on Environment and Development (1987), the sustainable development is the development that satisfies current wants without jeopardizing the capacity of future generations to satisfy their own.[3] The five Ps (People, Planet, Prosperity, Peace, and

Partnerships) are the core in the new agenda of SDGs. One of the important SDGs called "Hunger" which highlights the basic need of human beings kept at second number after "No Poverty" at the top. The Second SDG is "End Hunger Achieve Food Security and improve nutrition and promote sustainable agriculture".

This chapter throws light on direct and indirect measures of hunger, underdevelopment, and nutrition with their merits and demerits. It also talks on international, national, constitutional, legal, and policy frameworks. It focuses on national schemes and practices to combat hunger and malnutrition issues. SDGs consist of a set of eight targets and thirteen indicators. Out of eight targets, the first two targets are related to hunger and malnutrition. The other targets are mainly related to agriculture and production. The first target is about ending hunger and ensuring access to food for all by 2030. The second target is to end all types of malnutrition by 2030. The aim goes on to say that by 2025, stunting and wasting in children under the age of five will be reduced. The SDG-2 targets address the nutritional needs of elderly people, pregnant, and breastfeeding women, and teenaged girls. As per the UN, hunger is the time when people go days without eating because they don't have enough money, food, or other resources, or when they face extreme food insecurity.[4] Considering the above conditions, the continuous food depression for sustained period leads to several serious effects on the health. As a result of food insecurity, a person gets deprived of proteins, vitamins, minerals, and other nutrients required for a healthy life. If it is not addressed in time, it gets life threatening and gets manifested in following forms of malnutrition:

(a) **Stunting or Chronic Malnutrition:** Stunting is shortness of child for his or her particular age. It can cause lifelong physical and cognitive impairment.

(b) **Wasting or Acute Malnutrition:** Wasting is very low weight for his or her height. It can be seen as a severe hunger crisis, and it happens suddenly. Mortality risk is higher in wasted children. This condition is treatable.

(c) **Micronutrient Deficiencies:** It is also called hidden hunger. It is the deficiency of minerals and vitamins, which can cause deviation in healthy growth and development.

(d) **Overweight:** Obesity or overweight is having too much weight for that height. It is a result of poor diet which can lead to non-communicable diseases in later life of a person such as diabetes, hypertension, cardiovascular diseases (CVDs) and other lifestyle disorders.

Zero Hunger Progress and Trends

In India, zero hunger is still a major challenge to achieve (Fig. 9.1). Also, several countries from Southeast Asia, Africa, North America, and Australian continents are in the same category. So, achieving zero hunger is still a destination to reach. The trends in India are stagnant. Since 2015, food insecurity has increased and pandemic, climate change, growing inequalities are the factors accelerating the food insecurities. Worldwide 9.2 per cent population, i.e. 735 million faces chronic hunger in 2022 which is 122 million more than 2019 statistics.[5]

Fig. 9.1: India Statistics of SDG-2[6]

In the SDG rankings, India stands 112th position in 2023. Neighbouring countries like Sri Lanka and Bangladesh are above India in rankings, i.e. 83 and 101 rank respectively. The Pakistan stands behind the India at 128th rank. The overall score is 63.4

which is below the regional average. The SDG-2 performance is just above 50 per cent which is stagnated as per categorization of progress made by India.[6]

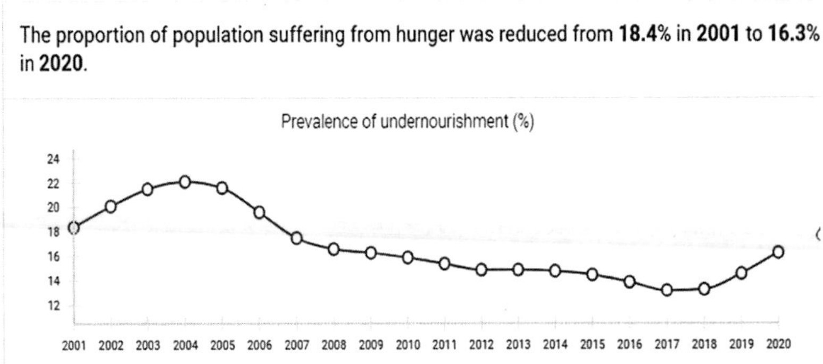

Fig. 9.2: India Statistics of SDG-2 as per SDG Database Country Profile[7]

Figure 9.2 shows the reduction in proportion of population undernourished in India.

Malnutrition Scenario

Considering the current food crisis, malnutrition is a global health concern. It is a major agenda point on many countries' health planning and policy making. Despite some progress made worldwide in malnutrition interventions, in many places of the world, it remains a serious public health risk. In 2022, stunting affected 22.3 per cent of the under five-year children worldwide, i.e. 148 million. The world is far away from the track to achieve the 2030 target of reduction of stunting by 50 per cent. Wasting amongst children is a red signal to the governments worldwide to accelerate their actions. The major cause of wasting is diseases and nutrients' poor diet. It compromises immunity, causes developmental delay and deaths. Wasting affected 6.8 per cent (45 million) of under five-year children worldwide in 2022. The world has made progress in bringing down wasting prevalence from 7.7 per cent in 2010 to 6.8 per cent in 2022. Still, it is not a considerable progress.[5]

NFHS-5 data shows wasting in under five-year children is of 19.3 per cent and stunting is 35.5 per cent in the same age group. However, it shows a little progress compared to NFHS-4, i.e. from 38.4 per cent to 35.5 per cent in stunting and 21 per cent to 19.3 per cent in wasting prevalence.[8]

The propportion of children under 5 years of age with stunted growth reduced from **50.0%** in **2000** to **31.7%** in **2022**.

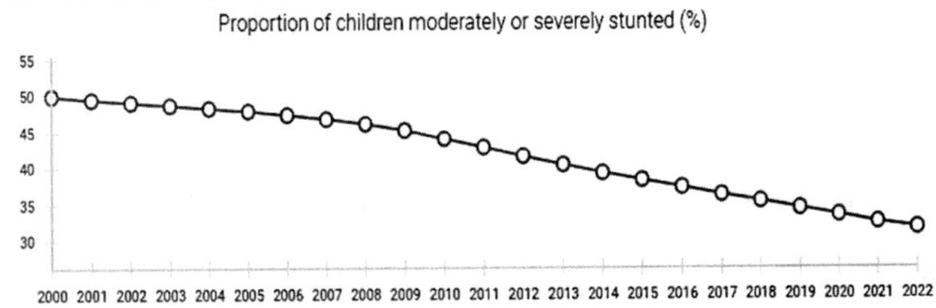

Fig. 9.3: India Statistics of SDG-2 as per SDG Database Country Profile[7]

In 2020, prevalence of undernutrition in India is 16.3 per cent considered, a cause of concern for consideration. It was observed stagnancy in performance of stunting and wasting i.e. 31.7 per cent and 18.7 per cent respectively in India (Fig. 9.3)[7]. Overall, it is considered as a major concern in the progress of SDG.

Number of children who were moderately or severely wasted reduced from **26,320.5** thousand in **2006** to **21,880.5** thousand in **2020**.

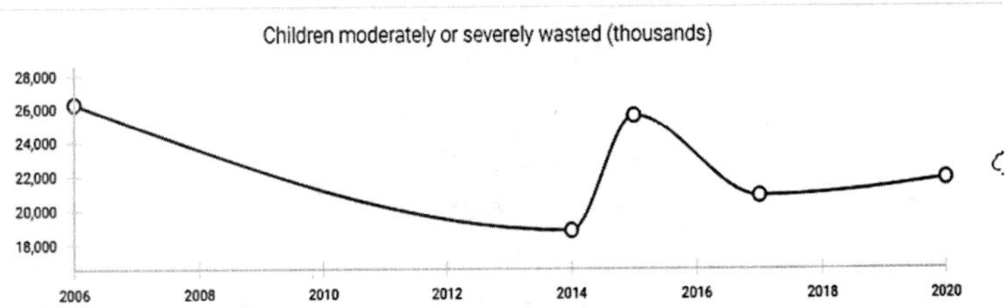

Fig. 9.4: SDG-2 Country Profile—India Statistics[7]

Severe wasting and moderate wasting reduction during 2006 to 2020 shows the fluctuation, it may be due to pandemic effect raising prevalence of wasting (Fig. 9.4).[7]

Measurement of Development and Nutrition: Indirect Measures

(a) Human Development Index (HDI)

The three fundamental pillars of human development—knowledge, health, and living standard—are measured by the Human Development Index (HDI). Gross national income per capita is used to assess living standards, life expectancy at birth is used to measure long and healthy lives, and the number of years of schooling is used to measure knowledge. The average score of all these constitutes HDI score, an easy way to compare one country from another. It is a composite index, which is used internationally, a most comprehensive indicator than per capita income.[9]

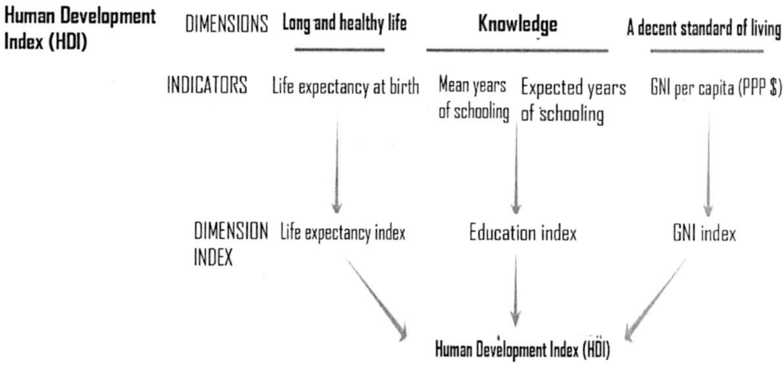

Source: UNDP 2011 HDI Report.[10]

Fig. 9.5: Calculation of Human Development Index

It reflects the accomplishments in most basic human competencies, i.e. enjoying a respectable quality of living, living a long life, and being knowledgeable. The HDI value ranges between 0 to 1. Maximum value towards 1 shows the progress of index. India ranks 132 in 191 countries with HDI 0.633 in 2021-22. Sri Lanka and Bangladesh are ahead of India in HDI ranking, i.e. 73rd and 129th positing respectively. Pakistan is behind India on 161 rank.[11]

(b) Global Multidimensional Poverty Index[12]

It is the counting-based international indicator, which is collected from more than 100 countries. The Oxford Poverty and Human Development Initiative (OPHI) at the University of Oxford and the Human Development Report Office (HDRO) of the United Nations Development Programme launched it in 2010. It gauges sporadically occurring shortages in standard of living, education, and health that has its impact on an individual's life and well-being.

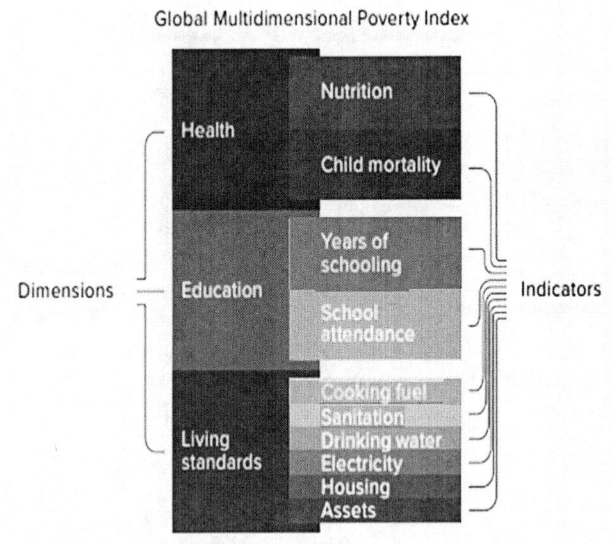

Source: HDRO and OPHI.

Fig. 9.6: Global MPI[12]

The MPI measures mainly the indicators related to the SDG-1 to end all kinds of poverty. It is interlinked with indicators related to SDG-1, 2, 3, 4, 6, 7 and 11. The global MPI is calculated for each household and person which measures deprivation according to ten parameters, including standard of life, health, and education (Fig. 9.6).[12] As per the global MPI report 2023, approximately 18 per cent or 1.1 billion out of 6.1 billion people in 110 countries, live in poverty. In Southeast Asia over, one-third of people are

Undernourishment	Child stunting	Child wasting	Child mortality
• Measures inadequate food access, an important indicator of hunger • Refers to the entire population, both children and adults • Is used as a lead indicator for international hunger reduction targets, including Sustainable Development Goal 2 (Zero Hunger)	• Go beyond calorie availability, consider aspects of diet quality and utilization • Reflect children's particular vulnerability to nutritional deficiencies • Are sensitive to uneven distribution of food within the household • Are used as nutrition indicators for SDG 2 (Zero Hunger)		• Reflects that death is the most serious consequence of hunger, and children are the most vulnerable • Improves the GHI's ability to reflect deficiencies of essential vitamins and minerals • Complements stunting and wasting, which only partially capture the mortality risk of undernutrition

Fig. 9.7: Multidimensional Nature of Four Indicators of GHI-14

poor, i.e. 389 million.[12] India is one of twenty-five nations that have reduced multidimensional poverty by half in the fifteen years between 2005-06 and 2020-21.[13] As per 2021 MPI report, India Ranked 66th across 109 countries.

(c) Global Hunger Index (GHI)

It is a well-designed instrument that tracks and measures hunger on all scales, including global, national, and local. It is mainly designed to call the world's attention towards the area where hunger level is higher and in need of major interventional efforts to reduce it. Each country's indicator is combined of four indicators namely undernourishment, under five-years child stunting, child wasting, and child mortality. It is a standardized calculation. GHI reflects calorie deficiency as well as poor child nutrition. All four indicators are part of set of the SDG indicators. The GHI calculation uses a 100-point scale, with 0 being the best result (no hunger) and 100 representing the worst.[14]

As per 2023 GHI report India ranks 111th amongst 125 countries with a score of 28.7. It is considered serious in GHI.[15]

(d) Global Food Security Index (GFSI)

It is defined as "the state in which people have physical, social, and economic access to sufficient and nutritious food that meets their dietary needs for a healthy and active life".[16] The World Food Summit's description above served as the basis for the creation of the Global Food Security Index (GFSI), which considered the three main concerns of food availability, cost, and quality across 113 nations. It is built using twenty-eight distinct indicators from both industrialized and developing nations, and it includes a qualitative and quantitative scoring approach.[16] The GFSI score is weighted from 0 to 100 where "0" is considered as the least favourable and 100 as the most favourable. As per the overall GFSI ranking, India stands at 68th position out of 113 countries with score of 58.9. India has shown improvement of 5.1 points in GFSI score from 2012.[17]

Anthropometric Measurement

This is one of the important aspects of measuring the growth of humans. Several popular anthropometric measurements include Head Circumference, Mid-Upper Arm Circumference (MUAC), Weight, and Height. Some of the comparative tools such as BMI, Waist Hip Ratio (WHR), Growth Charts of malnutrition among under-fives are used to understand the nutritional status across the world. Amongst the under five years, the following criteria are used to understand the nutritional status.

(a) Weight for Age

It is the most effective metric when used alone to evaluate physical growth. It is a widely used indicator for figuring out how to categorize malnutrition and how widespread it is. The WHO growth chart for weight for age (Z score, percentile) is commonly used to decide the nutrition status namely Severe Underweight (SUW), Moderate Underweight (MUW) and Normal Weight. In India, weight for age malnutrition (underweight) is 32.1 per cent as per NFHS-5.[8]

(b) Weight for Height

The status of acute malnutrition or wasting in children under five is often determined through calculation. There is a higher chance of morbidity and mortality when wasting is involved. The nutritional status (wasting) of children is determined using the WHO weight for height charts (Z-score, percentile) for three categories: Severe Acute Malnutrition (SAM), Moderate Acute Malnutrition (MAM), and normal. Wasting prevalence in India among under five-year children is 19.3 per cent.[8]

(c) Height for Age

When compared to weight, height provides a precise indicator of growth. Stunting or dwarfing is the term for low height for that age group. It demonstrates the longstanding malnourishment. WHO charts of height for age (Z score, percentile) are used to calculate the nutritional status (stunting) of children namely Severe Stunting, Moderate Stunting, and Normal. The stunting prevalence in under five-year children in India is 35.5 per cent. It is considered as major public health problem among under five-year children in India.[8]

(d) Mid-Upper Arm Circumference (MUAC)

Measuring the circumference of the middle of upper arm is a typical method used in the field to determine the nutritional condition of children. The mid-upper arm circumference is measured with the MUAC tape. MUAC is usually used to know the wasting status. The cut-off of MUAC less than 11.5 cm is considered as SAM, 11.5 cm to 12.5 cm considered as MAM and 12.5 cm considered as normal for the under five-years' child.

(e) Head Circumference

At birth, the head circumference is approximately 34 cm. The head circumference is typically increased and equalizes between six and nine months with chest circumference. Then, the circumference of the chest surpasses that of the head. It takes longer in youngsters who are malnourished.

(f) Body Mass Index (BMI)

Underweight, overweight, and obese people are typically categorized using a straightforward weight-for-height index. It is calculated by dividing the weight in kilograms by the height in meters squared (kg/m^2). Quetelet's index is the name of it.[2]

Body Mass Index (BMI) = Weight (kg)/Height^2 (m)^2

(g) Waist Hip Ratio

The halfway between the iliac crest and the lower border of the rib cage is where the waist circumference is measured. The Waist Heap Ratio (WHR) and BMI are related. It is an inaccurate measure of both total body fat and intra-abdominal fat mass.[2]

Legal and Policy Framework on Nutrition in India

In an effort to tackle undernutrition, the National Nutrition Policy (NNP) was launched in 1993. The strategy of NNP is using a multisectoral approach to eradicate all types of malnutrition. The implementation strategy involves intersectoral coordination between the centre, states, and district levels functionaries responsible such as policy makers, programme implementers related to health and nutrition, intended to increasing protein and micronutrients, malnutrition control activities. Making nutrition as per the requirements to reach people and monitoring progress. The NNP is made up of both indirect (long-term aims) and direct (short-term) tactics.[18]

(a) Direct Intervention

Nutrition intervention for especially vulnerable groups:

- Expanding the safety net through initiatives like the Public Distribution System, Oral Rehydration Therapy (ORT), Integrated Child Development Services (ICDS), and Universal Immunization Programme (UIP).
- Enhancing the tracking of 0- to 3-year-old children's growth.
- Reaching out to adolescents through ICDS.
- Improving the coverage of expecting mothers in order to lower the number of babies born with low birth weights.
- Enhanced nutrition for necessary foods.
- Increased consumption of inexpensive foods.
- Management of deficits related to micronutrients.

(b) Indirect Policy Intervention (Long Term)

Food security is defined as having 215 kg of food grains per person per year.

- Enhancing food habits via production and illustration.
- Raising the purchasing power of the impoverished in both urban and rural areas.

- Land reforms, health and family welfare, and nutrition and basic health knowledge.
- Food adulteration prevention.
- Nutrition surveillance.
- Programme monitoring.
- Research into many aspects of nutrition.
- Equal pay for women.
- Communication through established media for the execution of nutrition policy.
- Administration of minimum wages.
- Involvement of the community.
- Specifically, women's literacy and education.
- The advancement of women's status.

National Nutrition Schemes and Programmes in India

Many programmes are implemented to combat nutritional problems. The main issues and initiatives related to public health in India are listed below:

(a) ICDS Programme and Malnutrition

In accordance with the National Children Policy, Integrated Child Development Services (ICDS) were established in 1975. The six services of ICDS have strong nutritional components. It mainly deals with child malnutrition, which is major concern of India. Also, it works on adolescent health majorly anaemia control, etc. The population norm for Anganwadi is from 400 to 1,000 population. For 150 to 400 population, there is Mini Anganwadi and for 1,000 population, one Anganwadi at village level. The take home ration (THR) is provided to under five-year children and provides preschool education in developmental aspect. The Anganwadi *sevika* and helper are appointed at Anganwadi. Field supervision of Anganwadi is done through *mukhya sevika* (supervisor). Child Development Project Officers (CDPOs).

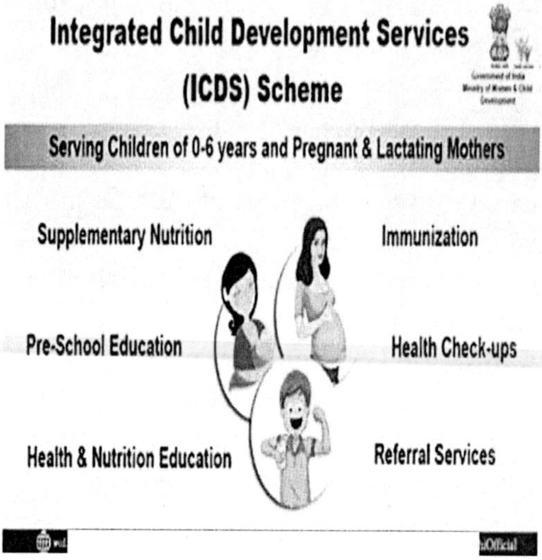

Fig. 9.8: ICDS Services

(b) Vitamin A Prophylaxis Programme

Overall Vitamin A Deficiency (VAD) prevalence is 17.54 per cent in India.[20] VAD is considered as major blind prevention control nutritional programme. Based on technologies created by the National Institute of Nutrition (NIN) in Hyderabad, the programme was introduced by the Ministry of Health and Family Welfare in 1970. As part of this programme, all children between the ages of 9 months and 5 years receive nine prophylactic doses of vitamin A.[21]

(c) Anaemia Mukta Bharat Strategy

Another widespread public health issue among children, teenage girls, and women in the reproductive years is anaemia. The prevalence of anaemia in children under five is 67.1 per cent. In women aged 15-49 who are not pregnant, it is 57.2 per cent. About 52.2 per cent of pregnant women of the same age have anaemia. To address this, the Government of India launched this flagship programme as a preventative measure against nutritional anaemia during the Fourth Five-Year Plan. The programme involves giving iron-folic acid tablets to children aged 1 to 12 as well as pregnant women and teenagers enrolled in school. Deworming is also a main component of Anaemia Mukta Bharat strategy. Campaigning Behaviour Change communication throughout year is core strategy of the programme. Testing, treating anaemia, and raising awareness regarding anaemia are other components of the programme.[2]

Iodine Deficiency Control Programme

The Government of India launched a national Goitre Control Programme in the Himalayan area in 1962. The objective was to assess the problem and replace normal salt with iodized salt to see the effect over the period. The issue was widespread; therefore, in 1986 the Iodine Deficiency Control Programme (IDD) was put into place with the goal of substituting iodized salt for whole edible salt.[2]

Mid-Day Meal Programme and Mid-Day Meal Scheme

This is an additional programme that addresses the nutritional needs of school-age children. Another name for it is the school lunch programme. It was launched in 1961 throughout the country. The PM Poshan Scheme, formerly the National Programme of Nutritional Support to Primary Education, has replaced the Mid-Day Meal Scheme. The Mid-Day Meal Scheme was introduced in 1995 and updated in 2004. The NIN in Hyderabad creates the model recipes, which are primarily meant for north and south Indian students, for school lunches. The general guidelines state that the meal should be an addition to home cooking rather than a replacement for it. Meals in schools should provide half of the required amount of proteins and one-third of the energy needed; there should be no difficult cooking involved. It is recommended to use parboiled or unpolished rice.[2]

Special Nutrition Programme

It was initiated in 1970 for women who were pregnant or nursing, and children under the age of six. It operates in impoverished rural areas, tribal areas, and slums. The additional meal provides each youngster with 10-12 gms of protein per day and 300 calories of energy. It is 500 kcal and 25 gms of protein for mothers. They receive it for a period of 300 days. Later, this programme gradually integrated with the ICDS programme.[2]

Approaches used in Malnutrition Reduction in India

Considering the magnitude of the problem and consequences of hunger, it is the need of hour to make an attempt of innovative practices with intersectoral participation to achieve SDG-2. The government is providing the services through Nutrition Rehabilitation Centre (NRC), and Village Health & Nutrition Day (VHND). Government of India (GOI) has developed a separate website to monitor the progress of SDG index. To tackle malnutrition in under five-year malnutrition organizations are working in close collabouration with GOI in different approach such as Community Based Management of Acute Malnutrition (CMAM).

One of the quasi experimental study design from Mumbai showed that wasting in children under three years of is reduced by 28 per cent in intervention area compared to 5 per cent in comparison area using CMAM approach. The success factors are considered in this CMAM study were encouragement and engaging with communities including delivery of customized information, supportive supervision of field staff, and complete management of other issues beyond acute malnutrition.[22]

Another position paper on CMAM has concluded that in CMAM approach SAM treatment must be accompanied by preventive interventions. Community Mobilization is important aspect in promotion of prevention undernutrition out of four pillars of CMAM. This paper also suggests the scaling up of CMAM for all forms of under nutrition and need of multisectoral approach in reduction of malnutrition.[23]

Conclusion

Malnutrition eradication is one of the important aspects of achieving SDG-2. Participation from multiple sectors is needed, including improved access to wholesome food, hygienic water and sanitation, high-quality health care, integrated illness management for children, optimal feeding practices for infants and young children, positive care practices, and increased community awareness of nutrition, health, and hygiene-related issues and practices.

Keywords

Hunger, SDG, malnutrition, CMAM, HDI.

NOTES

1. *Sustainable Developmental Goals*. United Nations. https://sdgs.un.org/goals
2. K. Park. (2023). *Park's Textbook of Preventive and Social Medicine*. Banarasidas Bhanot.
3. *Sustainable Developmental Goals*. (12 December 2023). United Nations. https://www.un.org/sustainabledevelopment/development-agenda/
4. *Action Against Hunger. What is Hunger*. https://www.actionagainsthunger.org/the-hunger-crisis/world-hunger-facts/what-is-hunger/
5. United Nations. (10 July 2023). *Sustainable Developmental Goals Progress Report 2023*. https://unstats.un.org/sdgs/report/2023/The-Sustainable-Development-Goals-Report-2023.pdf
6. *SDG Index and Dashboards. Sustainable Development Report 2023*. https://dashboards.sdgindex.org/profiles/india
7. United Nations. Department of Economic and Social Affairs. Statistics SDG Indicators Database SDG Country Profile India. https://unstats.un.org/sdgs/dataportal/countryprofiles/ind#goal-2
8. "National Family Health Survey-5 (2019-21)." *India Factsheet*. https://rchiips.org/nfhs/NFHS-5_FCTS/India.pdf

9. UNDP. *Human Development Report 2015*. https://sustainabledevelopment.un.org/content/documents/22212015_human_development_report.pdf
10. UNDP. (1 January 2011). *Human Development Report 2011*. https://hdr.undp.org/system/files/documents/human-development-report-2011-english.human-development-report-2011-english
11. UNDP. (2022, September 8). *Human Development Report 2021-22*. https://www.undp.org/sites/g/files/zskgke326/files/2022-09/hdr2021-22pdf_1.pdf
12. UNDP-OPHI. *Global Multidimensional Poverty Index 2023*. https://www.undp.org/sites/g/files/zskgke326/files/2023-07/2023mpireportenpdf.pdf
13. UNDP Press Release. (11 July 2023). *25 Countries Halved Multidimensional Poverty Within 15 Years, but 1.1 Billion Remain Poor*. https://www.undp.org/sites/g/files/zskgke326/files/2023-07/2023%20MPI%20press%20release_EN.pdf
14. *Global Hunger Index*. Methodology. https://www.globalhungerindex.org/methodology.html
15. *Global Hunger Index*. India. https://www.globalhungerindex.org/india.html
16. United Nations. *The Global Food Security Index*. https://www.unccd.int/resources/knowledge-sharing-system/global-food-security-index
17. Economist Impact. *Global Food Security Index 2022*. https://impact.economist.com/sustainability/project/food-security-index/reports/Economist_Impact_GFSI_2022_Global_Report_Sep_2022.pdf
18. Food Nutrition Board Government of India. (n.d.). *National Nutrition Policy 1993*. https://wcd.nic.in/sites/default/files/National%20Nutrition%20Policy.pdf
19. S. Kundu, B. Rai, and A. Shukla (8 May 2021). "Prevalence and Determinants of Vitamin A Deficiency among Children in India: Findings from a National Cross-sectional Survey." *Clinical Epidemiology and Global Health, Elsevier*. https://cegh.net/article/S2213-3984(21)00072-5/pdf
20. *Ibid.*
21. National Health Mission. *Vitamin A Supplementation*. https://nhm.gov.in/index1.php?lang=1&level=3&sublinkid=1452&lid=801
22. N. Shah More, A. Waingankar, S. Ramani, S. Chanani, V. D'Souza, S. Pantvaidya, A. Fernandez, and A. Jayaraman (30 March 2018). "Community-Based Management of Acute Malnutrition to Reduce Wasting in Urban Informal Settlements of Mumbai, India: A Mixed-Methods Evaluation." *Glob Health Sci Pract. 6*(1):103-27.

doi: 10.9745/GHSP-D-17-00182. PMID: 29602868; PMCID: PMC5878065.

23. M. Mathur, A. Halim, M. Gupta, B. Panda, and A. Syed (2018). "Community-based Management of Acute Malnutrition (CMAM) in India: A Position Paper." *International Journal of Research in Medical Sciences*, *6*(12): 4128-35. https://doi.org/10.18203/2320-6012.ijrms20184920

10

Water for People India

Assessing Interventions and Aligning with Sustainable Development Goal 6

Banasree Das, Ravikant Kumar, and *Sujata Tripathy*

The United Nations adopted the transformative agenda 2030 for sustainable development which was the way forward after the conclusion of The Millennium Development Goals (MDG) era ended in year 2016. The countries started to put their efforts into achieving the seventeen goals as per the new agenda. The agenda includes 169 targets for the next fifteen years. As per the UN Secretary-General Ban Ki-moon

> The Seventeen Sustainable Development Goals (SDGs) are our shared vision of humanity and a social contract between the world's leaders and the people. (United Nations, 2015)

The SDGs are focusing to change the problems of world and trigger to end the inequality, poverty, health and educational issues by protection of environment, ensuring prosperity and justice and service delivery and economic growth. SDGs also ensure that no one is left behind and which is essential.

In the year 2015, the United Nations adopted the goals, i.e. SDGs which is also known as Global Goals. The SDGs ensure reduction of poverty and protection of environment so that the people of this planet can enjoy the peace and economic prosperity. All the seventeen SDGs are converged the outcomes of each area to balance the socio-economic and environment.

As per the United Nations, the SDG targets have been set as per the below:

- By 2030, achieve universal and equitable access to safe and affordable drinking water for all.
- By 2030, achieve access to adequate and equitable sanitation and hygiene for all and end open defecation, paying special attention to the needs of women and girls and those in vulnerable situations.
- By 2030, improve water quality by reducing pollution, eliminating dumping and minimizing release of hazardous chemicals and materials, halving the proportion of untreated waste water and substantially increasing recycling and safe reuse globally.
- By 2030, substantially increase water-use efficiency across all sectors and ensure sustainable withdrawals and supply of fresh water to address water scarcity and substantially reduce the number of people suffering from water scarcity.
- By 2030, implement integrated water resources management at all levels, including through transboundary cooperation as appropriate.
- By 2030, protect and restore water-related ecosystems, including mountains, forests, wetlands, rivers, aquifers, and lakes.
- By 2030, expand international cooperation and capacity-building support to developing countries in water and sanitation-related activities and programmes, including water harvesting, desalination, water

efficiency, waste water treatment, recycling, and reuse technologies.

Support and strengthen the participation of local communities in improving water and sanitation management. (Goal Target: Goal 6: Clean water and sanitation | Sustainable Development Goals | United Nations Development Programme (undp.org))

In the Indian context, SDG-6 focuses on ensuring the availability and sustainable management of water and sanitation for all. India faces significant challenges in this regard, given its vast population, diverse geography, and varying level of development across different regions of the country.

Access to Clean Water

In current development scenario, Indian population still lacks access to clean and safe drinking water. Rural areas face challenges with contaminated (biological or chemical) water sources, leading to waterborne diseases. India's water bodies, including rivers, lakes, and groundwater sources, are facing pollution due to untreated sewage system, industrial discharge mixing with the water bodies, use of chemicals for agriculture purposes (pesticides and chemical composting), runoff of water carrying the pollutants and mixing with the water sources as well as water bodies. The polluted water not only affects the human health but also impacts aquatic ecosystems and overall biodiversity.

Sanitation

Accessibility of sufficient and improved facilities for sanitation is still challenging in various areas of India. Open defecation is still present in rural areas due to various reasons like lack of functional toilets or sometime due to behavioural practices which poses the health risk as well as environmental pollution and finally leading to poor health conditions.

Water Management

Efficient water management is very crucial for India in the current context as India is the largest groundwater-dependent country. especially given its agriculture-dependent economy and the growing water stress due to factors like climate change and overexploitation of water resources. There's a need for sustainable water management practices, including water budgeting, rainwater harvesting, watershed management, and efficient water resource management planning through Gram Panchayat Development Plan.

To address the water and sanitation related issues in India, the Government of India has launched several flagship programmes in mission mode like Jal Jeevan Mission, Swachh Bharat Mission with the aim of improving sanitation facilities including improvement of hygiene and providing piped water supply to all households. Community engagement especially at the grassroots level is crucial for the success of water and sanitation initiatives. Community-led approaches, such as the construction of community toilets, grey water management at community level, rainwater harvesting structures, water budgeting for judiciary usage of water can play a significant role in improving access to water and sanitation services.

Overall, achieving SDG-6 in the Indian context requires a multi-dimensional approach involving government action, People's participation in every stage of planning to implementation and post-implementation Operation and maintenance of created assets for long-term usage, technological innovations, and sustainable water management practices with ownership.

India has taken a positive and bold step to adopt, implement, and monitor SDGs at the national and subnational levels. NITI Aayog is playing a leading role in this endeavour. India's localization approach showcases a bold and remarkable strategic model for advancing the SDGs. The localization of SDGs is a strategic initiative by the Ministry of Panchayati Raj aimed at implementing the SDGs at the grassroots level through the PRIs. The approach clusters the seventeen global goals into nine themes tailored to the rural Indian context. The SDG-6 is reflected in theme 4 focusing on creating water sufficient villages and theme 5 focusing on "clean and green villages" of the localization of SDGs.

Implementation of India's localized SDG model addresses substantial demands for water, improvement of infrastructure, creates opportunities for market system development. Finally, the adoption of two key initiatives towards water and sanitation, the Jal Jeevan Mission and Swachh Bharat Mission, has greatly met the water and sanitation needs of local communities.

Through these interventions, Water For People contributes to advancing SDG-6 in India by improving access to clean water and sanitation services, promoting hygiene behaviour change, and strengthening institutional capacity for sustainable water and sanitation management.

Water-related Programmes in India

The important water-related programmes are:

- National Drinking Water Mission (NDWM) launched in 1986.
- NDWM was renamed as Rajiv Gandhi National Drinking Water Mission (RGNDWM) in 1991.
- The third-generation programme started in 1999-2000 when Sector Reform Projects evolved to involve the community in planning, implementation and management of drinking water-related schemes, later scaled up as Swajaldhara in 2002 and Jalanidhi.
- National Water Policy 2002 and revised in 2012 aligns with SGD-6 by emphasizing waste water management, water quality, integrated water resources management, conservation and sustainability, and access to safe drinking water for all (UNICEF India, n.d.).
- The Jal Jeevan Mission (JJM) was launched on 15 August 2019 (*The Economic Times*, 2019) aiming to provide tap water connection to every rural household by 2024 (Sreenidhi International School, 2023).

- Atal Bhujal Yojna (ABY) was launched with aims to ensure availability and sustainable management of water and sanitation for everyone, by promoting efficient water use community participation and sustainable groundwater management. The target is to improve water quality, increasing water use efficiency and ensuring sustainable withdrawals and supply of fresh water and groundwater recharge (Llausàs, 2022).

Linkage between Water for People's Strategy and SGD-6

Water For People vision, "a world where every person has access to safe water and sanitation services", is aimed at promotion of high-quality drinking water availability and elevated quality of sanitation services which is accessible to all, and sustained the provided services by building strong communities, businesses mechanism, and strengthened government systems. The organization's mission is to ensure that everyone has access to reliable and safe WASH services, especially in rural and marginalized communities, on a long-term basis. To achieve the goal, Water For People India collabourating with local communities, related departments of state and central government, and other stakeholders or partners working in the same field to implement sustainable WASH services that are congruent to the needs of target community. Water For People India working on water quality registered in 2008 as Water For People India Trust (WFPIT), raises funds for charity. It partners with the global headquarters to support state projects, providing oversight and technical assistance. In 2011, Water For People adopted a model based on universal and sustainable access, the Everyone Forever (EF) model. In many ways, the Everyone Forever model was the precursor for the Government of India's flagship programmes JJM and Swachh Bharat Mission (SBM) (Rising Kashmir, 2023). Water For People India has designed and implemented programmes across the states of West Bengal, Bihar, Maharashtra, Assam, and Odisha that include the most vulnerable communities to ensure access to quality services at households, schools, and hospitals in each block or district. Community ownership is the focus of programmes, including those for technical or engineering-driven interventions. To ensure quality service provision, we train local community members as service providers and local entrepreneurs or *jalbandhus* who provide services for water and sanitation. They are either accountable to the panchayat or work on a fee-based model through Points of Purchase (PoPs). West Bengal state government has adopted this model, and Water For People India works closely with district and block administrations that provide support for co-financing water systems, implementing programmes directly, or through partners. As a data-driven organization, our annual Level of Service (LoS) monitoring for water and sanitation and conducting annual survey for the Sustainable Service Checklist (SSC) inform the annual planning.

To date, Water For People India's efforts have resulted in an intermediate or high level of water access for 2.64 million people living in 71 blocks in 28 districts. We have installed approximately 3,100 community water points (new or renovated hand pumps and piped water supply systems). We have added water and sanitation facilities in 1,700 public institutions. We have also installed drip irrigation in twelve communities, which is more efficient than relying on flood irrigation. Despite successes over the past fifteen years, we realize that we need to exponentially scale up our work to achieve SDG-6 which emphasizes clean water and sanitation facilities for all. Therefore, because of intensive planning, the goal is to reach one hundred million people by 2030.

Water For People India's strategies are based on collabourative approaches and focus on systems strengthening to ensure sustainability. However, as we race to scale up our work, the sustainability of our work is severely threatened by factors such as climate change. Drinking water supply is almost entirely dependent on groundwater in both rural and urban areas. Climate change has caused erratic rainfall patterns, affecting both spatial and temporal availability of groundwater. In addition, in the areas where the organization work such as the Sundarbans, increasing incidences of cyclones and sea-level rise threaten to undo the gains of all the work, causing damage to water and sanitation infrastructure, salinity ingress, and severe flooding. Simultaneously, dry spells are increasing in parts of Birbhum, Nalanda, and Amravati districts, where the organization work. The Intergovernmental Panel on Climate Change (IPCC) Round 6 unambiguously states that climate change is real and almost irreversible, and that the situation is likely to worsen in coastal and Himalayan regions. Communities in these areas are the victims of climate change and have contributed little to the causes of climate change.

Water For People India recognizes that there is an urgent need to focus on and invest in both adaptation and mitigation. There is a need for significantly increased finance to tackle and strengthen systems for building resilience. Most importantly, for all actors to act in tandem, efforts shall be made to arrest the devastating impact of climate change. But, how do we do it? While we have recognized the impact of climate change on our work and have strategically added water resource management to augment our water, sanitation, and hygiene (WASH) interventions, we have not been highly successful at integrating climate change mitigation and adaptation activities into our work, which is needed to strengthen community resilience and reduce vulnerability.

Moreover, the motto of SDGs, "Leaving No One Behind" is aligned with Water For People India's destination 2023 strategy, It is also reflected in India's national development strategy of "Sabka Saath, Sabka Vikas, Sabka Vishwas, Sabka Prayas" (Everyone's support, everyone's development, everyone's faith, everyone's effort).

Water For People India is registered as a non-profit organization that strives to guarantee access to clean water and sanitation for all. In India, Water For People India has implemented various interventions aligned with SDG-6 to address water and sanitation challenges. Here are some examples of interventions:

(a) Community-Led Total Sanitation (CLTS)

Water For People India promotes CLTS approaches, which focus on empowering communities to become open defecation-free by facilitating behaviour change rather than solely providing infrastructure. This approach involves raising awareness about the importance of sanitation, conducting community meetings, and encouraging households to construct and use toilets.

(b) Water Supply Infrastructure

Water For People India aims to enhance access to safe and dependable drinking water by construction and establishment of proper maintenance mechanism of water supply infrastructure. This may include the drilling of boreholes, installation of hand pumps or piped water systems, and rehabilitation of existing water sources to ensure sustainability.

(c) Hygiene Promotion

Promoting good hygiene practices is essential for preventing water-borne diseases and improving overall health. Water For People India conducts hygiene education sessions in communities, schools, and health-care facilities to raise awareness about hand washing, safe water storage, and sanitation practices.

(d) Capacity Building and Training

Water For People India provides training and capacity building support to local government officials, community leaders, and water and sanitation committees. This helps strengthen their ability to manage water and sanitation facilities effectively, ensuring long-term sustainability of interventions.

(e) Monitoring and Evaluation

Water For People India focuses on robust monitoring and evaluation mechanisms to track progress, identify the gaps and find the feasible solutions along with measure the impact of interventions. This involves collecting data on water quality, sanitation coverage, and hygiene behaviours to inform decision making and improve programme effectiveness.

(f) Partnerships and Advocacy

Water For People India collabourates with government agencies, NGOs, education institutes and other stakeholders to advocate for policies and investments that prioritize water and sanitation access for all. By leveraging partnerships and engaging in advocacy efforts, they aim to create a positive environment towards sustainable water and sanitation service development in India.

Scale, Innovation, WRM for Sustainability and Forever Solution

Water For People India recognizes the need to exponentially scale up its efforts to reach the goal of providing clean water and sanitation services to 100 million people by 2030. This involves expanding its reach to more communities, districts, and states, while ensuring the quality and sustainability of the services provided. Scaling up involves leveraging partnerships, optimizing resources, and adopting efficient implementation strategies to maximize impact. Innovation plays a crucial role in tackling the challenges of climate change and ensuring sustainability of efforts. It aims to innovate across various aspects of work, including technology, community engagement, and financing models. For example, it can explore innovative water purification techniques, sustainable sanitation solutions, and resilient infrastructure designs to adapt to changing environmental conditions. Additionally, social innovations such as community-led initiatives and behaviour change campaigns can enhance the effectiveness and acceptance of its programmes. Water resource management is central to its sustainability efforts, especially in the face of climate change. It needs to prioritize the efficient and equitable use of water resources, considering factors such as groundwater recharge, rainwater harvesting, and watershed management. Integrated water resource management approaches will help it to ensure the availability of clean water for communities while minimizing the negative impacts of climate change, such as water scarcity and contamination. This involves working closely with target communities, government departments, partners and other stakeholders to reveal and implement sustainable water management practices tailored to each region's needs.

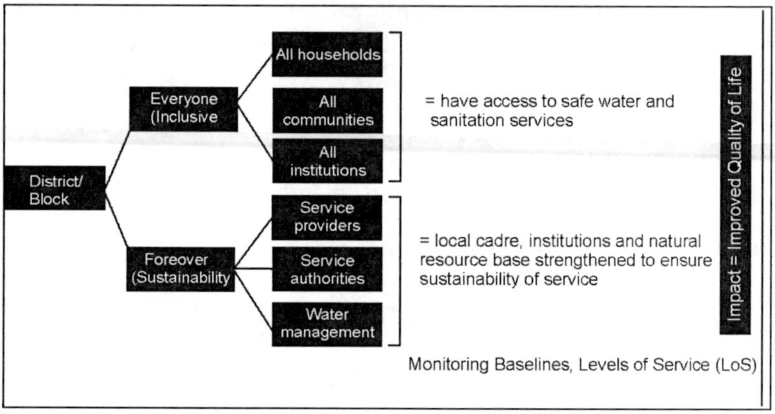

Water for People India's Intervention to Address SDG-6

SDG-6 is to ensure availability and accessibility of sustainable way of management for water and sanitation facilities to all. It can be enriched through practical case stories like leveraging local art for behaviour change. Water For People India Trust has effectively combined infrastructure development with behaviour change initiatives under the Swachho Nirapad Paribesh project in Birbhum. This project utilized traditional local art forms, such as performances by Baul singers, folk dancers, magicians, and puppeteers, to promote WASH practices. These artists, trained on WASH concepts, created engaging plays and skits that conveyed crucial hygiene messages in the local language, appealing to the community's cultural sensibilities. Their performances, which humorously addressed issues like safe water handling, open defecation, and handwashing, were instrumental in changing behaviours and improving public health. The project not only raised awareness but also provided these artists with a sustainable livelihood. The success of this initiative highlights the importance of integrating cultural and community-based approaches in achieving SDG-6 targets. It also demonstrates that behaviour change, facilitated through local and relatable mediums, is crucial for the sustainability of WASH infrastructure. This approach has been widely appreciated by the local communities and stakeholders, proving that cultural relevance is key to effective public health interventions.

Leveraging Local Art for Behaviour Change Approach: To Go Beyond Building Infrastructure

If infrastructure is the bricks and mortar of WASH, behaviour change is the cement that holds it together. In India, NGOs and communities have been instrumental in driving behaviour change, while the government has focused on building infrastructure. Behaviour change comes in at all stages of a WASH project, from creating demand, ensuring usage and O&M. Water For People India Trust has combined the two in the National Stock Exchange Foundation-supported Swachho Nirapad Paribesh project to provide sustainable WASH to "Everyone Forever" in Birbhum. It has leveraged local social art forms to trigger change and influence behaviour towards WASH in the Rajnagar and Khoyrasol blocks. The local art forms it has identified include traditional folk singers called the Bauls, folk dancers, magicians, puppeteers, street performers and drum players. These local artistes, who were struggling to get by on their traditional performing arts, have been able to earn considerably more while promoting good WASH behaviour supported by Water For People India Trust. "Birbhum district is known for its Baul performers music and traditional Adivasi dance. So our objective was to highlight the key WASH behaviour change among the community through the famous and accepted local art and culture" said an artist of Anandyo Lokyo Natyo Sansthan in Rajnagar. In both blocks, Water For People India Trust and the local communities identified singers, musicians and others who had the experience of performing local plays called *jatras*. The organization's team oriented them on WASH concepts and helped to write scripts for performances that the artists set to their tunes in the local language. This appealed to the hearts of local people on WASH related behaviour: to not defecate in the open, keep the surroundings clean, wash hands with soap after using toilets, and observe good hygiene practices. "In our group, we have actors, singers, drum (*dholak*) players and anchors who have the passion to perform plays before the crowd even at a short leveraging local art for behaviour change Approach—To go beyond building infrastructure notice" said artists of Jagriti Loknatyo Goshti of Khoyrasol block. In each block, the artists were assembled into performing troupes. The troupe in Khoyrasol was called Jagriti Loknatyo Goshti, and in Rajnagar, it was called Anando Lokko Natyo Santhan. In each group, there are ten-twelve artists. The artists were drawn from different *panchayat*s to help identify with the local communities. An agency called the Kathok Performing Repertoire trained these groups on how to work together to create plays/dramas. It oriented the on WASH and fashioned them into local critical change agents (communities) to become champions of positive WASH behaviour in their own community. The Goshti created musical skits on safe water handling, environmental cleaning, use of toilets everyday, hand wash with soap, menstrual hygiene management and so on. The 30-40 minute long plays humorously highlighted the importance of WASH. Water For People India Trust organized performances in villages where poor WASH behaviour was noticed. Both groups have performed more than ninty shows in their respective blocks and have earned appreciation from the community and *panchayat*s. A villager from Khoyrasol said,

> I really enjoyed the way the artists acted and sang to aware us on safe water handling and use of toilet with maintaining hygiene and shall follow the same at my place. I have recorded the entire play in my phone to further disseminate it to my friends in other villages through WhatsApp.

One of the Jagriti Loknatyo Goshti artists said,

> Whenever we walk through the village, where we have performed earlier, people recognize us and think, we might call them out for their inappropriate WASH behaviour. So, they become quite alert and try to improve themselves.

A female artist from the same group said when she performs in a village, women appreciate her skits and have improved their WASH practices. One Rajnagar artist said he influenced this family's behaviour. "Initially my wife used to fetch water in an unhygienically way but after seeing me act, she realized her mistake and changed her behaviour immediately." Another artist from Rajnagar said, "When we act as a person sick with cholera, dying in bed, it shakes up the audience." The artists have been felicitated by the various stakeholders in their respective blocks. The Khoyrasole group was invited by the local police station to perform their acts on "Save Life" as well as on WASH behaviour. This approach leveraging local art forms has increased the connect with local communities to change WASH behaviour. Even the artists feel that their involvement in this social development programme has given them importance and respect in the community However they strongly feel that beyond WASH other social messages which are ruining the society's development need to be focused too through this approach such as—stop dowry system, early girl childhood marriage, trafficking, etc.

Recommendations

Water For People India could focus on several areas to contribute to the improvement of SDG-6, which aims to ensure availability and sustainable management of water and sanitation for all. Here are some recommendations:

(a) Community Engagement and Empowerment

Water For People India shall continue to prioritize community engagement and empowerment in their projects. This includes involving target communities as well as stakeholders in decision making processes, to ensure building their capacities, to ensure their engagement in management and maintenance of water and sanitation infrastructure sustainably through planning and implementation process. And, also ensure post implementation O&M by ownership development.

(b) Integrated Water Resource Management

The adoption of integrated management system of water resources and consider the entire water source sustainability including water supply, sanitation, and waste water management. The adopted approach ensures the sustainable use of water resource management while addressing multiple challenges, such as water scarcity, pollution and ground water exploitation.

(c) Promotion of Hygiene and Sanitation Practices

Emphasize the importance of hygiene and sanitation practices, including handwashing by using soap, safe and managed sanitation facilities, and menstrual health and hygiene management. These practices are vital for reducing waterborne diseases and enhancing public health outcomes.

(d) Technology and Innovation

Explore innovative technologies and approaches for improving access to safe water and sanitation services, particularly in hard-to-reach or underserved areas. This could include the use of low-cost sanitation solutions, water treatment technologies, and digital tools for monitoring and evaluation.

(e) Partnerships and Collabouration

Foster partnerships and collabouration with government departments, partner NGOs, private organizations or sector partners, other stakeholders to accumulate resources, expert guidance and create networks. Collabourative efforts can help scale up impact and ensure the sustainability of interventions over the long-term.

(f) Monitoring and Evaluation

Establishment of strong monitoring and evaluation mechanisms to monitor the progress towards SDG-6 targets, identify challenges, and learn from successes and failures. This data-driven approach enables Water For People India to make evidence-based decisions and continuously improve their interventions.

(g) Climate Resilience

Integrate climate resilience considerations into water and sanitation projects to address the effects of climate change like changing in rainfall patterns and duration, increased period of extreme weather events, melting the glacier and rising sea levels. This may involve incorporating nature-based solutions, such as green infrastructure, to enhance resilience.

By focusing on these areas, Water For People India can make meaningful contributions to the achievement of SDG-6 and contribute to improving the lives of millions of people by ensuring access to clean water and sanitation services.

Conclusion

In conclusion, the linkage between SDG-6 and Water For People India interventions is profound and critical for achieving lasting impact in communities across India. Water For People India's interventions align directly with the objectives of SDG-6, which focus to ensure the access to clean and safe water and sanitation facilities to all, and their efforts play a crucial role in advancing progress towards this global goal.

Through community engagement and empowerment, Water For People India fosters sustainable solutions that address the root causes of water and sanitation challenges, by ensuring the interventions based on specific needs and priorities of local communities. By promoting integrated water resource management approaches, the organization contributes to the effective and sustainable management of water resources, while also addressing the prevalent challenges such as water scarcity and pollution.

Water For People India's emphasis on hygiene and sanitation practices not only improves public health outcomes but also contributes towards achieving SDG targets related to health and well-being. Through the adoption of innovative technologies and partnerships with stakeholders, including government agencies and the private sector, the organization leverages resources and expertise to scale up impact and ensure the sustainability of interventions over the long-term.

By incorporating climate resilience considerations into their projects, Water For People India helps the communities adapt to the impacts of climate change, ensuring that water and sanitation services remain accessible and reliable even in the face of environmental challenges.

In summary, Water For People India's interventions are instrumental in advancing progress towards SDG-6 by enhancing access to safe and portable water and sanitation, promoting sustainable practices, and building resilient inhabitants. Through their dedication and collabourative efforts, Water For People India continues to make meaningful contributions to the achievement of SDG-6 and the overall well-being of communities across India.

Keywords

SDG-6, WASH, climate resilience, community empowerment, water for people.

REFERENCES

Atal Bhujal Yojana. "Atal Bhujal Yojana." Ministry of Jal Shakti, Government of India, https://ataljal.hid.gov.in (accessed on 31 May 2024).

Goal Target: Goal 6: Clean Water and Sanitation | Sustainable Development Goals | United Nations Development Programme (undp.org))

Jal Jeevan Mission. "Jal Jeevan Mission." Ministry of Jal Shakti, Government of India, https://jaljeevanmission.gov.in/ (accessed on 31 May 2024).

Llausàs, A. (2022b). "Water Use in the Tourism Accommodation Sector." In *Encyclopedia of the UN Sustainable Development Goals* (pp. 913-25). https://doi.org/10.1007/978-3-319-95846-0_159

National Drinking Water Mission (1986). Proposal for Sustainable Drinking Water Solution. Government of India, https://www.cse.iitb.ac.in/~ctara/dilproposal/VishalMTP.pdf

Press Information Bureau. "Prime Minister's Address at the National Conclave on Natural Farming." Press Information Bureau, Government of India, 16 December 2021, https://pib.gov.in/Pressreleaseshare.aspx?PRID=1782283 (accessed on 31 May 2024).

Resources, SuSan, A. (n.d.-b). https://www.susana.org/en/knowledge-hub/resources-and-publications/library/sort/download_hits-ASC/filter/445?page=5

Rising Kashmir (8 June 2023). "Effective Implementation of Flagship Schemes can Transform Lives of Ordinary Citizens: LG Sinha". *Rising Kashmir*, http://risingkashmir.com/effective-implementation-of-flagship-schemes-can-transform-lives-of-ordinary-citizens-lg-sinha

Sreenidhi International School (8 June 2023). Sreenidhi International School.

The Economic Times (15 August 2019). "Launch of Jal Jeevan Misson". *The Economic Times*, https://economictimes.indiatimes.com/topic/UNICEF-India/4

UNICEF. "Water, Sanitation and Hygiene (WASH)." UNICEF, https://www.unicef.org/wash (accessed on 31 May 2024).

United Nations (30 December 2015). "Sustainable Development Goals to Kick in with Start of New Year." *UN News*, https://news.un.org/en/story/2015/12/519172

United Nations Development Programme. "Clean Water and Sanitation." United Nations Development Programme, https://www.undp.org/sustainable-development-goals/clean-water-and-sanitation (accessed on 31 May 2024).

United Nations Development Programme. "Sustainable Development Goals." United Nations Development Programme, https://www.undp.org/sustainable-development-goals (accessed on 31 May 2024).

United Nations. "Agenda 21." United Nations Department of Economic and Social Affairs, 1992, https://sustainabledevelopment.un.org/outcomedocuments/agenda21 (accessed on 31 May 2024).

United Nations. "The 17 Goals | Sustainable Development." United Nations Department of Economic and Social Affairs, https://sdgs.un.org/goals (accessed on 31 May 2024).

World Health Organization. "Sustainable Development Goals." World Health Organization Regional Office for Europe, https://www.who.int/europe/about-us/our-work/sustainable-development-goals (accessed on 31 May 2024).

Part III

11

Adopting Community-Based Participatory Research for Advancing Sustainable Development

Lessons from Indian Higher Education Institutions

Wafa Singh, Raisuyah Bhagwan, and *Manju Singh*

Today, India stands at the cusp of a complex developmental paradigm as it faces some of the most unprecedented social challenges in recent times. This reflects in the fact that India ranks 134 out of 193 countries in the Human Development Index (HDI), released by the United Nations Development Programme (UNDP) in its Human Development Report 2023/2024 (UNDP, 2024). Making matters worse are the challenges of social fragmentation, economic inequality, destruction of natural resources, youth unrest, etc., all of which are critical contributors towards unsustainable development. These multidimensional challenges have put the spotlight back on public institutions and their responsibility towards addressing the same, by way of adoption of innovative approaches (Tremblay *et al.*, 2017; Ahmadein, 2019). Considering the role and impact of public institutions in the society, a renewed approach to their social responsibilities is poised to have crucial implications on India's journey towards achieving sustainability.

It is here that Indian Higher Education Institutions (HEIs)—bearing the primary responsibility of knowledge creation and dissemination for public welfare—have an important role to play. Accordingly, they are now being called upon to leverage their core functions (of teaching, research and service) and resources (human, physical, and financial) to address critical social challenges (Tandon, 2017; Göransson, Donati and Wigren-Kristoferson, 2021). Their research function in particular, is expected to move from Model-1 knowledge production (traditional knowledge creation for disciplinary research) towards Mode-2 knowledge production (applied knowledge production for social benefit) for providing sustainable solutions to pressing societal problems (Gibbons *et al.,* 1994; Hall and Tandon, 2017). This has led to increasing calls for going beyond "traditional' research approaches, towards "new' knowledge production through innovative means.

It is in this context that Community-Based Participatory Research (CBPR), which is "action-oriented" and "community-based" has gained much popularity in the global academic discourse, including India (Hall and Tandon, 2017). As a collabourative and engaged form of research, CBPR entails the conduction of research based on social needs and results in the generation of knowledge solutions, which is locally and socially relevant (Molosi-France and Dipholo, 2022). The ability to generate local solutions to global challenges (thereby contributing towards achieving the United Nations Sustainable Development Goals (UN SDGs)), is what makes CBPR most pertinent in the current context (Hall and Tandon, 2017). This chapter, therefore, explores the conceptual framework of CBPR and its positioning amidst the sustainable development framework, while also outlining the Indian higher education policy scenario and institutional implementation in this regard. In doing so, the chapter carves out the emergent lessons, not only in terms of the potential of CBPR in attaining the sustainable development agenda, but also enlists aspects for strengthening and advancing its practice in Indian academia.

CBPR: The Theoretical Framework

(a) A Collabourative, Engaged Research Approach

Engaged research or community-engaged research is an umbrella term, used for a wide variety of research-based activities and methods (Mthembu, Chimbari and Macherera, 2023). These include community-based research, collabourative research, participatory action research, partnership research, community-based participatory research (CBPR), etc. (De Santis *et al.*, 2019: 151). Here, CBPR emerges as the most well-established method (initially applied in the field of health, and now expanding to other domains of human development), and has been gradually gaining prominence as a potential tool for providing sustainable solutions to critical societal challenges (Hall and Tandon, 2017). In particular, CBPR underscores research which is community driven, thereby foregrounding the importance of community agendas over researcher's agenda and also ensures that research is responsive to the community context (Neufeldt and Jansen, 2021, cited in Molosi-France and Dipholo, 2022: 116).

In essence, CBPR is described as a collabourative approach to enquiry, which involves working in collabouration with community members, researchers and other stakeholders in the research process, while recognizing each of their unique strengths (Machimana *et al.*, 2021; Sugawara *et al.*, 2023). It commences with a research topic that comes from, or is of importance to the community and stresses co-learning, capacity building and long-term commitment, with action integral to the research (Minkler, 2014). Use of CBPR methodology generates locally appropriate knowledge solutions, as well as disseminates new knowledge for generating awareness and taking actions to improve the situation in light of that knowledge (Hall and Tandon, 2017). Therefore, as a form of action-oriented research, CBPR aims to combine knowledge and action for social change (Hall *et al.*, 2016).

Here, Kelly and Given (2023) noted that such collabouration or working "with" the community, denotes the integration of community participation throughout the process. Further, Mutero and Chimbari (2021) argued that under such innovative research approaches, universities and different stakeholders coalesce in finding solutions to some of the community's intractable problems. As a result, CBPR emerges as a viable tool for advancing community engagement, that culminates in sustainable community development, in contrast to the more traditional approaches, which primarily take a top-down perspective (Sibhensana and Maistry, 2023).

Further, CBPR should not be considered as just another method of research, but as a means to enrich the scholarship of teaching and learning for students from different disciplines, by providing an opportunity to connect theory and practice through enhanced civic engagement (Molosi-France and Dipholo, 2022). Accordingly, Bidandi, Ambe and Mukong (2021) perceived CBPR as enabling students to become knowledgeable and active citizens in their respective communities, countries and also in the world.

(b) A Subset of the Community-University Engagement

In the face of the unsustainability crisis posed by socio-ecological systems and economic and political uncertainties, a variety of stakeholders are called upon to co-develop practical solutions for pressing social problems (Lepore and King, 2023). It is in this context that Community-University Research Partnerships (CURPs)—which provides the platform for the practice of CBPR—has emerged as a means to strengthen societal contribution of research, in various areas of sustainable socio-economic development (UNESCO Chair in CBRSR, 2015). Such research partnerships build on joint engagements between the university and the community, which generates opportunities to bring diverse resources to understanding the causes of, and solutions to wicked societal problems (UNESCO Chair in CBRSR, 2015; Lepore, Hall and Tandon, 2021).

Therefore, CBPR is one of the forms through which Community-University Engagement (CUE) (also known as

Community Engagement (CE)) is practised at HEIs (Tandon, 2014). CUE is a multifaceted, multidimensional umbrella term that may be applied to a vast range of activities, in relation to the role HEIs needs to play in a society (Escrigas *et al.*, 2014: xxxv). It emerges from the responsibility that HEIs have towards the society and the need for them to engage in issues of social concern, building on reciprocal collabourations between academic and civic cultures, and resulting in knowledge co-creation for public good and sustainable development (Boyer, 1996).

The Carnegie Foundation for the Advancement of Teaching defined CUE as:

> The collabouration between HEIs and larger communities for mutually beneficial exchange of knowledge and resources in a context of partnership and reciprocity ... to enrich scholarship, prepare engaged citizens, address critical societal issues and contribute to the public good. (McIlrath, 2014: 40)

Therefore, while CUE refers to the mutually beneficial collabouration between HEIs and communities for addressing shared societal concerns, CBPR emerges as a subset of CUE, where the university and the community enter into research partnerships, and are equal owners of the research process and its outputs (PRIA, 2014). Such partnerships also facilitate knowledge sharing, resource mobilization and expansion of opportunities for engaged research for advancing the sustainable development agenda (Leal Filho *et al.*, 2023). Therefore, CBPR as a form of CUE cannot only address the real issues of the communities, but can also be used to make practical recommendations to policy makers and strategists on possible avenues for sustainable socio-economic development of communities (Shabalala, 2023).

(c) An Effective Tool to Attain the UN SDGs

Being community-based and involving the values of participation and research for co-learning and co-generation of knowledge,

CBPR offers a valuable opportunity to address local issues, with respect to different aspects of SDGs such as water, sanitation, resource management, gender equality, etc. (Singh, 2021). Such "community-based" research offers the advantages of greater ownership of local problems, and can therefore help achieve sustainable and multidimensional "development", rather than unilateral "growth". Further, coherent and well managed CBPR partnerships and projects achieve a number of objectives, which directly contribute to the sustainable development agenda (Hall and Tandon, 2017). These include building networks and alliances, increasing empowerment, strengthening insight and identities, building organizational capacity and human, cultural and social capital and well-being, among others (Kagan *et al.*, 2017). In doing so, it contributes to the development of "sustainable communities", which are characterized as being fair, environmentally sensitive, harmonious, inclusive and well-run, with good quality services, and having a good economy (Kagan *et al.*, 2017). These arguments support the proposition that contextualized and localized actions, through engagement with societal actors, using an inter-disciplinary lens, is instrumental for the achievement of SDGs.

Globally, much evidence exists on the application of CBPR for achieving the UN SDGs. For instance, the Science Shops and the Responsible Research & Innovation (RRI) framework of Europe demonstrates a workable and practical example of how such collabourative and community-based research partnerships are furthering the sustainable development agenda (Tandon and Pandey, 2019). Further, the Knowledge for Change (K4C) international consortium (an initiative of the UNESCO Chair in Community-Based Research and Social Responsibility in Higher Education) develops capacities in CBPR for the co-creation of knowledge on issues related to UN SDGs, through collective action by academics and community actors (like *panchayat*s, municipalities, district administration, community organizations, etc.) (Lepore, Hall and Tandon, 2021). In doing so, the K4C programme aims to attain the locally prioritized SDG targets, by producing socially relevant and actionable knowledge (UNESCO Chair in CBRSR, 2022). Another evidence of such collabourative and engaged research was documented by Burman (2019), who demonstrated its application in solving the wicked problems in rural South Africa, through mutual engagement and reciprocal knowledge co-generation between the University of Limpopo and Waterberg welfare society, resulting in sustainable social change.

Positioning of CBPR in the Indian Higher Education Policy Landscape

While social engagement and contribution to societal welfare through educative practices was always accorded due importance and value in Indian higher education, it was the Twelfth Five-Year Plan (2012-17) which for the first time advocated for socially relevant research to be a part of the core mission of HEIs (Planning Commission, 2013: 111). It was under the guidance of these directives that the University Grants Commission (UGC) rolled out a scheme for the "Establishment of Centre(s) for Fostering Social Responsibility and Community Engagement (CFSRCE) in Universities" in 2014 (UGC, 2014). This scheme promoted CURPs in general and encouraged CBPR in particular, for improving the lives of the communities (UGC, 2014). This laid down one of the very first foundations for the integration of CBPR in Indian HEIs. Consolidating this development further, was the launch of the K4C consortium in India in 2018, for training mentors (faculty members from select Indian HEIs & practitioners from community-based organizations) in CBPR, for building their capacities to work towards the attainment of SDGs (Lepore *et al.*, 2021). At present, K4C is actively functioning in twenty-two hubs in thirteen countries across the world, including four in India: Pandit Ravishankar Shukla University, Raipur; Manipal University, Jaipur; Christ University, Bengaluru; and Dayalbagh Educational Institute, Agra (Lepore *et al.*, 2024).

In the same year (2018), the Ministry of Education [formerly known as the Ministry of Human Resource Development

(MHRD)] launched the Unnat Bharat Abhiyaan (UBA) 2.0 for fostering transformational change in rural development by leveraging knowledge institutions (HEIs) for building an inclusive India (MHRD, 2018). To achieve this objective, the UGC convened a subject expert group, which drafted the guidelines for fostering social responsibility and community engagement in Indian HEIs, in January 2020 (which was later revised in December 2022) (UGC, 2020, 2022). These guidelines placed an added emphasis on CURPs and CBPR, where research questions are framed in partnership with the local community, so that the "new knowledge solutions" thus produced, can appropriately and effectively address local challenges (UGC, 2022). Building on these ideas further, the UGC (in January 2022) launched a pan-India initiative for capacity building of academics in Indian HEIs as master trainers in CBPR (Press Information Bureau, 2022). This national programme is coordinated by seven UGC designated regional centres (HEIs) across different geographical zones in India (Press Information Bureau, 2022).

Finally, and most importantly, the major push for CBPR as a form of "socially relevant research" came from the National Education Policy (NEP) 2020 (drafted by Ministry of Education), as it acknowledged the contribution of higher education towards securing sustainable livelihoods and holistic social welfare. To do so, NEP 2020 outlined the importance of developing active and cross-disciplinary research communities (through practice based/experiential learning), to address the contemporary challenges in the spheres of climate change, water and sanitation, education and health care, air quality, energy and infrastructure, etc. (MHRD, 2020). For achieving this objective, it called for bringing together expert opinion and local/indigenous knowledge (rooted in local history, art, language and culture), thereby outlining the pathway for advancing the practice of CBPR in Indian HEIs (MHRD, 2020).

Best Practice Models of CBPR in Indian HEIs

The following section presents some of the institutional best practices with respect to the practice and implementation of

CBPR, emerging from three different HEIs belonging to different geographical zones and HEI category. These are:

(i) Pandit Ravishankar Shukla University (PRSU), Raipur Chhattisgarh (central India, state public university),
(ii) Amrita Vishwa Vidyapeetham (AVV), Kollam, Kerala (south India, private deemed university), and
(iii) Manipal University Jaipur, Rajasthan (north India, state private university).

(a) Pandit Ravishankar Shukla University (PRSU)

The Centre for Women's Studies at PRSU entered into a tripartite agreement with the State Planning Commission (SPC) of Chhattisgarh and Participatory Research in Asia (PRIA), (a non-governmental organization (NGO)), to constitute the "Sangwari" CBPR Hub (one of the Indian hubs under the K4C initiative) (Venugopal *et al.*, 2024). In the Chhattisgarhi dialect, the word *sangwari* means "friend", and symbolizes the harmonious relationships between HEIs and community for achieving common developmental goals. The objective of the hub is the co-creation of knowledge on SDG-5 (focusing on gender equality and women's empowerment), with equal participation of the community and the academia (Venugopal *et al.*, 2024).

As part of this effort, the hub introduced a certificate course on CBPR in 2018. The learning objectives of the course include understanding and practising theories and strategies of CBPR, for improving the quality of life of the people living in rural and slum areas, especially indigenous women (Centre for Women's Studies, 2018). As part of this course, students undertake CBPR on issues of women's empowerment jointly agreed by local tribal community and the SPC (Centre for Women's Studies, 2018).

As an important strategic partner, the SPC suggests and supports the research to be undertaken under the course, linked to local contextual issues and commits to using the research findings to devise local solutions to the challenges, in line with the UN SDGs (Centre for Women's Studies, n.d.). The topics researched by the students as part of the course include, role of women in local governance, assessment of women and child health care services provided by Anganwadi centres, impact of skill development schemes on economic empowerment of women, etc. (Centre for Women's Studies, n.d.). Furthermore, the hub has also been engaged in conducting numerous workshops on diverse topics such as techniques in CBPR, Participatory Safety Audit (PSA), ways to connect higher education and community, women's safety, etc. (Centre for Women's Studies, n.d.).

Lately, the hub has been engaged in conducting meaningful CBPR projects with the neighbouring communities. One such project focused on the aspect of rural maternal health in tribal areas. With support from community research partners, such as the members of the *panchayat*, community health workers and traditional birth attendants, the project sought to investigate the depth and richness of community knowledge cultures, and how it differed from academic knowledge cultures (Venugopal *et al.*, 2024). The project findings not only helped academics to strengthen their own understanding of maternal health, but also emerged to be of crucial significance for policy makers, in utilizing the findings while drafting maternal health schemes (Venugopal *et al.*, 2024). An important and a natural outcome of this process was the validation and legitimization of community knowledge not only in governmental policies, but also in academic publications (Venugopal *et al.*, 2024).

(b) Amrita Vishwa Vidyapeetham

Amrita Vishwa Vidyapeetham has been one of the few universities in India, which has put "societal engagement" as one of its primary focus areas. One of its key initiatives in this direction was the establishment of the "Live-in-Labs" programme in 2013 (Amrita Vishwa Vidyapeetham, n.d.). As a multidisciplinary experiential learning programme, it applies research and development for the deployment of sustainable solutions for current challenges that are faced by rural communities in India (Ramesh *et al.*, 2016). Using the tools of CBPR, the programme enables participants to study, observe and interact with rural populations while living in rural communities to gain a better understanding of challenges in the areas of agriculture, education, gender equality, skill development, livelihood, energy and environment, etc. (Amrita Vishwa Vidyapeetham, n.d.).

Leading over 150 projects in twenty-one states across India, the programme has impacted over 60,000 rural residents, with the academics clocking approximately 200,000+ hours of work in the field aimed at sustainable development of rural communities (Amrita Vishwa Vidyapeetham, n.d.). In addition to CBPR, the programme also employs a Rapid Translational Research & Implementation (RTRI) model; a multidimensional framework which facilitates the development and effective implementation of sustainable technological solutions for fostering rural development, through engagement with local communities (Ramesh, Mohan and Menon, 2016). The measurable outcomes of the programme include enhancement of knowledge, development of tools, conduction of trainings, expansion in outreach and collabourations and most importantly, fostering ownership, resulting in sustainability of locally devised and cost-effective solutions (Ramesh *et al.*, 2016).

An example of a CBPR project undertaken by the academics at the university was the Jeevamritam initiative, which involved co-designing and co-developing of a community-based drinking water solution (Ajith *et al.*, 2022). This research project built on synergetic cooperation between faculty, students at the university, the community and a local NGO, and demonstrated a successful public private partnership (PPP) model in establishing sustainable drinking water solutions (Ajith *et al.*, 2022). This model comprised of four foundational principles of

(i) engagement with the community for creating awareness, using Participatory Rural Appraisal (PRA) tools,
(ii) co-designing sessions with the community,
(iii) creation of a PPP model of ownership and cost sharing, and

(iv) community empowerment to facilitate sustainable social change (Ajith *et al.*, 2022).

(c) Manipal University Jaipur (MUJ)

As another Indian hub under the K4C programme, MUJ has taken great strides forward in the promotion and application of CBPR to achieve both academic learning and social development objectives (Manipal University Jaipur, n.d.) In doing so, MUJ aims to address the local challenges and attend to immediate social requirement by conducting needs based research, such as CBPR, and thereby contribute to socially relevant knowledge production (Manipal University Jaipur, n.d.). Among the many credible CBPR initiatives undertaken, one particularly noteworthy one is the work being done by architectural studios at MUJ (Yadav and Sharma, 2023). By way of undertaking design-based projects, these studios aim at understanding local problems, challenges and developing design-based solutions at multiple levels of neighbourhood, city, and regional scales (and is currently being operationalized in the cities of Jaipur, Ajmer, Pushkar and Bagru) (Yadav and Sharma, 2023).

Furthermore, MUJ has endeavoured to apply CBPR methodology in diverse areas of sustainable community development, such as conversion of waste to wealth, creation of inclusive public spaces and exploration of mutually beneficial solutions for immediate agro-environmental concerns (Yadav and Sharma, 2023). While equitable CURPs in all such efforts benefitted the community through the provision of sustainable solutions to social challenges, it provided the academics with an opportunity to understand the practical nuances of real-time situations, and develop critical social competencies in the bargain (Yadav and Sharma, 2023). These efforts demonstrate MUJ's commitment to serve as a knowledge producer, through investment in collabourative research and social innovation, while being driven by the overarching objective of benefitting the society, by aligning with the local needs and aspirations (Yadav and Sharma, 2023).

A prominent example of one such initiative undertaken by the MUJ hub involved the exploration of local, community waste management practices, with the objective of improving the same, through collabouration and partnership. In line with these ideas, this project involved the community (including trained community action group members and local councillors) and university academics as co-researchers in the process (Yadav *et al.*, 2024). Findings from this CBPR initiative reflected on some of the challenges in successfully conducting such research approaches in an academic setup. The study outlined the power inequalities which plague such research partnerships, which gets worsened by academic rigidities, and the non-acceptance of "other forms of (community) knowledge" as a valid source of knowledge (Yadav *et al.*, 2024). The study, therefore, proposed several recommendations to bridge this divide between community and university knowledge cultures, such as establishing sustainable and respectful partnerships between the university and the community, building capacities of academics for understanding the value and practice of CBPR, utilizing the local networks and access advantage that local NGOs offer in such cases, etc. (Yadav *et al.*, 2024).

Discussion

The aforementioned account on the practice and potential of CBPR, supported by evidence of its institutional implementation, necemssitates discussion on three crucial discussion pointers:

(i) requisites for successful conduction of CBPR projects,
(ii) emergent benefits for the stakeholders involved, and
(iii) the challenges which imbue such practices and the modalities to address them. Each of these are discussed as follows:

(a) Requisites

It is important to note that a practice like CBPR, which envisages a deviation from the business-as-usual approach to research, cannot be carried out in isolation. Based on the institutional examples, the following three important requisites emerge, which are key to facilitating CBPR practices:

(i) Supportive National Education Policies

As evident from the contextualization presented in the preceding sections, support from the national educational policy sector for CBPR is instrumental in ensuring its acceptance and adoption by HEIs. Much of the growth in the practice and popularity of CBPR in the Indian context can be attributed to the supportive national policies and guidelines, such as NEP 2020 and the UGC guidelines on fostering social responsibility and community engagement, respectively. In addition to creating a favourable pitch for CBPR, this policy push provides the much-needed incentive for academics and institutions to adopt the practice as part of their regular functions, in the absence of which, they mostly prefer to continue with status-quo and traditional research approaches.

(ii) Institutionalization of CBPR

Institutionalizing CBPR is essential for establishing it as a valid and accepted institutional research practice. Along with creating an enabling institutional environment in favour of CBPR, institutionalization also ensures necessary support for the practice, with respect to its integration within the higher education functions of teaching-learning and research, securing availability of funds, provisioning of logistic support, etc. Another important component of such support involves ensuring that the faculty and students engaged in the practice are appropriately incentivized and compensated for investing their time and efforts in such projects/ initiatives. Establishment of institutional CBPR hubs at PRSU and MUJ (as part of the K4C initiative) is an example of a positive step in this direction.

(iii) Fostering Mutually Beneficial and Respectful Community University Research Partnerships (CURPs)

Collabourative, respectful and mutually beneficial partnerships with communities, community workers, NGOs and practice-based organizations are the cornerstone of CBPR interventions. As documented through the institutional examples, all CBPR efforts build on collabouration between academics and community members, who participate as equal partners in the process. Valuing, respecting and acknowledging community knowledge culture(s) comprises the basic premise of such partnerships, which is also crucial for conducting CBPR initiatives in its true spirit. Finally, the aspect of mutual benefit also underlines such partnerships, wherein each partner derives benefit out of the collabouration, although the nature of the benefit may differ from one stakeholder to another. This is evident from the practice of CBPR carried out in different HEIs (as discussed earlier) where strong community partnerships built the foundation of the research process, where all partners derived mutual gains.

(b) Benefits

While the evidence emerging from the institutional examples of CBPR implementation points at several emergent benefits, three key ones are enlisted as follows:

(i) New Knowledge and Multi-faceted Learning

Through collective synergy and mobilization of diverse stakeholders, coupled with their respective expertise, networks and knowledge domains; CBPR offers a major advantage in terms of production of "new knowledge". This knowledge, emerging from the synthesis of academic (sciences, humanities, commerce, etc.) and community knowledge(s) delivers benefits that a single knowledge system would not be able to offer. It also results in multi-faceted learning, which transcends academic and classroom boundaries, and is more experiential, applied and practical. Further, the practice of CBPR also results in the development of new competencies and skills by research partners (belonging to academia and community), such as the ability to work in partnerships, to listen, reflect, communicate, think critically, and undertake action for transformative social change.

(ii) Attainment of UN SDGs

The institutional examples of CBPR also sheds light on the diverse areas in which this research approach has been applied, spanning rural maternal health, community-based drinking water solutions, urban design, agro-ecology, waste management, etc. While these aspects touch upon pressing and immediate social concerns, they also align with one or the other SDGs, such as SDG-3 (good health and well-being), SDG-6 (clean water and sanitation), SDG-11 (sustainable cities and communities), SDG-9 (which includes aspects of infrastructure creation), SDG-13 (climate action), etc. While these are global goals, CBPR projects targeting local issues related to the latter, offers the advantage of localization of SDG targets, which is major step forward towards achieving the global goals of sustainability.

(iii) Enhanced "Social Value" of Research which is Community-engaged

In light of the increased expectations entrusted upon HEIs and its research function to provide sustainable solutions, there have been a flurry of research initiatives at HEIs under the domain of sustainable development. However, what makes CBPR unique among other similar research efforts is that it is "community-based" rather than "community-placed", and acknowledges the contribution, knowledge and wisdom that the community stakeholders offer, in co-creating sustainable solutions to social challenges. This enhances the social value, authenticity and contextual relevance of the research process, one which is gradually gaining more respect and acceptance in academia. This is evident by the increasing number of academic publications dedicated to the practice of CBPR at HEIs. Further, the impact of such research and its findings also feeds into the government policy circles, who have begun to engage with HEIs carrying out CBPR in local contexts, for incorporating their feedback into drafting of national/regional developmental schemes.

(c) Challenges and Corresponding Recommendations

In addition to the benefits that CBPR brings along, it also emerged that, like any other practice, it is imbued with difficult challenges, with a significant ground to cover, to further consolidate its position in Indian HEIs. Three concerning ones, and the modalities to address them are discussed as follows:

(i) Ambiguities in the Understanding and Practice of CBPR

Considering that CBPR is a new addition in the vocabulary of Indian HEIs, and is in its nascent stages of development, there is a lack of clarity with respect to its concept and practice. This emerges as a major hindrance to its successful implementation, and within its true spirit. With much of "applied research" with a social impact quotient (but no community collabouration) being popularly practised by research centres at HEIs, the same is often considered as synonymous with CBPR or community engaged research. This lack of understanding on what the practice entails, its principles and values, along with the absence of competencies in carrying out this form of collabourative research, presents a major challenge with respect to the implementation of CBPR.

Therefore, there is an urgent need for investing in more capacity building opportunities for academics to develop their understanding on both the theory and practice of CBPR, along with its application in different educational disciplines and departments, including interdisciplinary opportunities in CBPR. While a step forward in this direction has been taken by the UGC, by way of its Master Trainers Programme for training academics in CBPR, there is an urgent need to multiply such efforts at the regional and institutional levels, so that more opportunities can be explored, scaled and replicated within a reasonable period of time.

(ii) Operational and Practical Challenges

Being field based, and involving multi-stakeholder partnerships, CBPR also presents dynamic challenges during field interventions. Some of such challenges may involve entering the communities, gaining their trust and building rapport, manoeuvring through power differentials within communities and/or between the research partners, sustaining the momentum of the research process, etc. These challenges also bear testimony to the kind of intricate competencies that researchers engaging in such processes must develop to successfully endure the emergent challenges, and address them effectively.

Therefore, there is a need for academics to "prepare for the field", and for this, it is essential that they have a prior knowledge of the research location, its demographics, cultural practices, local institutions, and also ability to network with community leaders or influential stakeholders who can facilitate community collabouration. Most importantly, since a good percentage of the emergent challenges may be sudden or contingent, for which no amount of preparation may be sufficient, the development of self as community-based researchers is crucial. This envisages the adoption of a reflective and accommodating mindset, involving learning of new aspects, re-learning of established facts from a novel and "different" perspective, and unlearning of facets that one may have been traditionally trained in.

(iii) Lack of Knowledge Sharing on Best Practices

Another striking challenge that emerges from the Indian context and the practice of CBPR in Indian HEIs is that despite institutions emerging as model cases for the practice of CBPR, unfortunately, they have been limited to becoming isolated islands of excellence. While they are doing good work in pockets, the transformative learnings that have emerged, have not been widely disseminated and shared, as would have normally been desired. As a result, there have not been many opportunities for knowledge sharing, inter-institutional learning or brainstorming, or even inter-institutional partnerships for undertaking joint CBPR projects. This lack of knowledge sharing platforms, portals or opportunities not only limits the practice, but also contributes to the negligible demand or interest in the same.

Therefore, along with putting in efforts at the institutional and field level to strengthen the practice of CBPR, equal attention needs to be given to creating more opportunities for knowledge sharing on the topic. This will not only popularize the practice and encourage replication and contextualization of best practice models, but will also create the much-needed market demand, resulting in a ripple effect. The summative impact of such efforts would result in advancing and consolidating CBPR within and among various Indian HEIs.

Conclusion

CBPR offers a unique and an exclusive opportunity to make research at HEIs, "socially responsible, engaged and contextually relevant". In framing locally usable research and co-creating "new knowledge", CBPR is instrumental in achieving the desired goals of sustainable social transformation, through the attainment of SDGs. As further, as an approach to "responsible research", CBPR also contributes towards the development of critical twenty-first century skills in researchers, thereby helping them emerge as active, innovative, ethical and socially responsible global citizens. Therefore, the significance of CBPR in bringing "value and responsibility" back into higher education in general and its research function in particular, stands uncontested.

The growth of CBPR in the Indian context bears testimony to the fact that Indian higher education realizes the importance of "responsible educative practices" and is committed to delivering its social responsibilities. However, in order to meaningfully integrate this practice as part of mainstream higher education, concerted efforts are needed, both at the conceptual and practical level, including support from all relevant stakeholders. Such efforts need to focus on creating a facilitative environment for CBPR, maximizing CBPR opportunities in HEIs, developing of competencies, and popularizing the practice, for generating its demand. This is essential to ensure that this "responsible research" approach which holds much promise for achieving sustainable social change—can be effectively advanced for shared benefits.

Keywords

Community-Based participatory research (CBPR), responsible research, sustainable development, sustainable development goals (SDGs), community engagement.

REFERENCES

Ahmadein, G. (2019). "Obstacles and Opportunities for Achieving the SDGs at Higher Education Instititutions: A Regional Arab Perspective." In: GUNi (ed.) *Implementing the 2030 Agenda at Higher Educational Institutions: Challenges and Responses*. Barcelona: GUNi, 15-22.

Ajith, V., A.S. Reshma, R. Mohan, and M. Vinodini Ramesh (2022). "Empowering Communities in Addressing Drinking Water Challenges using a Systematic, Participatory and Adaptive Approach and Sustainable PPP Model." *Technological Forecasting and Social Change, 185*: 1-17. Available: https://doi.org/10.1016/j.techfore.2022.121970 (accessed on 23 January 2024).

Amrita Vishwa Vidyapeetham, n.d. *Live-in-Labs*. Available: https://www.amrita.edu/school/sustainable-futures/academics/live-in-labs/(accessed on 9 February 2024).

Bidandi, F., A.N. Ambe, and C.H. Mukong (2021). "Insights and Current Debates on Community Engagement in Higher Education Institutions: Perspectives on the University of the Western Cape." *SAGE Open, 11*(2): 1-11. Available: https://doi.org/10.1177/21582440211011467 (accessed on 2 December 2023).

Boyer, E.L. (1996). "The Scholarship of Engagement." *American Academy of Arts and Sciences, 49*(7): 18-33. Available: https://doi.org/10.2307/3824459 (accessed on 3 December 2023).

Burman, C.J. (2019). "Engaging with Complexity: Making Sense of 'Wicked Problems' in Rural South Africa." *Journal of Higher Education Outreach and Engagement, 23*(9): 199-217.

Centre for Women's Studies (2018). *Certificate Course in Community-based Participatory Research*. Available: https://www.prsu.ac.in/backend/web/ theme/course/20122021030635Syllabus%20CBPR.pdf (accessed on 9 February 2024).

Centre for Women's Studies, n.d. *The SANGWARI CBPR Hub*. Available: https://prsu.ac.in/admin/theme/news/26052020065851.pdf (accessed on 9 February 2024).

De Santis, J.L., S.P. O'Connor, K. Pritchard, Z.E. Franco, S.M. Ahmed, and D.A. Nelson (2019). "The Collective Power of We: Breaking Barriers in Community Engagement through Dialogue." *Innovative Higher Education,* 44(2): 149-160. Available: https://doi.org/10.1007/s10755-018-9454-y (accessed on 3 December 2023).

Escrigas, C., J.G. Sanchez, B.L. Hall, and R. Tandon (2014). "Editors Introduction." In: GUNi ed. *Knowledge, Engagement and Higher Education: Contributing to Social Change.* Hampshire: Palgrave Macmillan, pp. xxxi-xxxix.

Gibbons, M., C. Limoges, H. Nowotny, S. Schwartman, P. Scott, and M. Trow (1994). *The New Production of Knowledge: The Dynamics of Science and Research in Contemporary Societies.* London: Sage.

Göransson, B., L. Donati, and C. Wigren-Kristoferson (2021). "Introduction to the Special Issue on Universities and Social Innovation." *Technological Forecasting and Social Change, 173*: 1-4.

Hall, B. and R. Tandon (2017). *Community-based Participatory Research and Sustainable Development Goals.* Available: https://unescochair-cbrsr.org/ pdf/ resource/BHALL_Community_Based_Research_ENG_Dec13.pdf (accessed on 30 November 2023).

Hall, B.H., R. Tandon, W. Lepore, W. Singh, A. Easby, and C. Tremblay (2016). "Theoretical Pedagogical Framework for Community-based Research." In: R. Tandon, B.H. Hall, W. Lepore, and W. Singh (eds.) *Knowledge and Engagement: Building Capacity for the Next Generation of Community-based Researchers.* New Delhi: PRIA, pp. 7-39.

Kagan, C., R. Lawthom, O.D. Clennon, J. Fisher, J. Diamond, and K. Goldstraw (2017). "Sustainable Communities: University-community Partnership Research on Social Dimensions of Sustainable Development." In: W. Leal (Ed.) *Sustainable Development Research at Universities in the United Kingdom.* New York: Springer, pp. 245-62.

Kelly, W.B. and L.M. Given (2023). "The Community Engagement for Impact (Cefi) Framework: An Evidence-based Strategy to Facilitate Social Change." *Studies in Higher Education*, pp. 1-19. Available: https://doi.org/10.1080/03075079.2023.2238762 (accessed on 29 November 2023).

Leal Filho, W.T. Dibbern, L. Viera Trevisan, E. Coggo Cristofoletti, M.A.P. Dinis, N. Matandirotya, J. Sierra, K. Shulla, G. Buttriss, P. L'Espoir Decosta, M.F. Mbah, and M. Sanni (2023). "Mapping Universities-Communities Partnerships in the Delivery of the Sustainable Development Goals." *Frontiers in Environmental Science, 11*: 1-12. Available: https://doi.org/10.3389/fenvs.2023.1246875 (accessed on 28 January 2024).

Lepore, W., B.H. Hall, and R. Tandon (2021). "The Knowledge for Change Consortium: A Decolonising Approach to International Collabouration in Capacity Building in Community-based Participatory Research." *Canadian Journal of Development Studies, 42*(3): 347-70. Available: https://doi.org/10.1080/02255189.2020.1838887 (accessed on 30 November 2023).

Lepore, W., B.L. Hall, and R. Tandon (2024). "Introduction." In: W. Lepore, B.L. Hall, and R. Tandon (eds.) *Bridging Knowledge Cultures: Rebalancing Power in the Co-construction of Knowledge*. Leiden: Brill, pp. 3-17.

Lepore, W. and L. King (2023). "Weaving Knowledge Systems: Challenges and Possible Solutions through Community-engaged Research in Canada and Nordic Countries." In: M. Singh, P. Bhatt, W. Singh, and K.S. Pareek (eds.) *Community Engagement in Higher Education: From Theory to Practice*. Abingdon: Routledge, pp. 58-71.

Machimana, E.G., M.M. Sefotho, L. Ebersohn, and L. Shultz (2021). "Higher Education Uses Community Engagement-partnership as a Research Space to Build Knowledge." *Educational Research for Policy and Practice, 20*(1): 45-62. Available: https://doi.org/10.1007/s10671-020-09266-6 (accessed on 2 December 2023).

Manipal University Jaipur. n.d. *K4C: MUJ-PRIA hub*. Available: https://www.unescochair-cbrsr.org/pdf/whec/MADHURA_MUJ_PRIA_Hub.pdf (accessed on 9 February 2024).

McIlrath, L. (2014). "Community-university Engagement: Global Terms and Terrain." In: Guni Ed. *Knowledge, Engagement and Higher Education: Contributing to Social Change*. Hampshire: Palgrave Macmillan, pp. 39-44.

MHRD (2018). *Unnat Bharat Abhiyaan 2.0*. New Delhi: Ministry of Human Resource Development. Available: https://unnatbharatabhiyan.gov.in/public/uploads/downloads/downloads-6122.pdf (accessed on 3 December 2023).

MHRD (2020). *National Education Policy 2020*. New Delhi: MHRD. Available: https://www.education.gov.in/sites/upload_files/mhrd/files/NEP_Final_English_0.pdf (accessed on 24 November 2023).

Minkler, M. (2014). "Community-based Participatory Research." In: Brydon-M. Miller (ed.) *SAGE Encyclopedia on Action Research*. Los Angeles: SAGE, pp. 152-56.

Molosi-France, K. and K. Dipholo (2022). "Community-based Participatory Research: A Ladder of Opportunity for Engaged Scholarship in Higher Education." *Journal of Contemporary Issues in Education, 17*(2): 111-122. Available: https://doi.org/10.20355/jcie29514 (accessed on 29 November 2023).

Mthembu, Z., M. Chimbari, and M. Macherera (2023). "Facilitating Community Engagement: Researchers' Lived Experiences in Rural Communities in the Kwazulu-Natal Ecohealth Programme, South Africa." *Cogent Social Sciences, 9*(1): 1-15. Available: https://doi.org/10.1080/23311886.2023.2225833 (accessed on 29 November 2023).

Mutero, I.T. and M.J. Chimbari (2021). "Partnership Dynamics in University-Community Engagement: A Case Study of the TibaSA Multidisciplinary Research Team in uMkhanyakude district, KwaZulu-Natal, South Africa." *International Journal of African Higher Education, 8*(1): 117-38.

Planning Commission (2013). *Twelfth Five Year Plan (2012-2017): Social Sectors*. New Delhi: SAGE Publications India Pvt Ltd. Available: https://www.education.gov.in/sites/upload_files/mhrd/files/document-reports/XIIFYP_SocialSector.pdf (accessed on 24 November, 2023).

Press Information Bureau (2022). *UGC Launches Training of Master Trainers in Community-based Participatory Research*. Available: https://pib.gov.in/PressReleasePage.aspx?PRID=1790047 (accessed on 1 December 2023).

PRIA (2014). *PRIA's Engagements with Higher Education Institutions: Initiatives in Community-based Research*. New Delhi: PRIA. Available: https://unescochair-cbrsr.org/unesco/pdf/resource/PRIA_Engagement_with_Higher_Educational_Institutions.pdf (accessed on 3 December 2023).

Ramesh, M.V., R. Mohan, and S. Menon (2016). "Live-in-Labs: Rapid Translational Research and Implementation-based Programme for Rural Development in India." Paper Presented at the *016 IEEE Global Humanitarian Technology Conference (GHTC)*. Seattle, USA, IEEE, 164-171. Available: https://doi.org/10.1109/GHTC.2016.7857275 (accessed on 9 February 2024).

Shabalala, L.P. (2023). "The Role Higher Education Plays Towards the Development of Sustainable Socio-Economic Opportunities for Mapungubwe World Cultural Heritage Site Communities." *Academica Turistica, 16*(1): 73-87. Available: https://doi.org/10.26493/2335-4194.16.73-87 (accessed on 23 January 2024).

Sibhensana, B. and S. Maistry (2023). "Conceptualising Public-private partnerships for Social Innovation through Community Engagement in Higher Education Institutions." *South African Journal of Higher Education, 37*(1): 185-205. Available: http://dx.doi.org/10.20853/37-1-5669 (accessed on 26 November 2023).

Singh, W. (2021). Using Community-based Participatory Research for Building Youth Consciousness on Democracy in Everyday Life in India. In:

B. Broucker, R. Pritchard, G. Melin, and C. Milsom (eds.) *Sustaining the Future of Higher Education*. Leiden: Brill Sense, pp. 117-37.

Sugawara, C.L., H.W. Kim, K. Modić Stanke, V. Krasniqi, and S. Basic (2023). "The Role of Community-University Engagement in Strengthening Local Community Capacity in Southeastern Europe." *International Journal of Educational Development, 98*: 1-11. Available: https://doi.org/10.1016/j.ijedudev.2023.102747 (accessed on 26 November 2023).

Tandon, R. (2014). *Fostering Social Responsibility in Higher Education in India*. Available: https://unescochair-cbrsr.org/unesco/pdf/Fostering_Social_Responsibility.pdf (accessed on 4 November 2024).

Tandon, R. (2017). *Making The Commitment: Contribution of Higher Education in Achieving the SDGs*. Available: https://unescochair-cbrsr.org/ pdf/resource/Making%20the%20Commitment_SDGs-Sep_2017_final. pdf (accessed on 11 November, 2023).

Tandon, R. and P. Pandey (2019). "Disciplines, Professions and the Sustainable Development Goals (SDGs): Challenges in Higher Education in India." In: GUNi ed. *Implementing the 2030 Agenda at Higher Education Institutions: Challenges and Responses*. Barcelona: GUNi, pp. 47-53.

Tremblay, C., W. Singh, and W. Lepore (2017). "Mutual Learning and Empowering Support: The Role of Networks in Achieving Global Engagement." In: GUNi ed. *Towards A Socially Responsible University: Balancing the Global with the Local*. Girona: GUNi, pp. 391-401.

UGC (2014). *XII Plan Guidelines for Establishment of Centre for Fostering Social Responsibiity and Community Engagement in Universities*. New Delhi: UGC. Available: https://www.ugc.ac.in/pdfnews/4750386_Guidelines-for-Establishment-of-CFSRC.pdf (accessed on 24 November 2023).

UGC (2020). *Fostering Social Responsibility and Community Engagement in Higher Education Institutions in India: National Curriculum Framework and Guidelines*. New Delhi: UGC. Available: https://www.ugc.ac.in/e- book/UNNAT%20BHARAT%20ABHIYAN.pdf (accessed on 24 November 2023).

UGC (2022). *Guidelines for Fostering Social Responsibility and Community Engagement in Indian Higher Education Institutions in India 2.0*. Available: https://www.ugc.gov.in/pdfnews/4187860_Revised-Final-Guidelines.pdf (accessed on 9 February 2024).

UNDP (2024). *Human Development Report 2023/2024*. New York: UNDP. Available: https://hdr.undp.org/system/files/documents/global-report-document/hdr2023-24reporten.pdf (accessed on 3 November 2024).

UNESCO Chair in CBRSR (2015). *Institutionalizing Community University Research Partnerships*. New Delhi: PRIA. Available: https://unescochair- cbrsr.org/unesco/pdf/CURP_Guidelines.pdf (accessed on 3 December 2023).

UNESCO Chair in CBRSR (2022). *The Justice Imperative: Knowledge Democracy, Higher Education and The SDGs*. Available: https://www.unescochair-cbrsr.org/wp-content/uploads/2022/05/Report_HE-and_SDGs_Barcelona.pdf (accessed on 9 February 2024).

Venugopal, R., P. Shrivastava, A. Chakraborty, and A. Varoda (2024). "Bridging Knowledge in Maternal Health Care in Rural Communities: Experiences from the Sangawari K4C hub, Chhattisgarh, India." In: W. Lepore, B.L. Hall, and R. Tandon (eds.) *Bridging Knowledge Cultures: Rebalancing Power in the Co-construction of Knowledge*. Leiden: Brill, pp. 99-115.

Yadav, M., M. Banerjee, S. Hirani, and M. Sharma (2024). "Understanding Community Waste Management through Service-Learning: Experiences from the Manipal University Jaipur K4C hub, India." In: W. Lepore, B.L. Hall, and R. Tandon (eds.) *Bridging Knowledge Cultures: Rebalancing Power in The Co-Construction of Knowledge*. Leiden: Brill, pp. 116-32.

Yadav, M. and M. Sharma (2023). "Establishing Community-University Collabourations: Experiential Learning Initiatives at Manipal University Jaipur." In: M. Singh, P. Bhatt, W. Singh, and K.S. Pareek (eds.) *Community Engagement in Higher Education: From Theory to Practice*. Abingdon: Routledge, pp. 181-96.

12

Practical Partnership Between TVET in Denmark and Kenya

Niels Larsen

This chapter is about a partnership between three vocational centres in Denmark and one in Kenya working with co-learning within the umbrella of SDG and the subject of carpentry and joinery woodwork. The aim was to get more experiences and reflection on how it was possible to work cross-culturally between the Global North and the Global South and to develop a didactical model for this kind of work.

The Transition to be a Green Institution

The transition to more sustainable societies requires a shift in skills, knowledge, attitudes, and competencies. The education sector is important for this transition and greening technical and vocational education and training (TVET) plays a key role in providing the workforce with this knowledge, skills, and competencies to facilitate the transition to a greener economy and open and engage with the complexity for a more sustainable and greener societies. TVET is the part of education that is directly connected to the labour market and the production sector, and it is the only sector of education that clearly connects the learning world with the working world. Furthermore, green skills are becoming increasingly important for all sectors and occupations range from basic cross-cutting competencies to new occupational profiles. Greening TVET worldwide in the Global North and Global South is therefore a top priority of UNEVOC (UNESCO International Centre for Technical and Vocational Education and Training).

In Denmark the Danish Ministry of Education is very committed to promote sustainability within the Danish TVET institutions. Greening TVET has over the years also gained an increased attention among the Danish TVET institutions themselves, and many have started to prioritize integration of sustainability and the SDGs. DEG: the Danish parastatal for all TVET institutions in Denmark also wishes to inspire all schools to use the SDGs as a basis both for development of educational activities as well as for a whole school approach.

It was within this perspective and in a more global context two Danish NGOs : FIC (Forum for International Cooperation) Denmark and the UN Worldwide Regional Centre of Expertise (RCE) made an application to CISU pool (funded by the Danish Ministry of Foreign Affairs) with a project called: USHIRIKA FITI or "practical partnership" with the overall goal: "to promote and strengthen interest and global engagement in sustainability, international development, and the sustainable development goals (SDGs)" among students and teachers in technical and vocational education in Denmark.

In this article, the author will mainly recall the didactic model (IVAC) that was used in this case. It means that all part of the practical intervention of IVAC will be told in the empirical part where I have used a qualitative questionnaire to the Danish TVET students (Analyses). After the analysis, the author will give a short discussion focusing on the pedagogic in ESD and TVET, followed by a short overview of the whole project and a presentation of the Bricks/IVAC didactical model.

The Project Interventions

The implementation of the project had the following interventions.

(a) Intervention 1

Has engaged primary fifteen carpentry and joinery students and six teachers from following Vocational Training Centers in Denmark: NEXT, in Copenhagen, Rybners, Esbjerg and Herningsholm in Herning (Jylland) directly in a partnership with students and teachers from Comboni Polytechnic in Gilgil, near Naivasha in Kenya.

(b) Intervention 2

The teachers in both Denmark and Kenya have together with students had developed an education module that embrace ESD and GCED (will be referred to as sustainability modules or Bricks/ IVAC model), a module which can now be used for education of students during the project and after the project has ended, so it can be useful for other TVET institutions.

(c) Intervention 3

Fact finding mission for a teacher/manager-delegation to Kenya where they were able to exchange ideas, learning and experience with their Kenyan counterparts, discuss and prepare pilot projects and prepare for the following travel of students from Denmark and a stay for ten days.

(d) Intervention 4

A student exchange trip to Kenya, where the students experiences challenges in the Global South at first-hand and get involved in finding and creating sustainable solutions to local community challenges in a slum area in Gilgil. The teachers and students participated in the different intervention and functioned as important dissemination intermediaries to promote interest and engagement among the other target groups. The participating students disseminate later their experiences to other young students and gave inspiration on how to become engaged in development cooperation and work for a more sustainable world—e.g. through volunteer work or internships in Denmark or in the Global South—where they get to use their craftmanship and skills hands-on.

(e) Intervention 5

A teacher-student delegation from Kenya going to Denmark for a week stay and work together with their new Danish friends and experience the needs for skills in local areas in Denmark within carpentry and joinery. But very unfortunate the Kenyan students never came to Denmark because they didn't get the VISA from the Danish ministry of foreign affairs (Danish Immigration Service).

During and after the stay in Kenya, the Danish students, teachers, and a journalist made news and stories in Danish newspapers and on social media and made it possible to disseminate the project outcome.

The Three Partners behind This Project

(a) Forum for International Cooperation (FIC)

It has carried out more than twenty development projects in East Africa. FIC's projects and programmes in Kenya have especially been aimed at addressing labour market challenges where the primary areas of intervention have been focused on

1. improving working conditions and labour rights in cooperation with local trade unions and
2. creating employment opportunities for young, disadvantaged men and women in cooperation with local youth organizations and TVET-institutions.

(b) Regional Centre of Expertise (RCE) Denmark

It has been established by the United Nations University is a regional network that promote ESD. Globally there are currently more than

175 RCE's. Denmark has one RCE that functions as a national and international powerhouse for practical research, development, and dissemination of ESD within different educational fields such as researchers, teachers at different levels (like TVET), educationalists, and in businesses and NGOs. The network furthermore supports and develops collabouration across research and practice and supports and develops collabouration across organizations and disciplines. During the project both a representative from the Danish RCE and a Kenyan (RCE Greater Nairobi) was involved as both a project coordinator and expert in ESD in Kenya.

(c) Comboni Polytechnic

It is a local based and private owned polytechnic school in Gilgil near Nakuru, Kenya was addressed as a good match with the Danish schools—partly because they also have educations within woodwork, partly because they also are trying to increasingly integrate the SDG's more into the whole-school approach, and partly because they have a close connection with the local community. The school has started to work on minimizing waste of their activities and the goods and products produced by students benefit the local community. They matched the whole project very well from start to finish.

The Bricks/IVAC model

This didactic model takes an approach in ESD and has originally the IVAC part has been used in a health project in Europe but is very useful in this project. Bricks/IVAC refer to a combination of knowledge (different Bricks and IVAC of processes) IVAC-part, see Simovska & Jensen (2009)

The model is illustrated below: *The collabouration model: Bricks/ IVAC in the USHIRIKA FITI project©.2023.*

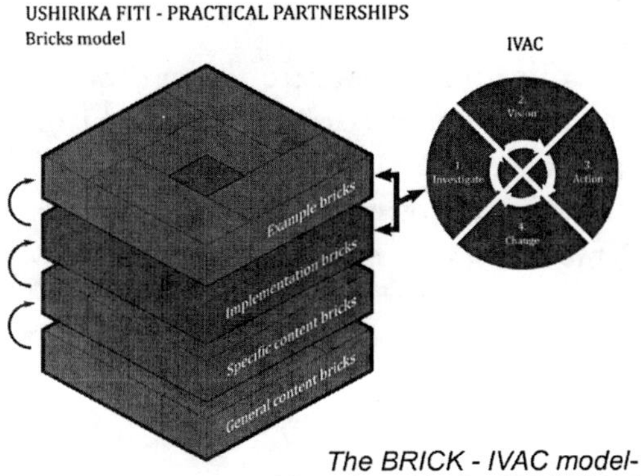

The BRICK - IVAC model- Developed in the USHIRIKA FITI project.

Explanation About Bricks/IVAC Model

The idea ofThe Bricks /IVAC model is to offer a methodology for ESD in TVET. The model integrated a more *informative/part* (the bricks) and a more *process-oriented part*: IVAC.

The model expands the learning environment by encouraging the students to go out in the local society, which enables a new kind of learning experience vital for the work of greening and authentic TVET.

The model works with different main topics that must be considered during and before the IVAC process can start:

- The four pillars in the sustainability and how they will be integrated in the work: Social, environment, cultural and economic.
- The seventeen SDGs are a main concern, and in every interaction or intervention try to find out which goals will mostly be integrated.
- Global citizenship is an ongoing issue in the exchange project where young TVET student will meet other students from another part of the world.
- The Ushirika Fiti project will always make engagement and participation, how can that be strengthen in the intervention?

(a) Specific Content Bricks

This Brick contains and elabourate the subtopics that relates the general knowledge about sustainability to fit into carpentry and joinery education which can match especially SDG-11 and SDG- 12, e.g., sustainable construction and techniques, production and housing (informal), entrepreneurship and innovation, waste materials, resource scarcity and resource efficiency. Through the "translation" of the general knowledge to the student's specific field of vocation the chance of engagement increases.

(b) Example Bricks

These bricks have a double function. Showing examples of sustainability or intercultural activities and engagement in a global, national, or local context. And showing specific examples and cases on pilot modules and student products from partnership institutions to inspire, share knowledge and at the same time create documentation on the knowledge creation in the project.

(c) Implementation Bricks

These bricks are about the actions in the project. What is being done at the partner institutions and what each institution wants to do with this project. The IVAC model, which is "beside" the main bricks is a core methodology of the implementation Bricks because training the IVAC process can support the students life skills and entrepreneurial education towards sustainable production, consumption, and lifestyle. IVAC processes can also support the kind of multifaceted and holistic learning processes being important in ESD and GCED.

IVAC Approach

The IVAC model is process-oriented part with the following phases: Investigation-Vision-Action-Change (IVAC) approach. This model represents an approach that supports school-community collabouration, pupil's participation, and action-oriented teaching. To develop the "students' ability to act, initiate and bring about positive change" the four elements of the IVAC model are vital to address when working with a participatory approach in education

(Simovska & Jensen, 2009). IVAC can also be seen as a kind of action learning circle supporting entrepreneurial education and part of the process should be to go out and investigate needs and challenges in the local society (like in the slum—or informal housing) to which carpentry or joinery can bring ideas to solutions and change.

When doing the IVAC processes students and teachers works in collabourative learning processes elabourating how to move carpentry and joinery education in Denmark and Kenya to an increased engagement in the local and global transformation towards a more sustainable living and working life.

The IVAC[1] approach

Investigation	**Vision**	**Action**	**Change**
Investigating of theme for the work: Like investigation in a slum area Why is this issue important to us? What is its significance to us/ others, now and/or in the future? What influence do live conditions have for the local dwellers In the slum? What influence are weexposed to and why? How were things before and why have will we try to change? How will it affect the different sustainable approaches? What is the history before?	What material do you like to use as carpenters and joinery work? Which alternatives are possible? What will be our main idea og ambition for a new and alternative product? How are the conditions in other areas of Kenya or Denmark cultures? Which alternatives do we prefer and why? What kind of participation and engagement do we like to happen? How can it fit to a new future work life in the area we work?	What possible actions, and product could achieve the changes? Which barriers might prevent us carrying out these actions? Which barriers might prevent actions from resulting in change? Which actions will initiate? How will we evaluate these actions? Will the actions be done alone or together with other peers and what is the benefit of this? What skills are important in the action? And why?	What changes will bring us closer to the vision? Not only about more sustainability but also change within us, in the local community—what is the main approach to local leaders (elders) and local politicians in Gilgil Naivasha in society?—like Kenya How is the change related to the seventeen-development goal? Can the change be related to a new IVAC process? Can we refer the change to different quality criteria? And in what way? Is the change related to new skills or competences?

Analysis

The evaluations process has been done with many methods like observations, interviews, informal communication, and questionnaire by internal approach.

The analysis can be related to the different steps in the IVAC process and in the way the cultural meeting was experienced by the participants.

Investigation

The visit to the primary school in the slum area gives rise to wonder, amazement, but also a lot of questions from the Danish students. How can there be so many in one class? It is difficult to see what the teachers are writing on the blackboard as it is very worn. How can we improve the tables and benches that the students sit on? How can the maintenance benefit all students? The school's recess area is very bare and in the school yard itself there are small beds that are fenced off with barbed wire so that students can't step on them. Some classrooms have very worn floors. How do students feel about the school? What is the perception of the school's buildings and surroundings by the teachers and the head of the school?

What do the students think needs to be improved? How can it be sustainable even after the Danish team has gone home?

The entire investigation phase helps the apprentices from both Kenya and Denmark to understand what kind of school they will be working at and what can be renovated in the ten days they spend at the school together. For the Danish apprentices, it was the first time they had been to a school in Africa. The students at the primary school were very eager to ask about different issues and conditions in Denmark.

During the tour of the classrooms, the Danish students talked to the Kenyan teachers about what was missing at the school. Some of the teachers talked about the lack of activities for the children during their breaks—one of the Danish and Kenyan girls picked up on this—and thought that a playground and "Tarzan tracks" could be made. For many of the children, a homemade ball, where they had used a t-shirt and wrapped string around it, so it became a cloth ball, especially the boys played with during recess. For the Danish-Kenyan group that later worked on the sports/playground, this gave them the idea to make a multifunctional wooden structure that could be used both as shade, because the sun was very bright, and something that could serve as a playhouse. The idea also came about because the Kenyan apprentices could tell how they themselves played as children when they were in school as children.

Vision

The visions come about after a thorough investigation of the conditions at the school. We arrive in April and the schools have been up and running since January and after the vacation in December. At the time we arrive, it's very hot, it hasn't rained for a long time, so it's very dusty everywhere.

During the tour around the school, there were clear signs that the school was not in the best condition. The floors in the classrooms were worn, many blackboards were no longer usable for writing on, but the tour of the school had given some ideas about what could be done, ideas and visions that were now to be discussed in the mixed groups, where there were both Kenyan and Danish students as well as a teacher from Denmark in each group and only one teacher from Comboni.

For some of the groups, the renovation of the office building and kitchen was predetermined. Here, several students remark that they had not been involved in figuring this out and that the renovation of the headmaster's office might not benefit all the children at the school. However, a group of students still got together to talk about how the exterior renovation of the school's office and part of the kitchen should be done.

Other groups had ideas to work on improving classrooms by disassembling school desks and benches and rebuilding them to fit new, larger tabletops. Since materials needed to be saved to make it more sustainable, the majority of the desks/benches were reused and reassembled. Here again, there was good input from the Kenyan students, who knew how to reassemble the table/bench sets and, not least, how nails can be reused without simply buying new ones. Several note that it was especially the Danish students who were active in the idea phase. Some of the Danish students thought it was because the Kenyan students had not yet been selected at this point, so there was uncertainty about which group they belonged to. Already during the first visit to the school during the investigate/research phase, many of the participants (Danish/Kenyan) had ideas and wishes about what could be renovated at the school. One of the more exciting ideas was when one of the groups saw the dusty and very dry "lawn" behind the school. The area was completely empty, with no playground equipment, so the idea initially came in the form of a "Tarzan court" so that more children could play at the same time and not just the boys who had a homemade ball. Therefore, the group started by brainstorming what could be, and all ideas were written down. "After that, we were good at grabbing each other's ideas and building on them, so we eventually came up with a great project", as one of the group members describes it. Another girl wrote: "There were both Danish and Kenyan students in this phase, and this phase worked really well". In this phase, the Kenyan participants showed good input on how they themselves played when they were in school and as children.

The project to renovate the principal's office and the school's kitchen façade was commissioned by many, so there were no challenges in terms of creativity. It was a challenge for the carpenters, among others, who learned a lot of carpentry.

For those who worked in the classrooms to stabilize the tables/bench sets, everyone was involved in the idea phase, where they specifically talked about how they could reuse the furniture, but first disassemble it and save nails that could then be used again when assembling the furniture. They got the idea when they saw how many students had very little space on the tables. Along the way, the classroom group came up with new ideas to renovate the boards and floors.

In summary, it can be said that it was mostly the Danish participants who were involved in the idea phase, one says that the Kenyan students did not have much experience with outdoor carpentry.

Action

"It was an insanely cool experience to work in different conditions than what you are used to", writes one of the participants. Even though it was very hot and there had been a drought for a long time, so it was quite dusty, which made the work process more challenging, all students were very hardworking. Some mention that because of the challenges and the lack of tools, they had to think outside the box. As one writes: "So the creative part of the brain was put to work". Several point out that they have now really learned how to use a hammer! In this phase, the Danish students also learned that in Denmark you are not allowed to work with varnish, so it was very much the Kenyans who did this part, knowing that it was not healthy for them. Some of the Danish participants note that the Kenyan students worked hard, sometimes harder than them. Some also write that communication could sometimes be a problem, especially when it came to the more specific terms in carpentry and joinery, but that they often figured it out in the end. Some write that they didn't learn anything new professionally,

but that this was outweighed by the good cooperation they had with the Kenyans. Others found a role in the group they work with. For example, one mentions that she acted as a mediator between the workshops involved in the playground group. Other mentions that he learned a lot from being the leader of the group he worked in. Most mention that the process went much better at the end of the programme, where they had learned each other better and therefore had the energy to joke around together. One writes: "I learned so much about the carpentry profession, but also about the work culture in Kenya". Another writes: "I learned pretty quickly that everything had to be done with a hammer and nails. We didn't have the luxury of a screwdriver and some screws ... first, it's not sustainable as it doesn't hold up well and secondly, it took longer." The big challenge, some mention, was the lack of materials, but it was therefore a "fun" challenge for some to adjust themselves to work with the materials they had.

It can be concluded that the Danish students learned to be creative in the work process when solving challenges in alternative ways without using the tools and materials they were used to. And they also learned a lot from the Kenyans during the work process. However, there are some differences between the Danish students who have just started the programme and the more experienced students.

The Collabouration with the Kenyans

[There was a tendency for the Danish students to talk more about the Kenyan way of being, than the actual collabouration, which is the co-learning that takes place when they are together, some also talk about what the Danish students could teach the Kenyan students, but not the other way around.]

All participants from Denmark mention that Kenyans are nice to work with. They are very talkative, and at the same time, some mention that they would have liked to know their Kenyan friends before the trip, but that there had also been more social activities along the way. Several mention names of Kenyans with whom they have developed a good personal relationship. The Kenyans are praised as nice, wonderful people and many would have liked to have more Kenyans in each group so they could have gotten to know more people. One writes: "The Kenyans wanted the project as much as we did, and that seemed nice". Others say that they learned a lot about Kenyan culture and the differences and similarities between the countries.

The Danish students experience Kenyans as very hospitable and welcoming. It was also good to be able to play football with them. It was also good that they were good at English, so they were easy to talk to, some of the Danish student's remark.

Others say that the Kenyans were very curious to learn about them as people and how we live in Denmark.

One writes:

> The collabouration with the Kenyans was great, both professionally and personally. Professionally, we learned something from each other, personally we had a great time, talked about everything, and just generally enjoyed ourselves when we were with them. Working with them was the coolest part of the trip.

As a main conclusion, the Danish students would have liked to know the Kenyans more before coming to Kenya. They would have liked to spend more time with them—not only at work, but also in their free time. In the beginning, the collabouration was a bit slow, but during the days they spent together and got to know each other, the collabouration improved and there was time for more laughter and jokes.

Interview with Two of the Male Kenyan Students

How do the Kenyan students perceive the collabouration with the Danish students? I got the opportunity to ask a couple of Kenyan students about this.

We first talk about the teamwork they have had with the Danes and they told me that Danes talks a lot, whereas Kenyans are more willing to get on with it together. But they also told me that the Danish students are very helpful. They also share the work between them, not only the craftsmanship but also the intellectual work. The Danes are more attentive and focused and well educated already, the two Kenyans notes.

The Kenyans say also that the Danish students are more superficial in the communication, especially in their relationships with the Kenyans, so they find it difficult to get personally close and get to know the Danes more deeply. They now discuss whether it's a lack of trust, so they don't dare to open to each other. On the other hand, they also say "Europeans are more open". This is something they have learned from the Danish team: to open and trust each other more.

The two male Kenyans think they work harder than the Danish students. "We are more robust and powerful", they say with a smile and continue: "Physical strength is more important for us than in Denmark".

"But at the same time, the Danes are more precise with their carpentry work and are more technically advanced than us", say the two Kenyan students. Overall, they find that Danes work more from models and use advanced tools.

They have both been happy that the project with the Danes took place in the local community in a school in the slum area. This has meant that both they and the Danes have seen how other people lived outside the school. They also suggest that Comboni themselves continue working on the project after the Danish students leave and went home.

We finish the interview and talk about what they understand by sustainability. One of the first in their mind was the famous female Kenyan professor Wangari Mathai, who was not only a champion of women's rights, but also laid the foundation for trees to be planted everywhere, especially in schools, which is part of the Greenbelt Movement that she started. She is one of Kenya's best-known conservationists and was awarded the Nobel Peace Prize. They look up to her and as carpenters, they will also be committed to planting trees and recycling wood. They are also both committed to stop pollution.

Change

Thinking creatively, collabourating across cultures, schools, "working together on the task at hand", writes one when pointing out the personal changes. Other students talk about getting to know new people in a task with common goals. The "good" conversations point was that they were on an equal base in the work task and, therefore, had a common starting point. Carpenters learn something about carpentry that they didn't know before. Working in wood, some think, is a good step towards working towards sustainability. "The wood, even if it is cut into boards or planks, lives and breathes—absorbing CO_2 and decomposing it", one told me. Both teachers and students told that social sustainability is what has meant the most in terms of change in this project.

One writes that the way to a better future is through the schooling and knowledge the children receive. "Where in Denmark we are very concerned about climate and the environment, in Kenya there is more talks about social sustainability and the development of society", he continues.

For many, the result of their work at the school in Gilgil was satisfying because they could see and feel that the students and teachers there were happy.

"When we finished at the school, I could feel a good change between us students and teachers. Not only us Danish students and teachers, but also the Kenyan ones. If you look at social sustainability, I think we have done a great job and have developed a good relationship with the Kenyans", writes one of the Danish students.

The biggest change for the Danish students was seeing how happy the Kenyan students were with what was done at the primary school, especially the upgrade of the sports/playground with new props. Several mentioned that it will benefit the children and teachers for a long time in Kenya.

Discussion

This project case illustrates new trends and development of new competencies in the TVET curriculum like intercultural competences and green skills, but also in the pedagogical approach which has been under prioritized in many years.

The curriculum and the pedagogical approach can be seen at the micro-level, like the curriculum, development on competencies, the TVET school, (like the Comboni Polytechnic in Gilgil from this case), but also TVET providers like primary and secondary schools.

At the Meso-level we have the national bodies, associations (individual trade unions, individual employers (like Comboni, who is a catholic TVET institution) and sectorial champers (who might set up indicators for competencies or assessment).

Finally we have the macro-level: Ministries, umbrella organizations representing several groups, nationally and internationally (UNESCO/UNEVOC Network) and trade organizations.

The discussion in this paper, will mostly be on the micro-level. At this level I am especially interested in how the pedagogic is expressed by Lucas, Spencer, and Claxton (2012). In their paper the TVET pedagogic is defined as: "the science, art and craft of teaching and learning vocational education". More simply I would say: that vocational pedagogy is the sum of the many decisions which vocational teachers take and discuss with their students when they teach. "Adjusting their approaches to meet the needs of learners and to match the context in which they find themselves".

As Spencer and Claxton mentioned TVET teaching is:

- Routine expertise (being skillful).
- Resourcefulness (stopping to think to deal with the non-routine).
- Functional literacies (communication, and the functional skills of literacy, numeracy, and ICT).
- Craftsmanship (vocational sensibility; aspiration to do a good job; pride in a job well done).
- Business-like attitudes (commercial or entrepreneurial—financial or social—sense).
- Wider skills (for employability and lifelong learning).

I will add, from the above case the following:

Intercultural understanding and working with co-learning in authentic projects like they did in the Case study. But also:

Knowledge about sustainable craftsmanship. Including—Greening TVET—as the IVAC model shows.

Co-learning is when people from different countries work together and learn together on a specific project which can be new for both partners. It is about learning from a new third perspective so to say, where they are both equal from the starting point. In this case both the Danish and the Kenyan TVET students did not knew the project input and output from the beginning when they started the IVAC process. They had to learn the bricks and the investigation, vision, action, and the change aspect in a new authentic context which was a slum school in a remote area. Not even the Kenyan students did know the school and the local area. The Bricks/IVAC model also shows the knowledge part of sustainability. In relation to this the case fulfil the intention with the SDG, goal number 4, 7 about:

> To ensure that all learners acquire the knowledge, and skills needed to promote sustainable development, including, among others, through education for sustainable development and sustainable lifestyles… and "citizenship and appreciation of cultural diversity and of culture's contribution to sustainable development (SDG).

Furthermore, the case meets a beginning of a broad range of relevant competencies for the twenty-first century, such as:

- *Basic competencies*, including literacy, numeracy, and digital literacy at a high enough level so that people can adapt to changes in their jobs and society.
- *Self-regulation*, social and emotional competencies such as conscientiousness, responsibility, empathy, self-efficacy, and collabouration.
- Most of all it also "meets Professional, technical, and specialized knowledge and competencies" needed to meet the demands of specific occupations, but also, with the potential to be "transferable and applicable in new, yet unknown fields".

Finally the case shows how teaching and learning practices in greening Education for Sustainable Development (ESD) requires that key topics—like climate change, disaster risk reduction, biodiversity, poverty reduction, and sustainable consumption can be introduced early on. Participatory teaching and learning that is centred on the student motivate them to engage personally with sustainability issues and hopeful solutions. A problem-based and project-based learning approach like the Bricks/IVAC approach to ESD provides students the opportunity to address sustainability issues while also developing communication, problem-solving and team-working skills and some other teaching and learning practices for ESD.

Conclusion

Both teachers and students from Kenya and Denmark, was satisfied with the whole project. In the whole process, there has been some challenges in implementing the sustainable model and prepare the pilot process before the students meet each other in Kenya. It has been a challenge for the Danish students that the process not always was predictable because the project has some changes because of local circumstances. For example, was it decided very late that the actual co-learning was not possible at the slumdwellers houses but had to be at the local primary school, before the actual work could begin.

But during the ten days stay in Gilgil it was a success and students and teachers was quite excited about the results and the close cross-cultural meeting with the pupils at the local school.

For both the Danish and the Kenyan students they wanted the stay to last longer together with their new friends. The project has been a success in many ways: Not only among the kids from the local school but also for the Danish and the Kenyan students and their institutions.

But the project ended in a very sad disappointment way. Although the Danish Foreign ministry funding agency, the U CISU Funds has supported the whole project another agency in the same ministry, The Immigration Service (in a strange way and with no real and validated argument did not gave visa for the Kenyans to come to Denmark. It means that it was not possible to implement Intervention 3 in the project.

Keywords

TVET pedagogic, co-learning, green skills in TVET, model for development of ESD competencies, intercultural understanding in TVET.

NOTE

1. Inspired by Venka Simovska and Bjarne Bruun Jensen (2009): Conceptualizing Participation: The Health of Children and Young People. World Health Organization Regional Office for Europe.

REFERENCES

Larsen, Niels (Ed.) (2023). *Bæredygtig Udvikling of Professionsdidaktiske Nedslag: VIA University College (Sustainable Development and Didactic Perspective in a University College Context*: *VIA University College.*

Lucas, B. & C. Claxton (2013). *Pedagogic Leadership: Creating Cultures and Practices for Outstanding Vocational Learning*, London: 157 Group.

Lucas, B., E. Spencer, and C. Claxton (2012). *How to Teach Vocational Education: A Theory of Vocational Pedagogy*, London: City & Guild.

Simovska, V. and B.B. Jensen (2009). *Conceptualizing Participation: The Health of Children and Young People.* World Health Organization Regional Office for Europe.

_______(2009). *Shape Up: A School Community Approach to Influencing the Determinants of Childhood Overweight and Obesity.* Lesson Lernt. Barcelona: P.A.U. Education.

Skills Commission (2010). *Teacher Training in Vocational Education.* London: Policy Connect.

UNESCO-UNEVOC: Jan Peter G. de Otero Jens Liebe Tristan Cole BIBB: Vera Hark Michael Schwarz (2022). Trends in New Qualifications and Competencies for TVET Perspectives of the European UNEVOC Network.

UNEVOC Network (2022). Handbook ETF Europa. Eu (2012). Proposed Indicators for Assessing Technical and Vocational Education and Training.

Xibin Han·Qian Zhou·Ming Li·Yuping Wang (Eds.) (2024). *Handbook of Technical and Vocational Teacher Professional Development in the Digital Age.*

Yang, K. (2022). *TPACK-based Integrated Competency Training Framework for Vocational Teachers.* Training Report from Shenzhen Polytechnic.

13

Role of Local Governments in Accelerating Sustainable Development Goals in India

Achievements, Challenges, and Strategic Actions

Jaya Bhalla and *BK Pandey*

The Sustainable Development Goals (SDGs) adopted by the United Nations in 2015 are a universal call to action to end poverty, protect the planet, and ensure prosperity for all by 2030. India, as a signatory, has committed to these goals, recognizing their importance in shaping a sustainable future. Local governments, as the closest level of governance to the people, play a crucial role in the realization of these goals. Their ability to implement programmes, manage resources, and engage communities directly impacts the success of SDG initiatives. Localization of the SDGs is crucial because it involves adapting the global goals to local contexts, providing a framework for local development policy, and enabling local and regional governments to support the achievement of the SDGs through bottom-up action. Localizing the SDGs matters because, although the goals are global, their realization depends on implementation at the local level. Consequently, local and regional governments must be integral to the 2030 Agenda.

This chapter explores the integral role of local governments in India in accelerating SDG achievement, assesses their contributions and challenges, and proposes strategies for enhancing their effectiveness. The paper analyses the crucial role local governments are playing in translating SDG targets into practical initiatives at the grassroots level. It argues that coordination efforts between national and local agencies are necessary to facilitate SDG implementation in Indian context and the monitoring tools and frameworks is essential to measure the impact on SDG progress. It discusses the challenges such as resource limitations and capacity along with strategies for overcoming them.

Objectives

- This chapter underscores the crucial role of local government institutions, such as *panchayats*, *block panchayats*, and *zila parishads*, in enhancing the effectiveness and accelerating the achievement of SDGs, through literature review and success stories. It examines how these local governments contribute to achieving SDG targets in a time-bound manner.
- It analyses the role of Niti Aayog, The Ministry of Panchayati Raj (MoPR) and MOSPI, district administration, municipalities, *gram panchayats* in successful local government initiatives in India that have accelerated SDG progress.
- It examines strategies and measures for localizing SDGs, evaluates progress made so far, reviews emerging challenges such as resource limitations, and the need for improved coordination among stakeholders.
- The paper finally suggests ways to enhance vertical integration between national and sub-national governments for improved policy coherence. It provides recommendations on how the Indian government can further include local governments in the achievement of SDGs.

By addressing these objectives, the paper aims to provide a comprehensive understanding of the role of local governments in achieving SDGs in India and offer actionable insights for improving the localization process.

Literature Review

(a) Progress in SDG

According to the SDG India Index 2023-24, India's overall composite score improved from 57 in 2018 to 66 in 2020-21 and further to 71 in 2023-24. Notable progress has been observed in Goal 1 (No Poverty), 8 (Decent Work and Economic Growth), and 13 (Climate Action), which are now in the "Front Runner" category. The Index reflects the alignment of national priorities with global goals and highlights India's advancements in SDG implementation. However, challenges remain in achieving a more nuanced localization of SDGs, necessitating a focused approach to integrate SDG concepts into local governance effectively.

(b) Local Government in SDG Localization

Local government institutions, such as municipalities and *panchayats*, are instrumental in advancing specific SDGs. Local governments are responsible for various essential services and development projects that align with SDG targets, including clean water supply, waste management, and sustainable urban planning. The vast and diverse socio-economic, cultural, and environmental landscape of India necessitates a tailored approach to SDG localization. This process involves adapting global objectives to address specific local challenges and opportunities. Localization is crucial for effectively addressing multidimensional poverty and inequality, and it requires a comprehensive, whole-of-society approach. Key elements of successful localization include effective multi-level governance, inclusive decision making, and active participation of subnational governments. Local governments are pivotal in the effective localization and implementation of SDGs, bridging global policies with local realities.

Dempsey *et al.* (2011) emphasize that "local governance is crucial for translating global SDGs into actionable plans tailored to local needs". They argue that local governments, through their proximity to communities, are uniquely positioned to address specific challenges and implement sustainable development initiatives effectively. Tandon and Pritchard (2020) highlight successful examples of local government practices in Germany and Kenya, noting that "Germany's municipalities have effectively integrated SDG targets into their local development plans, resulting in measurable advancements in renewable energy and social inclusion". Similarly, in Kenya, local governments have played a key role in advancing SDG-6 (Clean Water and Sanitation) through community-based water management projects, demonstrating the impact of local governance on sustainable development.

Mutasa *et al.* (2019) provide a case study on community-based water management in Kenya, stating, "Local communities have shown significant improvements in water access and quality through participatory management approaches aligned with SDG-6". This illustrates the effectiveness of local governance in addressing specific SDG targets through community involvement and management. Schweitzer and van der Haar (2021) identify key challenges faced by local governments in SDG localization, such as "limited financial resources and insufficient capacity", which hinder effective implementation. They advocate for "enhanced support and capacity building to address these challenges and improve local governance for SDG achievement".

Vetter *et al.* (2020) discuss opportunities for strengthening local government capacity, noting that "investments in training and resources can significantly enhance local governments' ability to implement and monitor SDG initiatives". They emphasize the need for "targeted capacity-building programmes to support local governments in achieving SDG objectives".

NITI Aayog's approach to SDG localization includes integrating SDG targets into national and state-level planning. The 2019 report by NITI Aayog states, "A" "whole-of-government' strategy is essential for effectively localizing SDGs, involving coordination across various ministries and levels of government" (NITI Aayog, 2019). This approach highlights the importance of aligning national policies with local implementation efforts.

The Ministry of Panchayati Raj (MoPR) supports SDG localization by providing state-specific guidelines for Gram Panchayat Development Plans (GPDPs). According to the Ministry of Panchayati Raj (2023), "GPDPs that reflect SDG targets enhance local governance and accountability, ensuring that development initiatives are aligned with national and global objectives" (MoPR, 2023).

Khare and Srinivasan (2020) examines the capacity and roles of local governments in India in achieving the SDGs. The authors argue that local governments are crucial for implementing SDGs due to their proximity to grassroots issues and their ability to integrate SDG targets into local planning processes.

Patel (2021) highlights the experiences of local governments in both urban and rural settings in India. It provides insights into successful strategies and challenges faced by local authorities in aligning their plans with the SDGs.

Rao and Sinha (2022) explore how Panchayati Raj Institutions (PRIs) contribute to sustainable development. The paper highlights case studies of successful PRI interventions and discusses the challenges faced in achieving SDGs at the local level.

Kumar and Mehta (2019) this paper focuses on capacity-building efforts for local governments, particularly *gram panchayats*, to effectively localize SDGs. It assesses the impact of various training programmes and resources on the ability of local governments to implement SDG-related projects.

Singh and Sharma (2020) Sharma analyse how SDG targets are integrated into local government plans across different Indian districts. The chapter provides case studies illustrating both successful integration efforts and areas needing improvement.

Kumar and Joshi (2018) examine the role of both urban and rural local bodies in implementing SDGs. They provide case studies from various states to illustrate different approaches and outcomes. "The success of SDG localization in India depends significantly on the empowerment of local governments through capacity building and decentralized decision making."

Bhat and Desai (2021) analyse challenges and opportunities in SDG localization across different states in India, focusing on both successes and shortcomings, challenges and opportunities in SDG localization across different states in India, focusing on both successes and shortcomings. "Local governments in India face diverse challenges in SDG localization, including financial constraints and limited administrative capacity, but there are significant opportunities for growth through innovative practices and collabouration."

Patel and Shah (2019) present case studies from Gujarat and Karnataka, highlighting how local governments in these states are addressing SDG-related issues such as clean water and sanitation. "Effective local governance in Gujarat and Karnataka has been instrumental in advancing SDG targets, especially in sectors like water management and sanitation."

Gupta and Agarwal (2022) focus on the role of *gram panchayats* in rural areas, detailing how these institutions are working to achieve various SDGs and the impact of their efforts on local development. "*Gram panchayats* play a crucial role in translating SDG targets into actionable plans at the grassroots level, though they face challenges related to resources and governance."

Mehta and Sharma (2021) explore the role of urban local bodies in achieving SDGs, examining how these bodies are integrating SDG targets into urban planning and development initiatives. They hold that "Urban local bodies in India are increasingly recognizing the importance of SDGs in shaping sustainable urban development, though they face challenges related to infrastructure and funding". Subramanyam (2022) in "Urban Governance and Sustainability: Case Studies from Indian Municipalities", explores various case studies of urban governance and sustainability initiatives across Indian municipalities, including Darjeeling. It provides insights into successful practices and challenges faced in implementing sustainability projects at the municipal level.

Subramanyam (2021) in "District-Level Success in SDG Implementation: Lessons from Kerala" focuses on the success stories from districts in Kerala, such as Alappuzha, and analyses the strategies and approaches that led to their achievements in sanitation and community engagement.

These studies and articles provide concrete examples of how local governments in India are contributing to SDG achievement through innovative projects and community engagement. They serve as valuable references for understanding the impact and potential of local governance in advancing sustainable development.

Research indicates that capacity building for local governments is crucial for effective SDG implementation. According to Sharma and Mukherjee (2022), training programmes and workshops organized by national and state agencies are essential for equipping local officials with the skills needed to align local policies with SDG targets. Additionally, monitoring mechanisms such as the SDG India Index provide valuable insights into progress and areas needing improvement.

Case Studies Highlighting the Role of Local Governments in the Indian Context

Numerous local government initiatives in India have demonstrated significant progress towards SDG targets. Case studies of successful projects highlight how local governments have tackled challenges creatively and effectively. Innovative approaches, such as community-driven sanitation programmes or green infrastructure projects, have set benchmarks for SDG achievement. Collabourations with NGOs, businesses, and civil society organizations have further amplified these efforts, showcasing the potential for local governments to lead transformative change.

In Dharavi, one of Mumbai's largest informal settlements, local governments have taken innovative steps to address SDG-related challenges such as sanitation and housing. This case study illustrates how local authorities have engaged with community members to develop solutions tailored to the unique needs of Dharavi's residents (Bhide, 2018). Efforts include upgrading sanitation facilities, improving waste management systems, and providing affordable housing. The involvement of local communities in decision making processes has been crucial in ensuring that the initiatives are effective and sustainable, demonstrating the significant role that local governance can play in achieving SDG targets in densely populated urban areas.

In Rajasthan, several *gram panchayats* have successfully implemented projects aligned with SDG-6 (Clean Water and Sanitation). These local governments have managed resources efficiently and engaged communities in initiatives to improve water access and quality. Notable projects include the construction of water storage facilities, installation of hand pumps, and promotion of rainwater harvesting techniques (Singh, 2019). By addressing water scarcity and improving sanitation infrastructure, these *gram Panchayats* have made substantial progress in enhancing the quality of life for rural populations and achieving the targets set under SDG-6.

Kerala's local self-government institutions have made significant strides in aligning their health and education initiatives with SDGs, particularly SDG-3 (Good Health and Well-being) and SDG-4 (Quality Education). The decentralized approach in Kerala has enabled local governments to tailor health programmes to community needs, leading to improved health outcomes. Initiatives include the establishment of primary health centres, immunization drives, and health awareness campaigns. In the education sector, efforts such as upgrading school infrastructure, providing training for teachers, and ensuring equitable access to education have contributed to higher literacy rates and better educational outcomes in the state.

In Madhya Pradesh, district-level efforts have focused on promoting sustainable agriculture and enhancing economic opportunities for rural population, aligning with the SDGs related to agriculture and livelihoods. Successful strategies include the introduction of modern farming techniques, support for organic farming, and the establishment of agricultural cooperatives. These initiatives have not only increased agricultural productivity but also provided better livelihood opportunities for farmers, contributing to economic growth and poverty reduction in rural areas.

In Sikkim's Environmental Sustainability Efforts, the local governments have been at the forefront of implementing climate action initiatives, aligning with SDG-13 (Sharma, 2018). The state's proactive measures include extensive afforestation projects, promotion of renewable energy sources, and community engagement in environmental conservation. Sikkim has also banned the use of plastic bags and other non-biodegradable materials, demonstrating a strong commitment to environmental sustainability. These efforts have resulted in significant progress in mitigating the impacts of climate change and preserving the natural environment, showcasing the pivotal role of local governance in achieving environmental sustainability goals.

Municipalities in Tamil Nadu have been pioneers in adopting innovative approaches to address urban challenges and promote sustainable development.[1] These efforts contribute to SDG-11 (Sustainable Cities and Communities) and SDG-7 (Affordable and Clean Energy). Several municipalities in Tamil Nadu have implemented solar street lighting projects to enhance energy efficiency and reduce reliance on non-renewable energy sources. These projects not only improve street safety but also contribute to reducing the carbon footprint of urban areas. Municipalities have introduced smart waste management systems that utilize technology to optimize waste collection routes and monitor waste levels. These systems improve operational efficiency and reduce environmental impact.

Adoption of solar street lighting and smart waste management systems led to increased energy efficiency, reduced environmental impact, and improved urban infrastructure. These initiatives highlight the potential of innovative solutions in advancing sustainable urban development.

These case studies highlight the diverse and impactful roles that local government bodies in India play in advancing the SDGs, adapting global goals to local contexts, and addressing specific challenges through innovative and community-driven approaches.

The literature underscores the pivotal role of local government institutions in the localization of SDGs in India. Effective coordination between central and state agencies, district-level administration, and PRIs is essential for aligning global objectives with local needs. While progress has been notable, continued efforts in capacity building, stakeholder engagement, and focused implementation strategies are necessary to enhance the effectiveness of SDG localization and ensure timely achievement of the targets by 2030.

The above review synthesizes key literature on the role of local government in SDG localization, focusing on, district administration, PRI engagement, capacity building, and progress monitoring. These sources provide a comprehensive view of how local governments in India are working to localize and achieve SDGs, offering valuable insights into both successful practices and ongoing challenges.

Strategy and Measures to Promote Localization of SDG in India

(a) ***Multi-Stakeholder Engagement:*** The successful localization of SDGs requires active participation from government bodies, civil society organizations, the private sector, academia, and local communities. This collabourative approach ensures that strategies are inclusive and cater to the needs of all stakeholders.

(b) ***Data Collection and Monitoring:*** Timely and accurate data collection is essential for tracking the progress of

SDGs. India is strengthening its data infrastructure and monitoring mechanisms, with the SDG India Index and Dashboard serve as a primary tool for assessing progress at both national and sub-national levels. The Index measures performance on 113 indicators aligned with the Ministry of Statistics and Programme Implementation's National Indicator Framework (NIF).

(c) ***Capacity Building:*** Enhancing the capacity of institutions and stakeholders is vital for effective SDG implementation. Capacity-building efforts focus on improving knowledge, skills, and resources necessary for achieving and monitoring SDGs.

(d) ***Utilizing Innovation and Technology:*** Leveraging technology and innovation can accelerate SDG implementation. Initiatives such as Digital India, the Smart Cities Mission, and the Atal Innovation Mission aim to tackle sustainable development challenges through technological advancements.

(e) ***Financing SDGs:*** Securing funding and mobilizing resources are crucial for SDG localization. India explores various financing mechanisms, including public-private partnerships and international collabourations, to support SDG initiatives.

(f) ***Awareness and Advocacy:*** Raising awareness about SDGs and advocating for their importance at the grassroots level are essential for public support and engagement. Awareness campaigns, educational programmes, and community activities play a key role in fostering a sense of responsibility towards achieving SDGs.

(g) ***Addressing Challenges:*** Localizing SDGs involves overcoming challenges such as poverty, inequality, and environmental degradation. Coordinated efforts and innovative solutions are needed to address these issues effectively.

(h) ***Coordination by National Institutions:*** While local governments are central to achieving SDGs in India, their effectiveness is significantly enhanced by the support and coordination provided by national institutions. NITI Aayog advocates for a "whole-of-government" and "whole- of-society" approach to SDG localization. This approach emphasizes that the responsibility of localizing SDGs is shared across all ministries. Many ministries' work directly impacts rural areas and intersects with the functions of PRIs, requiring coordinated efforts to integrate SDGs effectively at the grassroots level (NITI Aayog, 2019).

NITI Aayog, the Ministry of Panchayati Raj (MoPR), and the Ministry of Statistics and Programme Implementation (MoSPI) have been instrumental in coordinating efforts to achieve the SDGs. NITI Aayog has facilitated the integration of SDGs into local planning processes, working closely with state and local governments to align their strategies with national goals. The MoSPI plays a critical role in monitoring and evaluating SDG progress. It coordinates efforts to collect accurate data and reports on SDG indicators, ensuring that local governments' contributions are effectively measured and tracked. These agencies have been tasked with coordinating planning, monitoring, and statistical functions at the central and state levels (NITI Aayog, SDG India Index Baseline Report, 2018; Press Information Bureau, pib.gov.in). This approach highlights that SDGs are interconnected, encompassing economic, social, and environmental dimensions, and necessitates collabouration among diverse stakeholders, including line ministries, public agencies, PRIs, and others.

Role of NITI Aayog in Localizing SDGs

NITI Aayog (2019) underscores the necessity of a "whole-of-government" approach as outlined in the 2030 Agenda declaration. The SDG India Index, launched in 2017, has provided momentum for this localization effort by highlighting the role of states, UTs, and *panchayats* as essential stakeholders in achieving SDGs. It has brought out the Document "Localizing SDGs: Early lessons from India" in year 2019. NITI Aayog has released a report titled "The Indian Model of SDG Localisation", highlighting the significance of India's approach to achieving SDGs by 2030. The report outlines four pillars of the Indian SDG localization model:

- ***Institutional Ownership:*** Emphasizing the importance of institutional commitment to SDG implementation.
- ***Review and Monitoring System:*** Establishing robust mechanisms for monitoring progress.
- ***Capacity Development:*** Enhancing the ability to integrate SDGs into planning processes.
- ***Comprehensive Societal Approach:*** Ensuring that SDGs drive inclusive growth and development.

The model prioritizes aligning SDGs with the needs of communities, especially vulnerable or marginalized groups, and promoting the principle of "Sabka Saath, Sabka Vikas" (Collective Efforts, Inclusive Growth). NITI Aayog's SDG India Index and Dashboard serves as the official tool for monitoring SDG progress.

Localization of SDGs in Rural India by MoPR

The MoPR has been pivotal in coordinating local institutions through the formation of an expert group for SDG reporting. This expert group helps ensure that local governments are aligned with SDG targets and provides guidance on best practices for implementation. The MoPR has also launched a scheme to involve elected representatives directly in SDG initiatives. This scheme aims to enhance local governance by empowering elected officials to take a more active role in planning and executing SDG-related projects. To advance the localization of SDGs in rural India, a dedicated Expert Group was formed to develop strategies and initiatives for integrating SDGs into PRIs. This Expert Group conducted extensive deliberations and submitted a detailed report, which has been accepted by the MoPR. The report, titled "Localization of Sustainable Development Goals in Panchayat Raj Institutions (Volume 2 M)", outlines comprehensive recommendations for engaging PRIs and relevant stakeholders in rural areas.

Identified SDGs for Grassroots Intervention

Among the seventeen SDGs, the MoPR has identified nine specific goals where direct intervention at the grassroots level is crucial. These goals are:

- Goal-1: No Poverty
- Goal-2: Zero Hunger
- Goal-3: Good Health and Well-being
- Goal-4: Quality Education
- Goal-5: Gender Equality
- Goal-6: Clean Water and Sanitation
- Goal-7: Clean and Affordable Energy
- Goal-8: Decent Work and Economic Growth
- Goal-10: Reduced Inequalities

Additionally, other goals such as SDG-13 (Climate Action), SDG-14 (Life Below Water), SDG-15 (Life on Land), and SDG-16 (Peace, Justice, and Strong Institutions) are also relevant and require focused efforts.

India's local government system is structured through three tiers of PRIs: the *gram panchayat* at the village level, the block *panchayat* at the intermediate level, and the *zila panchayat* at the district level.

Role of Gram Panchayats

In India, the *gram panchayats* (GPs) are entrusted with twenty-nine subjects that cover various SDGs to different extents, depending on the level of devolution in each state. The process of localizing SDGs within the PRIs involves multiple facets, including capacity building, the establishment of frameworks for targets and indicators, rigorous monitoring, incentivization, partnerships, collabourations, and convergence of efforts among various ministries and departments (NITI Aayog, 2019). The "Sustainable

Development Goals and Gram Panchayats" report (UNDP, 2017) emphasizes that GPs are mandated to address twenty-nine subjects listed in the Eleventh Schedule of the Constitution, many of which align with SDG targets. GPs across India have developed Gram Panchayat Development Plans (GPDPs) that synchronize with SDGs. By leveraging resources from various centrally and state-sponsored schemes, *panchayats* are working towards achieving these goals at the local level.

Participatory Planning

The *panchayats* are tasked with preparing comprehensive GPDPs that outline local socio-economic goals in terms of the SDGs. These plans guide the local development agenda and action plans to address specific community needs. The central government provides training, mentoring, and closely monitors progress to ensure that development milestones are achieved effectively.

The MoPR aims to achieve SDGs through the Rashtriya Gram Swaraj Abhiyan (RGSA) scheme. There are more than 2.65 lakh GPs in India with around 32 lakh elected representatives covering thirty-four states and union territories of the country. This initiative focuses on empowering elected representatives and functionaries to deliver on SDG targets through participatory local planning. Under this scheme, *panchayats* are encouraged to integrate Village Poverty Reduction Plans (VPRPs) into GPDPs, ensuring that poverty alleviation strategies are embedded in local development plans. This initiative seeks to strengthen local governance by engaging elected officials in planning and execution, ensuring that SDG efforts are well-coordinated and responsive to local needs. The scheme provides a platform for elected representatives to contribute to and oversee SDG implementation, thereby increasing accountability and local ownership.

People's Plan Campaign (PPC) has been, launched to prepare GPDPs, mandates the incorporation of VPRPs. This integration ensures that local development plans address poverty reduction and align with SDG objectives. The MoPR has been instrumental in developing state-specific guidelines for GPDPs to align local planning with SDG targets. This approach integrates thematic goals into local development plans, facilitating the convergence of resources and actions (MoPR Guidelines, 2024).

The twenty-nine subjects that are the responsibility of the GPs cover the SDGs with varying levels of devolution in different states. The localization of SDGs necessitates robust planning and implementation at the local level, facilitated by PRIs. By leveraging these resources and schemes, local governments can better navigate challenges and accelerate progress towards the SDGs.

Role of District-Level Administration

Research by (Subramanian, 2023) emphasizes the critical role of district administration as the primary interface between the government and local population. The study notes that India's progress towards development goals is closely tied to the effectiveness of district-level administration. Districts are pivotal in tailoring initiatives to meet specific local needs, thereby ensuring contextual relevance and responsiveness. The assessment of SDG performance across Indian states, using data from the National Family Health Survey, highlights notable progress in districts such as Udaipur in Rajasthan. Udaipur achieved the highest number of indicators on target, reflecting substantial strides in SDG attainment. The study identifies that around fifty-four districts in Rajasthan, Madhya Pradesh, and Chhattisgarh are on track to meet seventeen to twenty-three indicators, indicating significant progress toward achieving SDGs in these regions.

Role of Municipality

SDG-11, which focuses on sustainable cities and human settlements, is particularly central to this process. Its inclusion in the 2030 Agenda resulted from extensive advocacy by the urban community and recognizes the importance of the subp-national dimension of development. Linking SDG-11 with the urban aspects of the other sixteen goals is essential for effective localization of the SDGs.

Former UN Secretary-General Ban Ki-moon (2012) emphasized this by stating, "our struggle for global sustainability will be won or lost in cities". Cities and regions are ideally positioned to translate the broad and abstract 2030 Agenda into concrete actions that fit their specific contexts, helping citizens understand how local actions contribute to achieving these goals. Local governments are crucial for translating global goals into actionable local plans, owing to their proximity to the community and their ability to address localized needs effectively. The roadmap for localizing the SDGs has been developed by the Global Taskforce of Local and Regional Governments, UNDP, and UN Habitat to assist cities and regions in delivering the 2030 Agenda. Raise awareness and advocate for the active role of local actors in the localization of the SDGs. Support local actors in making decisions that contribute towards achieving the SDGs.

Since the UN Conference on Environment and Development in Rio de Janeiro in 1992, local governments and civil society have gained considerable experience in implementing sustainable development at the local level. As stated by the South African Local Government Association (SALGA), "Local spaces are ultimately the key site of delivery and development and, as such, local government is central to the success of sustainable development".

Mission Mode Approach

For effective implementation, localizing SDGs within PRIs should be approached in mission mode. This highlights the critical importance of the initiative from the highest levels of government and ensures that it receives the necessary attention and resources. Mission mode implementation provides clear objectives and accelerates progress by focusing on defined targets and outcomes. This approach aligns with various flagship schemes already executed in mission mode, reinforcing the need for a concerted effort to achieve SDGs at the local level.

While various flagship schemes are taken up in mission mode, localizing SDGs in PRIs taken in mission mode would get the required thrust and attention. Mission mode status would communicate the importance from the highest level and attract attention to clearly defined objectives.

Challenges Faced by Local Governments

Localizing SDGs in PRIs is a function of Capacity building, framework of targets and indicators, monitoring, incentivizing, partnerships and collabourations, convergence in working of ministries/departments. Despite their pivotal role, local governments face several challenges that hinder their ability to fully realize SDG targets. Resource constraints, including financial limitations and a lack of skilled personnel, often impede the implementation of ambitious projects. Capacity gaps and policy barriers further complicate their efforts. Additionally, engaging communities and ensuring active public participation remain ongoing challenges.

Addressing the following issues is crucial for enabling local governments to effectively contribute to the SDGs.

- ***Resource Constraints:*** Issues related to financial and human resources.
- ***Capacity Gaps:*** Challenges in technical expertise and administrative capacity.
- ***Policy and Regulatory Barriers:*** Analysis of policy limitations and regulatory challenges.
- ***Public Engagement:*** Difficulties in engaging communities and stakeholders effectively.

Strategic Actions for Leveraging Local Governments

To enhance the role of local governments in achieving SDGs, several strategic actions are recommended. Strengthening institutional frameworks and improving governance structures can provide a solid foundation for effective implementation. Increasing funding and resource mobilization is essential for supporting local projects and initiatives. Capacity building and training programmes can address skill gaps and enhance administrative efficiency. Fostering community participation through inclusive approaches and leveraging technology for better service delivery are also vital strategies. Capacity building and Information, Education, and Communication (IEC) initiatives play a significant role in enhancing stakeholder ownership and achieving SDGs. Progress should be monitored through a framework of targets and indicators that are relatable to local contexts.

Institutional Framework and Capacity Building

To effectively localize SDGs, capacity building for PRIs is paramount. The framework includes setting targets and indicators, establishing robust monitoring systems, and fostering collabourations with various stakeholders. The document "Localizing SDGs: Early Lessons from India" released by NITI Aayog in 2019 outlines initial experiences and lessons learned in this endeavour (NITI Aayog, 2019). It will necessitate strengthening institutional frameworks. The recommendations for improving the institutional capacity of local governments include Enhanced Funding and Resource Mobilization, Capacity Building and Training, Fostering Community Participation: Approaches for Enhancing Public Engagement and Involvement, Leveraging Technology and Innovation: Use of Technology to Improve Service Delivery and Monitoring.

Importance of PRIs and Capacity Building

The localization of SDGs is fundamentally reliant on the effective functioning of PRIs. Local action and people-centred approaches are essential for addressing issues that are best managed at the grassroots level. The capacity of PRIs to plan and implement development initiatives is crucial for the successful localization of SDGs. Effective capacity building and IEC strategies are vital for ensuring stakeholder ownership and engagement in SDG processes.

Conclusion

India's progress in attaining SDGs at the local level has been marked by notable advancements and innovative approaches driven by local governments. For instance, in Kerala, local self-government institutions have made significant strides in aligning their health and education initiatives with SDGs, improving health outcomes and educational access in line with SDG-3 (Good Health and Well-being) and SDG-4 (Quality Education). The state's decentralized governance model has enabled better resource management and community involvement, resulting in more effective and sustainable outcomes. Similarly, Rajasthan's GPs have successfully implemented water and sanitation projects, contributing to SDG-6 (Clean Water and Sanitation). These projects have improved water access and quality, demonstrating how local governance can effectively address specific SDG targets through tailored, community-focused initiatives.

In other regions, such as Madhya Pradesh and Sikkim, local governments have taken proactive measures to address SDG-related challenges. Madhya Pradesh's district-level initiatives in agriculture and livelihoods have promoted sustainable agricultural practices and enhanced economic opportunities for rural populations, aligning with SDG-2 (Zero Hunger) and SDG-8 (Decent Work and Economic Growth). Meanwhile, Sikkim has focused on environmental sustainability, implementing climate action initiatives that contribute to SDG-13 (Climate Action). The state's efforts in afforestation, renewable energy adoption, and community engagement have made significant progress in combating climate change. These examples highlight the critical role of local governments in driving SDG attainment through localized. Local governments are at the forefront of SDG implementation in India, with their proximity to communities allowing for targeted and impactful actions.

While challenges exist, strategic actions can significantly enhance their contributions to achieving the SDGs. By strengthening institutional frameworks, increasing resources, and fostering community engagement, local governments can play a crucial role in meeting SDG targets within the stipulated timeframe. Collabouration between all stakeholders, including national and state governments, civil society, and international organizations, is essential for supporting and empowering local governments in this critical endeavour.

NOTE

1. https://spc.tn.gov.in/tanii/

REFERENCES

Bhide, A. (2018). "Localizing SDGs in Informal Settlements." *Environment and Urbanization Asia*, *9*: 26-39.

Dempsey, N. *et al.* (2011). "Local Governance and the Role of Local Government in Achieving SDGs." *Urban Studies Journal*, *19*(5): 289-300.

Global Taskforce of Local and Regional Government, UN Habitat (2015). *Roadmap for Localizing the SDGs: Implementation and Monitoring at Subnational Level.*

Ministry of Panchayati Raj (2023). *State-Specific Guidelines for Gram Panchayat Development Plans.* Ministry of Panchayati Raj Publications.

Mutasa, M., *et al.* (2019). *Community-Based Water Management and SDG-6 in Kenya: A Case Study*. Water Policy.

NITI Aayog (2018). *SDG India Index Baseline Report.*

NITI Aayog (2019). *Localizing SDGs: Early Lessons from India.* NITI Aayog Reports.

Schweitzer, K. & G. van der Haar (2021). "Challenges in SDG Localization for Local Governments." *Development Policy Review*, *39*(2): 150-165.

Sharma, A. & S. Mukherjee (2022). "Capacity Building and Monitoring in Local Government SDG Implementation." *Journal of Development Studies.*

Sharma, R. (2018). "Sikkim's Green Initiatives: Role of Local Governments in Achieving SDG-13." *Environmental Development*, pp. 18-30.

Singh, K. (2019). "Rajasthan's Water and Sanitation Initiatives: Local Government Efforts and SDG Implementation." *Journal of Rural Development*, 374-91.

Subramanian, S. (2023). "Progress on Sustainable Development Goal Indicators in 707 Districts of India: A Quantitative Mid-line Assessment

Using the National Family Health Surveys, 2016 and 2021." *The Lancet Southeast Asia, 13*: 100-134.

Tandon, R. & W. Pritchard (2020). "Successful Local Government Practices for SDG Localization: Case Studies from Germany and Kenya." *International Journal of Urban and Regional Research, 44*(5).

United Nations (2012). "Meeting Coverages and Press Release, 'Our Struggle for Global Sustainability Will Be Won or Lost in Cities'."

UNDP (2017). *Sustainable Development Goals and Gram Panchayats: The Future We Want.*

Vetter, A. *et al.* (2020). *Opportunities for Enhancing Local Government Capacity for SDG Implementation. Public Administration Review.*

14

Impact of Participatory Structures at the Grassroots

A Case Study from Prathabaramapuram Village Panchayat, Nagapattinam, Tamil Nadu

Prabagaran, M. and *Inbarasan, K.G.*

Decentralized democracy is a need in a country like India due to its huge population. Decentralized democracy can be achieved by empowering citizens to exercise their rights wisely with various support systems in the grassroots (Piper, 2014). Effective citizenship is the actual capacity of the citizens to use their formal political and civil rights available to them. The democratic accountability of local governments is mainly feasible by two aspects, i.e. through building good institutions and enhancing participation of people in the process with the support of both political sphere and civil societies (Heller, 2012). It was experimented in the Prathabaramapuram Village Panchayat by duly following the process of decentralized planning as suggested by Ministry of Panchayat Raj, Government of India in the Village Panchayat Development Plan Preparation. This case study discusses various participatory forums and the support systems utilized for strengthening and initiating the forums through the political will, expectations and requirements in the village *panchayat*.

About Prathabaramapuram (PRpuram) Village Panchayat

Prathabaramapuram is a coastal village *panchayat* of Keelaiyur Panchayat Union, Nagapattinam District, Tamil Nadu situated about 10 km away from the district headquarters. This village *panchayat* shares northern border with Velankanni Special Grade Town Panchayat and Vellaiyar River, eastern border with Bay of Bengal, Western border with Chinnathumbur, Thalayamalai Village Panchayat and Vellaiyar River and southern border with Thirupoondi West and Thirupoondi East Village Panchayat. Nagapattinam lies between Northern Latitude 10.6620 degrees and 79.8420 degrees Eastern longitude. The village *panchayat* spreads over an area of 15 sq. km.

Participatory Forums in the Village Panchayat

The decentralized democracy is feasible through participatory forums available to the citizens and its engagements and nature of its functionality (Piper, 2014). The *gram sabha* in India is a constitutionally recognized forum primarily for socio-economic planning of the respective village *panchayat* (VP) and beneficiary selection forum for various schemes of the Government of India and state governments depending on the structure of the scheme guidelines.

The *gram sabha* is the participatory forum sometimes which is not possible towards catering to the needs of everyone in the village due to its own limitations including population and size of the VP, hesitation to interact by specific social categories such as women, children, differently-abled persons, etc. Hence to overcome some limitations and to receive everyone's perception in the VP planning process, Ward Sabha, Women's Sabha (Magalir Sabhai), Sabha for the Differently-Abled (Matruthiranali Sabhai), and Children's Sabha (Balar Sabhai) are required for enhanced participation of citizens. Further the participatory structures are also expected to achieve the Sustainable Development Goals (SDGs). This chapter discusses in detail about the participatory forums, its objectives, function and the outcome of the resolutions.

Women's Sabha (Magalir Sabhai or Mahila Sabha)

The concept of a "Mahila Sabha" first emerged in Maharashtra when SHG and women members of the community came together and called for a Mahila Sabha for their fight against alcoholism (PRIA, n.d.). Acknowledging the importance of such a platform, in 2003, Rajasthan issued circular for conducting Women's *sabhas* before the *gram sabha* meetings. It was then legalized by Maharashtra Village Panchayati Raj Amendment Act, 2012 in Maharashtra. Subsequently, other states followed. The SDG-5 discusses in detail about achieving gender equality and empowering women and girls and the Target 5.5. indicates to ensure full participation in leadership and decision making which is an integral part of this Women's Sabha (United Nations, 2012).

The main objectives of the Women's Sabha are to ensure the women share their demands and difficulties in a forum and also to know about the facilities and their rights. Further it will enhance their participation in *gram sabha* and their confidence level in discussing various issues concerning them in different forums and also to bring many women-related aspects during the plan preparation of the respective villages/VPs. (UN Women Asia and the Pacific, 2013).

Objectives of the Women's Sabha by the PRpuram VP

- To understand the views on women's issues and problems in PRpuram study area.
- To enable PRpuram as a Women-Friendly VP.
- To prepare gender budgeting for the PRpuram VP.
- To enhance the livelihood of women in the PRpuram VP.
- To achieve the Target 5.5 of SDG-5.

Mobilization, Participation and Conduct of Women's Sabha

An execution committee under the leadership of VP president was formed by the Panchayat Council to conduct Magalir Sabhai. The committee comprises four members including president, vice-president and two ward members. Except the president, the remaining members of the committee are women. The committee mobilized women for the Magalir Sabhai through SHGs discussions, interactions with MGNREGA workers and various officials of line departments including District Social Welfare Officer.

All women in the village were informed well in advance, i.e., seven days before the Magalir Sabhai through audio announcements. Due to awareness created by the executive committee, sixty-seven women participated in the Magalir Sabhai. The *sabha* was chaired by Ms. T. Ramya, Vice-President. Around ten resolutions were passed by the *sabha*.

Major Discussion Points of Women's Sabha

During the discussion, the women discussed many points focusing on livelihood and other issues faced by them. The prime points of the discussion was to create a women's collective to support the livelihood of women in PRpuram. Further, illegal preparation of alcohol in the village came into limelight during the discussion. They passed a resolution against it and some of them also reported about domestic violence. They also raised the requirement for the coaching female candidates for the competitive examinations. Along with that, they gave various inputs for the perspective plan of PRpuram VP including request livelihood shed for fisherwomen, drinking water issue in different wards, etc.

Outcomes of Women's Sabha

Women's collective named *thurigai* has been formed that took initiatives for the livelihood of the women. The list of livelihood related activities including preparation of scheme information boards, plastic segregation and processing and nursery activities. The PRpuram VP took initiative and arranged a coaching centre for all the students preparing for competitive exams including the female candidates. Domestic violence issue was addressed by the VP administration through counselling. The *gram sabha* and *panchayat* council have considered all the inputs and views of Magalir Sabha while preparing and approving the Village Panchayat Development Plan (VPDP). This decision making is ensuring to achieve target 5.5 of the SDGs.

Children's Sabha (Balar Sabhai or Bala Sabha)

According to the Eleventh Schedule of Constitution of India, child development is devolved to local governments. Hence their participation is required to ensure their development. The *bala sabhas* are the groups of children formed to discuss their demands and requirements in school or ward or village or village *panchayats* (Caritas India, n.d.). The *bala sabhas* included children between the age of 12-18 years. This *sabha* is an important component for the participation of children because they can form their views which were also mentioned in the Tamil Nadu State Policy for Children, 2021. The policy says that the *bala sabhas* shall meet four times in a year and the resolutions need to be discussed in the *gram sabhas* to take appropriate actions in various matters related to children (GoTN, 2021). As the children were affected by almost all the SDGs, involving them to understand their problems and providing solutions by involving them leads to achieve the SDGs at much faster rate.

The concept of Bala Sabha was noted from Kerala initiated by Kudumbashree. Its main thrust was to prevent the transmission of intergenerational poverty through capability enhancement of children (Kudumbashree, n.d.). The structure and functions of Bala Sabha can vary based on the local situations in the respective village *panchayats* like the availability of number of children, Institutions like schools, library, etc.

Objectives of the Children's Sabha by the PRpuram VP

- To understand the views of children in VPDP preparation process.
- To ensure the demands and requirements of children to be addressed by the PRpuram VP.
- To create civic sense among the children.

- To encourage participation of children in democratic process.
- To achieve the Target 5.5 of SDG-5 and Target 10.2 of SDG-10.

Structure of Children's Sabha

The volunteers from different areas were identified at ward level and they were provided professional training about the election rules to be followed in each ward to conduct the elections in a decentralized manner. They conducted elections at respective wards to elect children representatives from the wards. Further, the representatives are also elected from the schools to ensure representation at various aspects. The elected children were trained by professionals to enhance their participation and civic sense. Hence a total of fifteen representatives (nine boys and six girls) were elected.

Mobilization, Participation and Conduct of Children's Sabha

The VP administration facilitated and conducted the Balar Sabhai and also ensured to invite all the related line departments. The District Collector was also present as the Special Invitee during the Children's Sabha. The elected representatives led the discussions where a total of 322 children participated that include 153 boys and 169 girls from the VP. Around twenty-eight resolutions were passed by the *sabha* on various issues as discussed by the children among themselves.

Discussion Points and Outcomes

The children's *sabha* conducted in the PRpuram VP brought out major issues of children such as improving the infrastructure of schools in terms of constructing more classrooms, upgrading the existing toilet facilities and providing safe/purified drinking water facilities. The *sabha* discussed the need for having parks and playgrounds in the VP for encouraging the sports activities. The *sabha* indicated the requirement of self-defence training for the female kids and suggested to rename the hamlets/areas/streets which having caste based names. The District Collector keenly observed the *sabha* as the Special Invitee and encouraged the children to share their views in the participatory forums.

Sabha for Differently-abled (Matruthiranali Sabhai)

It is an important aspect to include and receive the views of the persons of differently-abled, wherever applicable. The same was stipulated in the guidelines for the VPDP Preparation by the Ministry of Panchayat Raj, Government of India. PRpuram VP is one of the largest VPs in Nagapattinam district. The need of the *sabha* for differently-abled was naturally raised and initiated by the VP president.

The functioning of this *sabha* was aligned with the SDG-10 which expresses to reduce inequalities in various means. Target 10.2 indicates the promotion of universal social, economic and political inclusion. The *sabha* was initiated to empower the persons of differently-abled to include them in the planning process and ensuring the entitlements and support from the VP. It is also important to note that the equal opportunities was created by the VP to them which is the Target 10.3 (United Nations, 2012).

Objectives of the Sabha for Differently-abled by the PRpuram VP

- To ensure the entitlements of the differently-abled persons in the study area.
- To create awareness among differently-abled persons about various schemes available for them.
- To ensure inclusiveness and views of differently-abled in the VPDP preparation process.
- To achieve target 10.2 of SDG-10.

Mobilization and Conduct of the Sabha for Differently-abled

All the differently-abled persons were informed well in advance, i.e., seven days before the *sabha* for differently-abled through audio announcements and worksite supervisors of MGNREGS by the VP administration. Due to awareness creation, sixty-seven differently-abled persons participated in the *sabha* and the numbers increased consequently. The District Differently-Abled Welfare Officer was invited and was also present for the *sabha*. Further, the VP administration arranged a transportation facility to pick up and drop them for attending the *sabha* for differently-abled. The *sabha* was chaired by Mr. Shanmuganathan who is a differently- abled person in presence of VP president and special invitees such as district differently abled welfare officer and special *tahsildar* also attended the *sabha*. Around twelve resolutions were passed by the *sabha*.

Major Discussion Points of the Sabha for Differently-abled

It is observed that many of them were unaware about the Unique Disability Identity (UDID) cards because of which they were denied many benefits under different schemes such as financial assistance, two wheeler/three wheeler vehicles and other disabled friendly equipment. To avail the entitlements and benefits, they are facing administrative delays due to lengthy procedures which lead to multiple visits for them in the district offices. With respect to the VPDP preparation, many unique points related to differently-abled were raised such as construction of disabled friendly toilets, ensuring disabled friendly infrastructure in all the infrastructure within the VP, etc.

Outcome of the Sabha for Differently-abled

A coordinator was appointed by the VP administration to ensure the benefits of the differently-abled persons through door-step assistance. A vehicle was arranged monthly once on need basis by the VP administration in consultation with District Differently Abled Welfare Office, Nagapattinam, to ensure the UDID application process, various benefits under schemes such as wheelchairs, walking sticks, etc. One of the differently-abled beneficiary of the Swachh Bharat Mission highlighted the matter regarding the partial construction of toilet facilities. That issue was addressed by the VP administration and the toilet was constructed and handed over to the beneficiary. Ultimately the SDG-10 and the Targets 10.2 and 10.3 were achieved by the VP to a limited extent through this *sabha*.

Ward Sabha

The wards are the components of the VP and the ward *sabha*s are similar to *gram sabha*s which are conducted at the ward levels. It is required when the population of the VP is very high and needs separate discussion for their wards. Hence, the ward *sabha*s were conducted in PRpuram to understand the requirements, demands based on detailed discussions among the local persons at the grassroots for the planning of their own requirements in the respective wards.

Mobilization, Discussion and Outcomes

The event of the ward *sabha* was informed to the concerned area at least three days in advance through ward member and work site supervisor. The *sabha* was chaired by respective ward members of each ward. The primary discussion point is the preparation of ward wise development plans and the same was presented to the *gram sabha* through the Gram Panchayat Planning and Facilitation Team (GPPFT) and VP council.

Gram Sabha

Gram sabha is a fulcrum of the VP and a constitutional body that comprises the persons registered in the electoral roll related to the village composed in the *panchayat* at village level as mentioned in Article 243 (b) of Constitution of India. In Tamil Nadu, as per various government orders, *gram sabha*s are made compulsory to be conducted in all the villages six times in a calendar year, i.e., 26 January, 22 March, 1 May, 15 August, 2 October and 1 November. GPPFT was formed initially with thirt-nine members including ward members, youth, volunteers, women, SHG members, farmers, social activists, government staffs in the village and MGNREGA workers. For the VPDP preparation and to coordinate various aspects of the plans in view of the different inputs received from various *sabhas* mentioned in the paper, a detailed report was prepared by the GPPFT to present it to the VP council. After deliberations in the VP council, it was placed in the *gram sabha* for the detailed discussions, deliberations and approvals (GoI, n.d.).

SDG Goals, Targets and Its Relevance

These participatory forums not only focus on one SDG rather it is also related to fulfil other goals such as SDG-5 (Gender Equality) by empowering women in a participatory forum (Magalir Sabhai and Balar Sabhai) to discuss various development aspects of the village related to women from their point of view. This intern also to an extent fulfils the Target 5.5 which is to "Ensure full participation in leadership and decision making" of women as well as girl children. Indirectly, Target 4.5 and 4.a of the SDG-4 Education is enhanced through the Balar Sabhai and the Matruthiranali Sabhai because the requirements of education and the required inclusive infrastructure was be identified and VP is working to achieve the target.

Further, SDG-10 and the Targets 10.2 shows the inclusivity indicator by promoting universal social, economic and political inclusion. The Ward Sabha was focussing on the inclusivity to ensure every person in the ward to participate in the planning process of the VP. The Matruthiranali Sabhai is exclusively prioritizing the requirements of the person who are differently-abled and supports them to achieve Targets 10.2 and 10.3 of the SDGs. All the participatory structures in near future supports to other SDGs. The SDG-13 and Target 13.b discusses about promoting mechanisms for raising capacity for effective climate change related planning and management which is feasible through these structures.

The SDG-16 (Peace, Justice and Strong Institutions) has twelve targets and the participatory forums which is being discussed is precisely related to the following targets of SDG-16.

- Target 16.6. Develop effective, accountable and transparent Institutions.
- Target 16.7. Ensure responsive, inclusive and representative decision making.

The targets about inclusive and representative decision making which are visible in the four participatory forums highlights the presence of different social groups of a village being represented. It also brought out the efforts made to discuss wide range of issues related to them from the perspective of inclusive development in the study area. Further, the points of discussions were put forth in the *gram sabha*, the constitutional structure to take necessary actions. The accountability and transparency in the VP has also improved through the discussions and responses from the officials and elected representatives in the participatory forums. The people also realized the operational limitations and problems of the functionaries of the VP to a certain extent through the discussions in the participatory forums. Ultimately, the initiation and/or activation of different participatory structures in the study area contributed significantly to achieve various targets of the SDGs directly and indirectly.

Conclusion

The initiatives and interventions in PRpuram VP highlight number of learnings to other VPs. It may be viewed as a model for rejuvenation of participatory structures at the local level, which they achieved through their activities in terms of planning and implementing various requirements of its citizens. The ultimate aim for a VP is to ensure economic development and social justice in its jurisdiction which was clearly visible through the outcomes of various *sabhas* and initiatives in the study area. One important factor to be noticed for the achievement is the professional support provided by Institute of Grassroots Governance, a development organization working in Tamil Nadu for strengthening local governance in India. In the development point of view achieving Goal-16 (Peace, Justice and Strong

Institutions) of SDGs is also achieved by following the Rule of Law and ensuring the responsive,inclusive, participatory and representative decision making at the grassroots in an accountable and transparent manner. This case study provides several learnings to other VPs in the state and the country, highlighting its experiences towards active involvement and participation of the diverse sections of the community towards ensuring local economic development and social justice.

Keywords

Gram sabha, children's *sabha*, women's *sabha*, *sabha* for differently-abled, community ownership, community participation, decision making, sustainable development, community empowerment, inclusive development, SDG implementation.

REFERENCES

Caritas India (n.d.), Enabling Children's Participation in Their Development: Nothing About Us Without Us. Retrieved on 22 August 2023, from https://www.caritasindia.org/enabling-childrens-participation-in-their-development-nothing-about-us-without-us/

Government of India (GoI). People's Plan Campaign (PPC), Ministry of Panchayati Raj. Retrieved on 21 August 2023, from https://panchayat.gov.in/peoples-plan-campaign-ppc/

Government of Tamil Nadu (GoTN). (2021). Tamil Nadu State Policy for Children 2021, Social Welfare and Women Empowerment Department, Retrieved on 20 August 2023, from https://dsdcpimms.tn.gov.in/landing/assets/images/pdf_file/pdf_19.pdf

Heller, P. (2012). "Democracy, Participatory Politics and Development: Some Comparative Lessons from Brazil, India and South Africa. *Polity*, *44*(4): 643-65. The University of Chicago Press on behalf of the Northeastern Political Science Association. https://www.jstor.org/stable/41684508

Kudumbashree initiative of Bala Sabha. Retrieved on 19 August 2023, from https://www.kudumbashree.org/pages/708

Piper, L. (2014). "How Participatory Institutions Deepen Democracy through Broadening Representation: The Case of Participatory Budgeting in Porto Alegre, Brazil." *Theoria: A Journal of Social and Political Theory*, *61*(139): 50-67. Retrieved from http://www.jstor.org/stable/24719938

Society for Participatory Research in Asia (PRIA). (n.d.). *How to Conduct Mahila Sabhas*. Delhi: PRIA. Retrieved on 20 August 2023, from
https://pria.org/knowledge_resource/1564115720_How%20to%20conduct%20Mahila%20Sabhas_English.pdf

United Nations. (2012). *The 17 Goals*. United Nations. https://sdgs.un.org/goals

UN Women Asia and the Pacific. (March 2013). Rajasthan's Pride: The Exemplary Functioning of Mahila Sabhas. Retrieved on 20 August 2023, from https://asiapacific.unwomen.org/en/news-and-events/stories/2013/3/rajasthan-s-pride-the-exemplary-functioning-of-mahila-sabhas

Part IV

15

A Solar Realization with Connections to SDGs

Guido-Henri De Couvreur

A Closer Look at Solar 2002

Solar 2002 is a demonstration project of the Flemish Community, in Belgium. In addition to being a visitor centre, Solar 2002 is a research and educational centre as well. Mondo vzw (NGO) strives to get alternative and sustainable techniques even more explicit and more extensive in the attainment targets of secondary education to lay a foundation for building a more ecologically responsible society. It is good to emphasize the fact that already by now, this Solar 2002 project/realization is recognized as an example by the United Nations Organization, and UNESCO. From this perspective, it is good to mention that this realization/project is involved in the next number of SDGs 3, 4, 6, 7, 10, 11, 12, 13, 14, and 16.

It has already been pointed out in Meer Rendement[1] that—if we want to have a future for nature and our descendants—we need to think (more than) ecologically as much as possible.[2]

Could one say that Solar 2002 is a mini model for society at large, as it were a new living paradigm on how our culture should evolve? In the current state of technology, there is a lack of knowledge still among designers, contractors, craftsmen, etc.

If, in the near or more distant future, we do not succeed in building houses and buildings not only ecologically but also "intelligently", will we have come a long way as "homo rationale"?

Some dream of nuclear fusion, but the largest fusion reactor (the sun) provides enough energy for thousands of years! With Solar 2002, one wants to show that this is possible already.

Several do something, hovering between minimally ecologically responsible and superficially ecological, to soothe their consciences. With an energy-saving light bulb, global warming will not be stopped or reversed. It takes more than that. Superficial ecology will not reasonably be enough. Roughly speaking, this gradation follows:

- Non-ecological
- Superficially ecological
- Deeply ecological

An important remark is at his place here. After all, we conclude that this solution does not exist for all people in a different place on earth.

1. What is presented here has to do with a welfare country because we have to emphasize them since these countries

are the most polluting ones in the world and take a lot of the natural commodities that are considered for the whole world.

2. This is about a country with a land-sea climate in the northern hemisphere.
3. What is developed here is not applicable, for instance in the equator situation, a tropical climate.
4. In each different location, there is a need for a specific solution. Difference between the tropical country and the North Pole. There is no universal solution!
5. Last but not least in this article, we will share some figures, measured over years to avoid superficial slogans or conclusions. To come out of the theoretical but to the concrete, physical.

Renewable Energy, a Vehicle for Local Development and Peace

Mondo vzw (NGO) has come to realize that renewable energy carriers are a solid basis to help bring peace to the world. Raising awareness of the various categories in the population is certainly the most important element in this curious matter; in other words, breaking the cycle of ignorance that we find in all social strata. There is a lot of work to be done to make builders, architects, engineers, design firms, technicians, teachers, policymakers, etc., aware that this domain should not remain a "natural necessity" (oh, the irony of the word) as it is now.

Large "energy companies", more specifically the "fossil fuel producers", several other companies, and even large industrial groups, have diligently started producing photovoltaic solar cells for the generation of electric power.

Large oil companies do not conceal the fact that, even if the use remains the same, oil is only available for a few decades. And yet many don't wake up and even complain that the fuel is too expensive and has to be cheaper (again). This is the strange logic of the widely praised "free market".

Doesn't the scarcity of a product determine its price after all? How can the price of a product be temporarily lowered if the "scarcity" increases? Do we believe in Santa Claus?

To alleviate the excessive wastage, it would even be justified to allow fuel prices to rise to reduce car use, waiting for nature-friendly renewable energy carriers to be supplied on a large scale. (Apart from the fact that many automobiles are becoming counterproductive in terms of mobility: traffic jams, traffic jams. Commuting is a lot of stationary traffic, another contradiction.)

Staggering amounts of raw materials (curiously called fuels) are currently being swallowed up by vehicles. CO_2 emissions, excess ozone, and products that convert into nitric and sulphuric acid in the air, which in turn affect buildings, torment the air and earth.

For example, Rik Pinxten gives an example of this issue and the principle of: "Think global, act local. Think local, act global".

Think globally, act locally. Let's say I want to buy an off-road vehicle in Flanders. The impact of such a choice increases my ecological footprint, and I thus increase poverty and the lack of raw materials in the poor areas of the world. I will use even more energy and resources and deny them, while on the modern road network in this part of the world, I don't need an off-road vehicle at all.[3]

What is Available in Flanders, Belgium?

Let's take a look at a Demonstration Project of the Flemish Region, Solar 2002, recognized by VIBE as a "bio-ecological top project". Is Solar 2002 a Passivhaus? Not according to the definition. Only partially. Incidentally, this is not a new building but a building that has been renovated after twenty-five years and now houses a seminar room, an office, and a permanent dwelling.

Co-ordinates and weather data[4] of Solar 2002

Continent	Europe
Land	Belgium
Municipality	Berlaar
Realization Name	Solar 2002
Realization of	Mondo vzw (NGO)
Coordinates—Northings	51°06′56″N
Coordinates—Eastings	4°37′42″E
Altitude (Above Mean Sea Level)	6 m
Azimuth (Solar generators)	0°
Wind-direction solar collectors	Z, 183°
Predominant wind direction	SW, 236°, (75%)
Average Annual Temperature	9.8°C
The average amount of precipitation water column per year	780 mm
Number of frost days	80 days
Number of degree-days below 18° C	3409°D
Average wind speed	3.0 m/s
The average amount of sunshine on	
A horizontal surface	2.55 KWh per square meter per day
The angle of inclination of solar thermal collectors (air)	60°
The angle of inclination of hybrid collectors (PV: electricity and heat)	30°

The demonstration project aims to be able to measure everything in living conditions with the behaviour of the residents, not a labouratory situation. To this end, the building is equipped with a metering system.

From Mondo vzw (an NGO) (see http://www.mondo.be) it may be said that the indoor environment is more than just the ecological impact. Comfort, temperature control, air quality, and air are important factors.

How much fuel oil has already burned out before the ship docks? Already 5 to 10 per cent for transport alone, add the conversion efficiencies, and one gets indeed higher values. In an average house—for heating, electricity, etc.—this value is well above 230 kWh per sq.m of a living area (230 kWh/m2a) per year (in secondary energy consumption). In primary energy consumption, this can increase by up to double: specifically, in this case, to about 460 kWh per sq.m per year. There is usually a lot of silence about this. It is often not spoken of.

In what follows, we will go a little deeper into technical aspects. This may be less interesting for less technical people but all the more so for professionals who know how to do it. It's a bonus. Those who do not wish to receive this bonus can move on to the next chapter.

Realization: Mondo Point of View in Solar 2002: A Case Study

- As a zero-balance energy building/house.
- With as many bio-ecologically responsible materials as possible.
- With its own water production and waste water treatment.

What is the Context of Solar 2002?

Mondo vzw (NGO) distances itself from the anthropocentrism that is especially prevalent in the Western world and in which people are placed centrally. Humans used to think they were the centre of the universe. In this view, people and people alone determine what is valuable.

Solar 2002 is a transformation of a philosophical body of thought into a real realization. Words are not just words but deeds.

Philosophy of Dealing with Nature

That philosophy becomes—the keeping of wisdom, in its etymological sense—to a way of life (lifestyle) of relating to nature around us. How? It should certainly not be inferred from this work that it gives philosophical shape to Solar 2002 has grown out of all the negative reports that have been made about the state of the earth. Be disseminated. It is not based on a certain doom- mongering.

In terms of prosperity, Flanders scores "high" at the world level but is lagging when it comes to dealing with nature. This knowledge is not our starting point. At the most, it is a confirmation that living differently is as harmonious as possible with nature, more than is desirable.

One of the exponents of our relationship with nature that led to a residential environment is a "waste problem". Together, "civilized countries" produce quite a bit of "waste".

Innovative Techniques and Special Points of Attention in Solar 2002

- Research centre in Flanders, with more than 52 measuring points, including solar irradiation: indoor and outdoor, solar collectors, and storage vessel temperatures. Indoor and outdoor humidity, water quality, CO_2 measurement, relative humidity, heat meters on heat pumps, and solar energy converters.

- Moisture-regulating thermal insulation with increased resistance to heat penetration.
- Heat recovery with high efficiency 90 per cent, CO_2 controlled (Not an option for an ordinary home, but in the seminar room. Can be used as an example for all public buildings!)
- Complete water extraction, up to drinking water level, from rainwater.
- Waste water treatment into clear water, the circle is closed, and the rainwater used—temporarily derived from the natural cycle—is transferred to nature and returned as quasi-drinking, but is not used as drinking water.
- Heat recovery is a by-product of electricity production, the heat is used as heating and/or as preheating of the renewed air.
- This creates the possibility of cooling PV panels (solar cells), which increases their efficiency and their lifespan (i.e., the cooler the solar cells, the more power they can deliver).
- Semi-automatic night-time cooling with cool outside air
- High-efficiency lighting.
- Zero balance on secondary energy on an annual basis for the energy in the building: as much energy is supplied to the public grid as is taken from the public grid on an annual basis.
- CO_2 neutral: all these techniques avoid tons of CO_2 spread over years.
- The wood used comes from close by, from harvests, and not from clear-cut forests.
- Materials with the lowest possible built-in energy, in the demolition phase of the house, the whole thing is returned to the earth as easily as possible recorded.

Electricity consumption in Belgium on an annual basis, of course, without electric heating, is, on average, 4,000 kWh/year per household; according to some, it should be reduced to 2,400 kWh/year. This is 60 per cent of the normal consumption. An average family will have to save a lot to fully cover its electricity consumption with the proceeds. That's not all! This is not a "dark green". Rather, between green and light green.

Consume Less: The Order is Important

There are priorities in rational energy consumption and energy before vision. As noted above, transport has a considerable impact on the energy management of a family, but also of a country, of a continent, of the world.

To achieve more savings, one can use one of the following or more methodologies in order of easy applicability:

- Monitoring: recording KWh meters weekly. This gives immediate feedback in which many wish to adjust their behaviour, according to a principle known as behaviourism.
- Shield the use of daylight at night where possible to reduce night-time heat losses.
- Optimal adjustment of the heating system: this is often neglected, so resetting is necessary.
- Thermal insulation of windows, doors, and exterior walls.
- Solar water heater for domestic hot water.
- Solar Thermal Conversion.
- Passive (windows).
- Active (solar collectors).
- Thermal and/or PV panels.
- Wind energy/water energy: no CO_2, possible environmental nuisance.
- Biomass (possible environmental nuisance and CO_2 neutral): the use of organic material such as plants to generate energy.
- Combined heat and power (CHP) for the simultaneous generation of heat with electricity as a by-product can still be used at a transitional stage.
- Fossil fuels: but depletion, environmental nuisance, and all kinds of emissions (but in the process of being phased out)!
- Nuclear (hopefully out of the game due to exit scenarios).

In the future, the above-mentioned energy carriers can be employed to ensure transport, this can be done in a non-polluting or less polluting manner.

Conclusion

Even one degree of less heating means about 7 per cent savings on heating energy.

Suggestion: Putting on one more sweater is possible.

Interim Conclusions

Aesthetic, functional, building biological, energetic, economic, and psychological aspects are often in conflict with each other. For example, a house with levels, living pits, and lots of glass can look very nice and stand out to the outside world, but how adapt this whole to the more fundamental needs of the people? The bio-ecological house can not only be a house but should also be a home.

The key architectural elements in Solar 2002 briefly:

- Greatest possible integration of the building into its surroundings.
- Rainwater collection and use down to drinking water level.
- Low energy consumptive.
- Threefold glazing or low-loss glass K 46.
- As few thermal bridges as possible.
- Thermal insulation (roof with a value of approx. 0.2 W/m^2K).
- Blinds insulated wooden shutters.
- Heating: passive, windows facing south and west, semi-passive solar system, additional heating in winter with heat pump, use of water under the house (15°C at the end of summer > 2°C after winter), heater connected to the underfloor heating can auxiliary heating in the event of a fault in the power supply.
- Cooling air through the crawl space that contains water that evaporates up to 20°C. At very high temperatures and

without cooling, the temperature does not exceed 24-25°C in the enclosures at 38°C outside temperature.

- Ventilation is done through ducts with special sound attenuation to avoid cross talk from room to room. No overwhelming noise from the diesel trains or no street noise at open windows. Fresh air and insect-free air.
- The air sucked in is mainly taken from the air behind the PV panels, so it is either preheated or heated on cold days. At that time, the panels get much greater efficiency, sometimes 40 to 50 per cent, instead of between 10 and 15 per cent. In this way, energy conversion as heat is also used, which is not the case with the tens of thousands of PV arrays scattered throughout the world.
- Behind the PV panels are extracted on the south side and released on the north side so that the PV panels remain cooled and are about 10°C less hot than non-cooled PV panels, which benefits both the yield and their lifespan.

In a warm period of the year, mechanical ventilation is in favour of natural ventilation with windows, which allows the building that can then be flushed with cooler night air. The upper roof windows are automatically controlled according to the inside and outside temperatures. The so-called "night flushing" is used here, and that is only possible because it is a "lightweight" building construction. Flexural walls, with a lot of insulation, and the "mass" is the floor. Which also serves as a heat buffer. In recent decades, architecture has been talking about "masses". But it cannot be cooled once it is warmed through, with unforced night-time cooling in a natural way.

Because this is a building on which the first floor also has an office and a multipurpose room to give seminars, presentations, lessons, and so on, the entire ventilation system is controlled with CO_2 sensors both on the upper and on the ground floor. With the presence of more people, i.e., more strain, more fresh air is supplied.

The refrigerator has an extra 4 cm PU insulation; despite this, the refrigerator remains one of the biggest consumers in all Solar 2002 because it is also on day and night, so to speak.

- The extraction of the kitchen air can be additionally controlled by the hygrostat present—which measures the humidity—and then achieve an increased airflow.
- The computers have low energy consumption, even to such an extent that the office without heating is now less likely to stay at the right temperature.
- Standby consumption: electrical consumers are switched off after use.
- Most sockets are measured on their consumption so that action can be taken if something can be improved.
- Low energy supply for the construction of the building materials, especially for the existing recycled materials.
- Selection of materials for the highest possible physical and psychological well-being: brick floor, white plastered walls, brick cabinets made of recycled brick, white wooden furniture, and elements that are difficult to move.
- Benches, with brick base with extra sleeping space for two people; under the benches, there is storage space for eight folding chairs.
- Control of noise (tractors, agricultural machinery, cars, etc.) and acoustics (sound and music). There is soundproofing in each room to provide the necessary peace and quiet. (Silence is a rare commodity in a small, industrialized country. Who can become wiser without silence?)
- Between the ground floor and the upper floor, there is a lot of recycled insulation material installed, approximately 25 cm. The wooden floors are laid floating to have as little impact noise as possible from the first floor downwards. Even though this is a wooden construction with the damping of the floors. The insulation In between until part and the sound-attenuated ducts for ventilation, there is almost no sound transmission between the top and lower floor.

- An additional advantage is that together with the roof insulation and the floor insulation of the upper floor, there is approximately 50 cm of insulation is located above the living area.
- In addition to recovered materials such as bricks, building materials have been used in their most natural appearance and have only been treated where necessary. Low gloss, the aspect structure of the materials was respected as much as possible. In the main, warm tones were chosen against white walls that make it possible to enter silence and emptiness. After all, a room that is too full does not allow you to be there. It is already full.
- The whole is metered at 52 measuring points, and the readout data is sampled every 5 minutes for immediate use—for example, in seminar lessons—and every half hour for statistical findings and scientific research. Also, for the continuous optimization of the entire installation.

• This whole Solar 2002 project and its realization have also provided the opportunity for volunteers to develop in this direction and to contribute to the more efficient use of all equipment and the dissemination of ideas.

Objectives of Solar 2002

- Translating the philosophical background of Mondo vzw (NGO) into practice: a new economic paradigm helps get off the ground.
- Showing a model that needs to be applied on a larger scale.
- Proving that the sun also in Belgium.
- Demonstrate that there are many more possibilities than is usually thought.
- How about the sun life does not reduce comfort, but increases comfort?
- Showing that goals can be achieved by intelligent means.
- To provide opportunities to apply aspects of Solar 2002 on a broader scale.

- Helping to initiate social change through this demonstration project.
- Demonstrate that it offers realization opportunities for applications in multiple countries.

Mondo vzw (NGO) attaches great importance to living in harmony with the environment as much as possible. In the concept realized in a zero-balance energy house with special bio-ecological characteristics, people want to treat that "environment" with respect. That is why a home should be as ecologically "neutral" as possible.

Features of Solar 2002

Ecologically Neutral

Solar 2002 contributes to this in various ways. Nature is being used not to make more use than is strictly necessary. To avoid the use of raw materials to be converted into irreversible substances that cannot be easily absorbed by nature; hence, wood is the most commonly used. It is renewable.

CO_2 Neutral

The house does not emit any CO_2. The residents and the visitors do, of course.

No fossil or other fuels are consumed.

This means no combustion processes for:

- Electricity generation,
- Heating,
- Food Preparation,
- CO_2 or other emissions: none.

Energy-neutral

On an annual basis, Solar 2002 is energetically self-supporting. The house only uses the radiation of the sun to produce energy: a zero-balance energy house. (At a later stage, it became a "positive" building, so more electricity was produced than was needed for domestic activities. This made it possible to power an electrically powered car). In concrete terms, this means that electricity will be supplied to the public grid in the summer. In winter and at night, electricity can be requested to compensate for the shortages of energy.

Why was there not opt for an autonomous solution? It is not a question of cutting oneself off from society, on the contrary, of contributing. When everything is connected to everything else on this planet earth—a typically religious idea—why then should one withdraw from a common electricity grid, a sign of solidarity? An example of collective self-centredness transcends?

For the energy management of the house, no use is made of the conversion of raw materials into energy. The sun delivers more energy to the earth in one day than we all consume in a full year. Is it evidence of ignorance and decadence that we still use valuable raw materials such as oil and natural gas, sometimes almost exclusively as fuels, for energy conversion? Unbelievable in a high-tech age, a rather decadent custom from the last century(s)? After all, these raw materials can be better used—with limited—to produce new products. Hopefully, this is a transitional stage, and in the coming centuries, only solar energy and derivatives will be used to produce materials.

In Solar 2002, all energy used already comes from the Sun.

Zero-energy balance: The annual yield of all energy systems is as much as is needed for daily use in the building: preparing food, heating, lighting, ventilating; for the consumption of the computers, the measuring installations, the water extraction, and the water purification, etc. To top it all off, transport with a solar-powered electric car, as mentioned above.

Energetic Comparison with Passive House

In recent years, there has been a tendency, especially in Germany, to build so-called Passive Houses. Solar 2002 goes a few steps further.

The 120 KWh/m2a, specific primary energy consumption (for space heating, hot water heating, domestic electricity, food preparation, refrigeration, computers, water purification, etc.) Solar 2002, 0KWh/m2a reduced: roughly 120 times less than the passive standard.

- This is not a new building but a renovation.
- Consumption also covers the energy consumption of the entire measuring plant for the research centre, which is considerable.
- The building houses office and seminar space for Mondo vzw (NGO).

H_2O Neutral

Similarly, when it comes to water, Solar 2002 treats the environment neutrally. The water required for use in the home is derived from natural borrows, with 100 per cent coverage. Rainwater is collected and stored in tanks.

The "grey" and "black" water is sprayed on-site in organic, completely converted into pure water, and is then released into nature and taken up again. Dealing with the earth in this way complies with the rule that presupposes sustainable development:

- All the water used comes from "heaven".
- No necessary connection to the (drinking) water supply network.
- Liquids and all food consumed are converted into water.
- In other words, "black" and "grey" water is transformed into water and ends up in a pond in which fish, aquatic insects, and plants live.

To put it bluntly, thanks to the industrial purification on site of food residues, excrement, bath, and kitchen water, etc., the water that falls from the sky and contains a lot of pollutants is returned to the earth purer. Perhaps 2 billion people on our planet would be very happy with this level of purity, too bad they don't have it!

It is impossible to be completely neutral when it comes to materials. Even without the comfort requirements, this is impossible because building always means interfering with nature.

During the renovation of this house, bio-ecological materials were, of course, used where possible. After demolishing the building, these can be connected to nature without much difficulty. Be returned.

However, the house is not completely neutral. The preparation of materials, for example, almost always involves transformations of raw materials beforehand. It is then important to weigh the energy and material content of the products. Baked bricks, for example, have a much higher built-in energy than stones that have been pressed exclusively. But the latter also has a certain built-in energy. That is why it is always necessary to consider whether it is not possible to reuse an existing material rather than to reuse it in a form, albeit less transformed, new to nature to evade it.

For Solar 2002, the choice was made for the adaptation of an existing house, not for a far-reaching ecological new construction project. In that sense, this realization cannot be compared to very low-energy new-build homes. And yet.

When assessing materials, the full life cycle should be considered. Materials are given to nature abstract. Products are produced in companies. During their "useful life", products require energy and/or maintenance. After use, products are disassembled, recycled, incinerated, or landfilled. Moreover, many of these transformation stages involve transport and, consequently, the consumption of energy again.

Ecological Garden

The non-profit organization VELT wants to promote the experience and construction of ecological ornamental greenery everywhere, both in private gardens and in public green spaces.

After all, "nature" does not only belong in reserves but can claim its rights everywhere: also, in gardens and parks, on the street and balcony, in the countryside and the city.

An ecological ornamental garden assumes that natural processes are supported. Plants adapted to the soil and region are chosen. People opt for beauty, for adapted garden art. That is what Solar 2002 was aiming for. An underlying goal was certainly to create a garden with as little maintenance as possible.

Plants that grow spontaneously in this environment are cultivated. The front garden is a soft transition from the "hard" street to the "soft" building. This prevents the building from falling like a "dagger" into the earth, which is often the case.

Techniques Used

- Solar Thermal
- Photovoltaic cells
- (Small) heat pump
- Heat pipe
- More insulation than usual
- Balanced ventilation
- Composting
- Positive regenerative water purification
- Purification pond
- Water extraction: nine filters to drinkable water
- Heat recovery
- Ecological garden
- Monitoring: 52 measuring points
- Basic solar heating
- Solar thermal collectors

The basic heating is provided by solar heating coming from some windows, from the thermal and hybrid sunroof.

Consequence: Draws from "Living with the Sun"

The whole of this life is abundantly complex. There is a link between the economy, nature conservation nature, nature conservation, habitation, environment, and people. It's a pity that so few take that into account. One of the biggest problems in many areas is overconcentration. And the constant growth of the population is also disadvantageous. Most of the problems we face, in virtually all cultures, are almost all inextricably linked to too many people in too small a place on our planet. The problem is that in the very foreseeable future, a large part of the world's population in large cities, even megacities, resides.

Many poor people live in the hope—as a legitimate demand—of earning an income in those big cities and thus surviving, at best, "living". The question is, how many people can live "crammed together" and still live a comfortable and dignified life without falling into a pool of pollution, aggression, and hostility? After all, as soon as human groups live too close to each other, hostility lurks around the corner. At the same time, the degree of contamination easily rises above the permissible biological standard so that at that time, people no longer have to conserve nature, nor can management speak.

In addition, when people do not have a meaningful, informative activity, boredom sets in, and criminal behaviour occurs quickly. For many, that "being busy" has been a paid job so far, but no one can guarantee this for the future. Robotization means fewer working hours and more free time. Filling that free time in a meaningful way is an important task for all kinds of associations. From an ecological and anthropological point of view, it is certainly not tolerable to continue to think in terms of unbridled growth, certainly not without taking the necessary measures or pursuing the principle of prudence concerning the health of all living beings. It belongs to nature and our nature that everything is connected in one way or another: nature conservation in the broadest sense.

In the case of unbridled, uncontrolled multiplication of cells, it is referred to as cancer, rampant cell proliferation. One may wonder whether large cities and unbridled economic systems do not apply in the same way. Isn't the same pattern developing in megacities with a lot of expansion economy and urbanization?

The economic thinking of the last 150 years has mainly focused on profit "short-term-thinking". This results in repeatedly asking the wrong question: "When will the invested capital be recouped?"

It has become the adagium in economic thinking that is not even economically justified in the long run. What if human activities make life impossible for humans and animals in a healthy way?

The economy is there for people and not like now: people are there for economic reasons. Interests are concretely expressed in terms of profit and power. That's why there are so many mergers. Profit for whom? In times of boom, people are looking for people to fill factories. They don't even ask themselves whether they are missing the mark. In short, the world turned upside down. We are all on the train of self-evidence. It turns out that it is not even necessary to ask questions. Blind pragmatism reigns supreme: lack of vision for the future, "solving problems as they arise". Can this be done in the context of sustainable management of natural resources, avoidance of pollution, and emission of hazardous gases? The result is irreparable effects: the feverish clearing of the rainforests, for example, which have grown over thousands of years to what they are or are today. Or the petroleum that we eagerly consume in a few generations, the massive squandering of natural substances, minerals, and raw materials. To burn them ingloriously—usually with low efficiency—with pollution on top. And what if the reserves are depleted? Irreversible. Is that what is meant by nature conservation? or management?

Another thorny issue of our endless consumption society is what we have come to call "waste", where it is a secondary raw material.

What does all this have to do with Solar 2002? The above was tried to be kept to a minimum or excluded in this project.

According to Mondo vzw (NGO), a human being can be a co-creator on the one hand and a caretaker, user, or caretaker of the Earth on the other beings.

A humane society is not only marked by a biological starting point—as far as health is concerned—nor by an ecological one. It takes more than that, especially the ethical. It is ethical that takes into account this biological and ecological, in other words, it implies the biological and the ecological, but is not fully absorbed in it. It requires a great deal of awareness to arrive at ethically acceptable behaviour.

The realization of Solar 2002, therefore, tries to improve the ecological and the biological to transcend it. In this way, try to point the way to another dimension, namely the human social level. With a somewhat obsolete word, one could speak of what is more just.

Speaking about solidarity no longer sounds popular in a culture of "cut-throat competition" where, according to some, everything is left to the "free market". But can anyone tell me whether it is ethical to interpret the fact that the well-to-do countries consume so much more? Solar 2002 aims to put an end to this situation, albeit as a modest example.

Mondo vzw (NGO) does not want to remain at the wailing wall, but Solar 2002 achieves zero CO_2 emissions. In twenty years, calculated at least 25 tons less CO_2 and no more other harmful exhaust gases due to the combustion of raw materials.

Even in a country where the sun. The solar roofs do not provide enough energy. With this, we want to make it clear that the sun does shine in this country. Thinking differently, that is what it comes down to.

The price of energy is not only determined by the land dust, wages, etc. A crucial factor is whether or not hidden subsidies or allowances make something financially attractive. This concerns the political, ecological choice that determines the price, often a forgotten or concealed theme.

In Mondo's way of thinking, the starting point for every design, including housing, is:

- The ecological
- The organic
- The social
- The economic
- The financial
- The aesthetic

And in that order! Only when one condition has been met, can one move on to the next one. In the best-case scenario, the reverse order is now used. The financial is becoming the decisive factor in the current collective self-centred thinking of our culture. "What can I earn financially from it?" is usually the underlying unspoken question. For Mondo vzw (NGO), there is more. What is the profit for nature, the earth, for the inhabitants of other continents, for our compatriots, for the non-human primates, for plants, for our offspring? Most of the time, people are now confusing the economy with the finances. After all, the economic is a category that is much broader than the financial. Why the short-sightedness? The Minister for the Economy is seldom the same as the Minister for Finance, and yet. Hundreds of times, I was asked the question: "Is that economically viable?" When what was meant was: "Is this financially feasible?"

Is it financial? Is it not important for Mondo vzw? On the contrary, a heavy price has been paid for the realization. But is there another way? Besides, what are we going to tell the 800 million people who do not even earn a euro a day? Heart Wrenching, isn't it? Here, too, Solar 2002 wants to set an example through everything of the sun's expensive energy-consuming transports. A good economy is in contradiction with the commercial interests of a collective of overly self-centred interest groups.

Mondo vzw (NGO) is also concerned about the social. It is not acceptable that renewable energy should only be for the well-to-do. That is why it is a clever idea to equip new-build homes more and more with solar collectors that are responsible for heating and/or electricity generation in the context of social housing. Recent social housing estates can be equipped with solar roofs, life-giving roofs instead of the dead roofs, so characteristic in our landscape. Is it such a foolish idea to take the lead in Europe in this area? A chance to turn the tide? "Wake up", Anthony de Mello is heard calling. It seems as if most of the world's population is asleep, walking around, sleeping, and not noticing any of this.

On the contrary, people are preparing for even more people. Unfortunately, people do not consider the fact that in the foreseeable future, any humane, ecological, and social life will become impossible.

Greater prosperity allows changing cultural values, for example, "well-being", a chance. Our time offers more time that should not be spent for a living. Think of it this way: "I'm wasting too much time with my job!" well, it is best not to comment. A big problem is that people do not have time to enjoy other things in life because of all the work and/or labour. Lots of material possessions one can collect, but transferring them to the hereafter is still not an option!

I would like to hear some Bertrand Russell wrote at the beginning of the twentieth century quoting:

> And what humane Man would prefer a large population, living in poverty and decay, to a smaller population with a happy and comfortable existence.

Let us then learn from the past to live in the present and into the future.

What are we waiting for?

NOTES

1. Guido-Henri De Couvreur, Meer rendement. Een menswaardige visie op een merkwaardig bestel. Lier, Mondo, 1992, More Efficiency.
2. Ibidem, p.120; 7.1.1.
3. Rik Pinxten, on the occasion of the publication of his book *The Small Revolutions*, at EPO in SOFIE MULDERS. There is again, room for forms of small resistance, in De Morgen, 26 February (2013): 6-7.
4. Which, unfortunately, sometimes spills over into collective selfishness where people, being informed, knowingly and knowingly act as they do, knowing that there are better behaviours than just taking care of themselves.
5. Anthony De Mello, *Consciousness, Risks and Possibilities of Reality, Amsterdam*, Samsara, 2004. Anthony de Mello was an Indian Jesuit priest and psychotherapist. A spiritual teacher, writer, and public speaker.
6. B. Russell, *Individual and Authority*, Katwijk, Sevire, 1979, p. 121.

REFERENCES

Bauer, C., & de M. Boer *et al.* (1981). *Energie.* Rotterdam: Shell The Netherlands.

Bellens, Geert (2005). *Health*. Antwerp: VIBE.

Bernhard, Krieg (1992). *Power from the Sun: Solar Cell Technology in Theory and Practice*, Elektuur Publishers.

Bodifée, Gerard (2007). *God, and the Rock: About Religion and Science Speak and be Silent*, Leuven: Davidsfonds/Ten have.

Bok, S.T. (1963). *The Origin of Life.* Utrecht/Antwerp: Het Spectrum.

Bourges, B., (ed.) (1992). *Climatic Data Handbook for Europe: Climatic Data for the Design of Solar Energy Systems*. Dordrecht: Commission for the European Communities/Kluwer, ISBN 0-7923-1716-5.

Bourges, B., & Centre d'Energétique, & Ecole de mines, *European Simplified Methods for Active Solar System Design*. Dordrecht: Commission for the European Communities/Kluwer, ISBN 0-7923-1230-9.

Braeckman, B., N. De Cock, & K. Drugmand (1987). *Thermal and Hygienic Behaviour of Building Structures, EBES.*

Bruyndonckx, J., *Solar Energy Already*? Hove, Self-managed.

Butti, Ken & John Perlin (1980). A *Golden Thread: 2500 Years of Solar Architecture.* Palo Alto: Cheshire Books.

Center for Environmental Philosophy and Bioethics UG, *Ripples in the Water, Environmental Philosophy Between Question and Answer.* Festschrift on the Occasion of the Sixtieth Birthday of Professor Dr Etienne Vermeersch, With Contributions by: Wouter Achterberg, Hans Achterhuis, Wim De Temmerman, Jaap Kruithof, Ton Lemaire. Hugo Van den Enden, Philippe Van Parijs, Freddy Verbruggen, Leuven/Amersfoort, Acco, 1994.

Chareyre, R. (1978). *La Maison Autonome*. Paris: Editions Alternative et parallèles.

Collard, B., A. Nihoul, A. De Herde, N. Lesens (1996). *Guide d'aide à la rénovation Bioclimatique.* Louvain-la-Neuve: Architecture et Climat.

Commission de Communautés Européennes, *Architecture solaires en Europe.*

Conceptions, Performances, Usage, Brussels/Luxembourg, 1991.

Daly, H.E. (ed.) (1980). *Economics, Ecology, Ethics: Essays Toward a Steady State Economy*. San Francisco: W.H. Freeman & Cy.

De Couvreur, G.H. (ed.) *What Does Religion Mean? Today? In a World Full of Technology*: Lier, Mondo, mcmxciv.

De Couvreur, G.H.M. (1992). *More Efficiency: A Humane Vision of a Remarkable System.* Lier: Mondo.

De Mello, Anthony (2004). *Consciousness, Risks and Opportunities of Reality*, Amsterdam: Samsara.

Duchâtelet, Roland (2004). *The Road to More Net Domestic Happiness: A Future for all Europeans*. Leuven: Van Halewyck.

Duffie, J.A., & A.B. Beckman (1991). *Solar Engineering of Thermal Processes.* New York: Wiley & Sons (19741)

fortmann, H. (1980). *Hindus, and Buddhists: Diary Entries and Travel Letters.* Baarn: Ambo.

Gräff, P. & P.A. Rauh, *Independent with Solar Energy: What is Already Possible and How to Proceed.* Baarn: Bosch & Keuning, X.

Grupp, M. (1981). *Switch! What Everyone Needs to Know About Energy.* Baarn: Anthos.

Harper, P. & G. Boyle, the editors of Undercurrents (1977). *Radical Technology.* London: Wildhouse.

Hastings, Robert, (ed.) (1999). *Solar Air Systems: Built Examples*. London: James & James.

Hastings, Robert, & Ove MØrck (eds.) (2000). *Solar Air Systems: A Design Handbook*. London: James & James.

Hendriks, Ch. F. *et al.* (1999). *Sustainable Building Materials.* Delft: Aeneas.

Ladener, H. (1995). *Solare Stromversorgung. Grundlagen*. Planung: Anwendung. Freiburg: Ökobuch.

Moore, F. (1993). *Environmental Control Systems: Heating Cooling Lightning.* New York/London/Paris: McGraw-Hill.

Moorman, B. (1981). *Wind Power: Weather Vane for Clean Energy from Polder Windmill to Wind Turbine*. Rotterdam: Futile.

N.N., *Ventilation of Homes.* Dl1 General Principles, 1994, WTCB. TV 192.

N.N., *Ventilation of Homes.* Dl2 Implementation and Performance of Ventilation Systems, 1994, WTCB. TV 203.

N.N. (1972). *How does That Work?* Vol.1: *The Technique Explained in Words and Images*. Utrecht/Antwerp: Het Spectrum.

N.N. (1980). *Polytechnic Pocketbook*. Arnhem: Royal PBNA.

N.N., *Seattle's Speech.* Soest: Kairos.

N.N. (1979). *Solar Heating and Cooling Demonstration: Project Summaries.* Washington, U.S.: Department of Energy.

N.N. (1995). *Solar Low Energy House of IEA Task 13*. International Energy Agency.

United States of America—Department of Energy (1979). *Solar Heating and Cooling Demonstration: Project Summaries*. Washington D.C.: X.

Vaes, Guido & Creffier, Willem (2000). *Water Guide For Architects. A Guide to Sustainable Water Use in and Around Private Homes*. Erembodegem: Flemish Environment Agency.

van König, F. (1980). *Wind and Energy*. Deventer/Antwerp: Kluwer. Van Mechelen, F. (1987). *Is Europe Dying Out?*. Leuven: Davidsfonds.

Vandeplas, P., *Solar Energy Course*. Syllabus: Study Centre for Nuclear Energy, Mol.

Vander Kerken, L. (1987). *People Want to be Happy*. Antwerp/Amsterdam: De Nederlandse Boekhandel.

Vandermeersch, P. (1987). *Ethics: Between Science and Ideology*. Leuven: Peeters.

Verbruggen, A. (1991). *Beyond Happiness: An Environmental Economic Essay*. Stichting Leefmilieu: Antwerp.

Verbrugh, H.S. (1974). *Medicine at a Dead End, The Prevailing Medical Model of Man as a Pre-scientific Ideology*. Rotterdam: Lemniscaat.

Worster, Donald (1996). *Nature's Economy: A History of Ecological Ideas*. Cambridge: University Press.

Zurel, F. (ed.) (1980). *New Illustrated Encyclopedia*. Amsterdam: Trendboek, 22 volumes.

16

Significant Approaches Towards Social Security Leading to Sustainable Development Goals in India

A Study

Soumen Sarkar

The term "social security" was first officially brought in a US legislation entitled Social Security Act, 1935. Under this Act, several welfare programmes initiated to cover the risk of old age, death and unemployment. Afterwards, the term "social security" was found to be used in 1938 by New Zealand government while passing an act that has however expressed a broader understanding of social security including more benefits for countrymen.

Subsequently, the International Labour Organization (ILO)[1] adopted the term "social security" and thus spread globally.

ILO through its various official proceedings, during the period 1952-82 had elabourated a detailed concepts and scopes of social security. This concept of social security, as then characterized (ILO, 1984) is given below:

> ... the protection which society provides for its members, through a series of public measures, against

> the economic and social distress that otherwise would be caused by the stoppage or substantial reduction of earnings resulting from sickness, maternity, employment injury, unemployment, invalidity, old age and death; the provision of medical care; and the provision of subsidies for families with children.

The above definition framed by ILO, actually expressed the then mainstream understanding about social security, and this conception remained till mid-1980s. Three points of this definition of ILO are noteworthy to discuss here below:

(a) according to this understanding, social security has to be organized largely by the state and/or public institutions.
(b) this definition presumed that the citizen of the country have already attained a considerable standard of living. And thus, the main ambition of social security is therefore to protect the members of society from a fall from their present standard of living, rather assisting them to achieve a higher level of the latter.
(c) the risks assumed in the ILO definition refer to a specific ecological and socio-economic setting found in developed countries. It does not cover risk insurance against environmental and medical contingencies such as droughts, earthquakes, floods, epidemics (Leliveld, 1991).

During the referred period, the ILO was the only international agency who dealt with the concept of social security, with academic depth and field experiences. ILO continued to lead international debates on social security for a long time and had also spearheaded in designing state-sponsored schemes. The aforementioned milieu has immensely transformed over the years and across the globe. Neither the definition nor the concept of ILO is nowadays accepted as a universal benchmark for framing social security systems. Moreover, keeping World Bank in the forefront, various other international and development organizations have become increasingly active on the subject.

Nobel Laureate Professor Amartya Sen and Jean Drèze identified two very aspects of social security those are—"Protection" and "Promotion" (Drèze & Sen, 2011). The former denotes protection against a fall in living standards/conditions through ill health/ accidents. While, the latter focuses on enhanced living conditions, helping everyone overcome persistent capabilities deprivation.

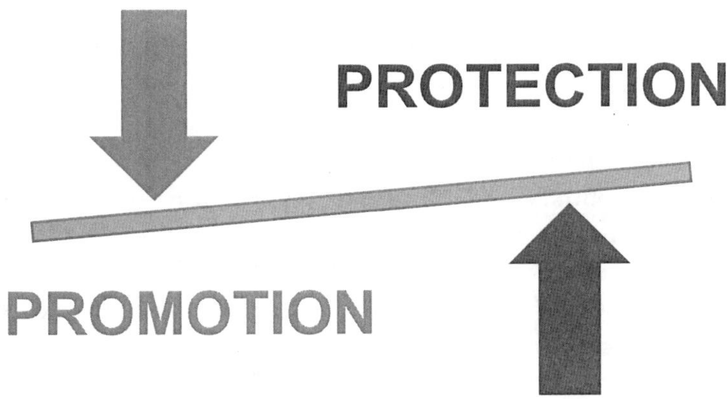

India's record in providing social security shows that a lower fraction of population enjoys "protection", is being further eroded with current pattern of economic growth. In relation to provisions aimed at "promotion", social security through nutrition, work allocation for all, recent evidence gives cheerful reasons with alert of being threatened with fund cuts and further shrinking. Thus, the objective has been shifted to risk coverage and guarantee schemes, which allow individuals to cope with exigencies viz. illness, accident, widowhood, disability apart from old-age and death. The focus was also turned to collective risks, viz., drought, floods, bad harvests, natural disasters, riots, etc. Thus, the concept of social security was evolved to cover both individual level risks and covariate risks.

Conventional Approaches Classifying Social Security Systems

One side, globally there is no such categorized framework established for social security system. On the other side, there is discrete lack of consensus within international community, regarding the actual definition of social security, since 1980s. However, German authors generally relied on an approach that classifies social security systems as either "Formal" or "Traditional". It sometimes further includes a third category, i.e., "Informal". While few other authors are found use different categories, viz., "Traditional Systems", "Private" vis-à- vis "State Based Systems" or "Collective Arrangements" (Leliveld, 1991). Among all these aforesaid classifications of social security system, the formal systems largely cover the state-sponsored or private firm led benefits, which are mostly contributory in nature, otherwise sponsored from taxes, and these systems are all linked to professional employment in various sectors.

On the contrary, the "Traditional" systems are usually anchored from the advance of various traditions in social groups. This traditional mode is more of solidarity and reciprocity, than that of its efficiency considerations that find their expression in moral codes and specific norms. The wages and allowance structure for land labour often itself contains important social security elements that are supported by specific insurance coverage. All these mentioned social security structures are however not usually integrated into the economy. Therefore, the "Informal" systems, or otherwise called as "Collective" arrangements, stands somewhere between the formal and traditional systems. Its existence is based on either for dilution of traditional systems due to transformation in socio-economic structure of the society and social forces, or as an alternative to address lesser coverage of the formal systems. As per the traditional systems, informal structures are too based on the fundamentals of solidarity and reciprocity, as discussed above. The general financial products, viz., savings and loan for associations and cooperatives are emphasized through informal SHG.

The aforesaid approaches referred so far, to categorize social security systems, have not been accepted by policy makers in international community for different reasons. First, it is difficult to distinguish between "traditional" and "informal" frequently, as such instance of the "informal" savings and loan groups already continuing in several countries within Latin America since eighteenth century. Second, paving on the sort of path dependency, this type of classification in social security basically assumes a quasi-automatic progress from the earlier traditional mode to this so-called formal social security systems primarily within developing nations.

Subsequently, the ILO formulated a three-phase dynamic model for describing the development of a social insurance system in order to contribute this sector with

(i) a paternalistic phase, through the introduction of
(ii) social insurance with limited coverage, and finally
(iii) on to the maturation of the social insurance system with universal character (ILO, 1984).

The research work on this sector accepts that divergence between the "traditional", "informal" and "formal" is not very effective in classifying the various social security systems, and can integrate a combination of these three elements. Ultimately, it is the divergence that is deficient in underlying theoretical assumptions, leading to confusing reference to sponsors of social security. Therefore, the long-standing argument for the need of a new classification system based on institutions finds rational endorsement, against the conventional approaches towards social security as discussed herein.

Constraints Towards Social Security

As per report of ILO (2014), around 73 per cent of global population is deprived of the need-based social security coverage. While in India, around 90 per cent of workers earn their livelihood depending on the unorganized sector, which lacks social security (Wadhwa, 2020). This vast excluded population remains most vulnerable to various unforeseen hazards and hinders the agendas towards poverty alleviations and inclusive growth of a society.

Globally, there are several constraints and challenges identified towards bringing population under social security coverage in various research works. One of the inherent problems as discussed in several related study towards coverage of rural population under social security schemes (especially to cover under insurance coverage), is their moral hazard which has been also realized during the household survey conducted under this research work.

The implementation of social security schemes either sponsored by the state or by the market faces practical difficulties in rural areas as these policies go beyond those of special relevance to urban areas. Following are the key reasons contributing to rural predicament:

- People living in rural areas are highly dependent on agricultural activities (even on single crop, viz., paddy) as their major source of livelihood income.
- A vast population is distant from market, inconvenient mode of access to formal institutions, and not able to bear high cost of transportation for daily life.
- There is no efficient financial or labour market that may substitute insurance markets in countries like India.
- The feeble voice and distracted political agenda of rural population. Even after six decades of realizing independence, rural population have not consolidated their voice for agenda towards inclusive development.

In rural areas, the main source of household income comes from agriculture and allied activities by small and marginal agri-land holders. Due to high dependence of unorganized agricultural production on season cycle and weather conditions, the income of rural household is generally unstable, demanding insurance coverage. In rural India, although there is very high requirement of insurance coverage for agriculture and allied activities, but inabilities of poor to pay insurance premiums on a regular basis are serious barrier. On discussion with Banking, Financial Services, and Insurance (BFSI) experts, it has been realized that rural areas are majorly exposed to various covariate risks, and this is the key hurdle towards providing viable insurance arrangements to cover income loss. While the majority of the population living in rural areas still has no access to state or market-based social security, the most important alternative—systems based on reciprocity and solidarity at the household or community level—are facing tremendous adjustment problems due to economic and social changes (Mishra, 2020). Moreover, in rural areas, the institutional development of insurance schemes is hindered by the existence of covariate risks, adverse selection problems and high unit transaction costs per contract (Noponen & Kantor, 2004).

People in developing countries are mostly exposed to various risks in their day-to-day life. Individual faces sudden risks like illness, disability, death, widowhood, riots and natural disasters, which adversely affect income consistency and disgrace quality of life. In urban or metro locations, people are having easy access to state or market-based insurance schemes. However, in rural areas, there is lack of insurance markets for life and assets, and no possible substitutes in the form of labour markets with lack of credit flow. It is an accepted fact that poverty is directly linked to availability of resources to generate an income for sustenance and improvement of an individual's standard of living. In a developing country like India, social security schemes assume significant importance towards poverty alleviation programmes. It tends to supplement the meagre income level of poor either by direct transfers or through schemes where labour can be traded for food or money. While the later opens scope that some community assets are built in the process.

Approaches Towards Social Security in India

The gradual collapse of joint family system across the country has underscored the necessity to develop a suitable policy that would help current participants in the unorganized workforce to develop a minimum retirement income for themselves. There is urgent need for evaluation of prudent options to compress the coverage gap has special significance to eastern and north-eastern region of India. As per Article 41 of Indian Constitution (1950) state

> within the limits of its economic capacity and development, make effective provision for securing

> the right to work, to education and to public assistance in cases of unemployment, old age, sickness and disablement, and in other cases of undeserved want.

Further, Article 42 says the state shall make provisions for securing just and humane conditions of work and for maternity benefits.

During 1995, Indian government launched the National Social Assistance Programme (Ministry of Rural Development, 1995). It was the first pensions programme for the poor in this country starting with of a pension of Rs. 75 per month. Later, under the Indira Gandhi National Old Age Pension Scheme and Widow Pension Scheme, central government contributed Rs. 200 and Rs. 300 per month respectively. Several states like Himachal Pradesh, Rajasthan and Bihar provided monthly pension of around Rs. 300 to Rs. 400, while the state of Tamil Nadu disbursed monthly pension of Rs. 1,000 to its eligible beneficiaries.

In 2004, Government of India appointed the National Commission for Enterprises in the Unorganized Sector (NCEUS) to look into social security and livelihood conditions of unorganized workers—employed either in unorganized sector or those in formal sector without any social protection. The aforesaid commission found that 8 per cent of India's workforces engaged in the formal sectors were enjoying social security coverage. Whereas over 91 per cent of workers, i.e., over 39.5 crore workers at that point of time, were exposed to vulnerability in the informal sector. NCEUS highlighted that there had been almost no growth in formal employment since early 1990s but there was growth in employment reported in unorganized sectors. NCEUS reported that 79 per cent of Indian workers engaged in unorganized sector manage their livelihood, depending on an average income of less than Rs.20 per day. These findings are clearly evident that the state's dividends of economic growth have been somehow bypassing majority of the unorganized working population in India. The NCEUS thus proposed

> legislation for a national minimum security package for unorganized sector workers, social insurance, social assistance for life and health cover, old age benefits to all workers within a period of 5 years, to be sponsored both by the centre and state governments, employers (wherever identifiable) and workers at a cost of less than 0.5 per cent of GDP after 5 years.

Indian policy makers had initially discarded these recommendations for statutory intervention to extend social protection to unorganized workforce. NCEUS suggested a provisioning of budget for social security schemes, and consequently central government allotted a notional amount of Rs.1,500 crore for the same.

Public Evaluation of Entitlement Programme conducted a survey through IIT Delhi in 2013. As per the survey report, "among nearly 900 rural respondents, selected at random from the official pension lists in 10 states, 97 per cent were getting their pension". During the survey, 76 per cent beneficiaries reported that they received pensions, through post offices or banking channel even after delays over a month. The report opined that although pension amounts are low, but this assured flow of income had its impact in supplementing an elder's resource to afford medicines, clothing, food and other basic necessities.

On review of several data available in public domain, it is found that India spends around 1.4 per cent of its GDP on range of social security schemes, which is lowest in the continent. As per print media reports, Government of India initiated a smart card, "Unorganized Sector Identification Number" (U-WIN), to unorganized workforce embossing unique identification number for accessing eligible social schemes across the country. Nonetheless, what these benefits will be, and what their legal guarantee is, that are still up in the air.

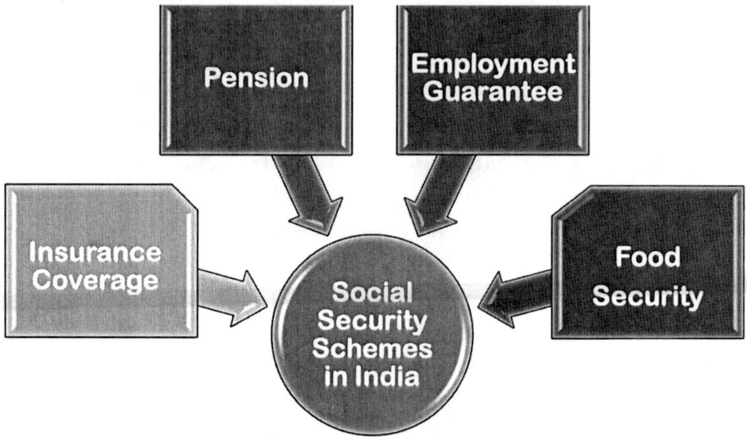

Objectives of Social Security Schemes in India

Considering the vulnerability of elder population retiring from unorganized workforce, policy makers across the world is primarily strategizing need-based social security schemes to ensure sustenance income for elder's within the coverage gap. Coverage Gap is basically a term used to indicate workforce who do not have access to any formal social security scheme for their old age income. World Bank reports that around 1/8th of the world's elder people live in India (Asli Demirguc-Kunt, 2014). Majority of country's elder population depends on financial support (i.e., by money transfer) from their children working elsewhere from native. In India, such coverage gap constitutes around 90 per cent (Wadhwa, 2020) of the estimated workforce of 400 million people.

For a longer period, India has not explicitly focused to make provisions for minimum social security coverage to its citizens. During the last decade, the Government of India had rolled out an employment generation programme, Mahatma Gandhi National Rural Employment Guarantee Scheme (MGNREGS), to enhance livelihood of rural population by providing legal guarantee of minimum 100 days wage employment to a family in a financial year. This employment guarantee scheme was launched in India following the intervention of Supreme Court while dealing with the "Right to Food" case. MGNREGS basically aims protection of unorganized workforce in rural areas against their vulnerabilities. The researcher believes that financial inclusion drives through Pradhan Mantri Jan Dhan Yojana (PMJDY), as linked to a scheme like MGNREGS, is complementing each other. As per government report[2], there is total 13.12 crore active workers (including 6.84 crore women workers) covering 4.03 crore rural households under the scheme during the current fiscal year, FY 2024-25. The scheme has so far generated 127.43 crore person-days and made total number of 20.27 crore Direct Bank Transfer (DBT) across the country (including 3.52 lakh persons), which has created assets value to the tune of Rs.4.03 crore during the current fiscal year, FY 2024-25.

The fundamental notion of policy makers in India always had one recurring pattern that always accentuate vulnerabilities and deprivation. While India's economic progress is claimed to be growing consistently, different think-tanks arguing to plough back considerable portion of state's revenue for extending need-based social security to the unprivileged sections of the country. During the last decade in India, a great deal of attention has been found both from the end of union government and respective state governments towards reformation of social security systems. However, the concern still remained around bureaucrats lobby in India's is what kind of social security scheme is suitable for implementation in rapidly changing economic phase and demographic challenges having impact in social environment in this developing nation. Like in the industrial regions, awareness among population is considerably higher and the households are generally covered by various schemes of social security, either sponsored by the state or the market forces. But in other locations, vulnerabilities are more as major population remains uncovered despite various efforts taken up through community development programmes.

India has certainly traversed most essential milestones for achieving United Nation's "Sustainable Development Goals" (SDGs) through its strategic thrust towards financial inclusion and its forward linkages to various welfare schemes. The launching of PMJDY on August 2014 has been a massive step towards bolstering financial inclusion agenda in the country. PMJDY has created further platform for launching three ambitious social security schemes, viz., "Pradhan Mantri Jeevan Jyoti Bima Yojana" (PMJJBY), "Pradhan Mantri Suraksha Bima Yojana" (PMSBY) and "Atal Pension Yojana" (APY). These three new Social Security Schemes (PMSBY, PMJJBY and APY) are undoubtedly laudable steps forward, as these schemes are expected to contribute towards the welfare of downtrodden workforce who are dependent on the unorganized sectors.

While celebrating 8th anniversary of launching these Jan Suraksha schemes, Finance Minister (FM) of India (PIB, May 2023) reported[3] that around 16.2 crore enrolment under PMJJBY, 34.2 crore enrolment under PMSBY and 5.2 crore enrolment of beneficiaries have been done under APY till 26th April 2023. Being specific to PMJJBY scheme, the FM of India reported that union government has provided supports to around 6.64 lakh households, who have received life insurance claims. The total payment of claim nationwide amounting to Rs. 13,290 crore as on 31 March 2023. Under PMSBY scheme, the FM of India reported that more than 1.15 lakh household have received accidental insurance claims that nationwide amounting to Rs. 2,302 crore.

Overall impacts of these strategies are giving positive outcomes to present government. As per the latest HCES report[4], India's rural poverty has substantially declined to 7.2 per cent in FY 2022-23 from that of 25.7 per cent in FY 2011-12, while the urban poverty level fell to 4.6 per cent from 13.7 per cent during the same period. NSSO reports that the inequality between top and bottom spenders has reduced across both rural and urban areas 2011-12.

Policy Suggestions

- During interaction with beneficiaries from varied group, a common demand for increasing the upper limit of pension amount has been noted. Beneficiaries were concerned about the value of such low pension amount, keeping in view of the market inflation. The existing maximum pension slab of Rs. 5,000 will have insignificant value to support livelihood of an individual on attaining the age of 60 years.

- Government of India shall move further to cover its entire population under social security schemes at least in certain areas. On this endeavor and considering low amount of annual premium for enrolment/renewal under PMSBY, the union government shall bring national policy to enroll all bank account holders mandatorily under PMSBY. This means all citizen of this nation, with an active bank account, will be covered under accidental insurance coverage by way of paying annual premium through auto debit mode through savings account. A regulatory policy or ordinance will rule out the present norms of obtaining official consent of an individual for enrolment or renewal as such enrolment will become mandatory for all citizens of India like many developing countries across the world.
- On discussion with various beneficiaries and bank employees, it is suggested that Government of India may bring an "auto enrolment policy" under PMJJBY in order to cover its beneficiaries under the life insurance policy on payment of low annual premium. The union government may bring regulatory policy of auto enrolment under PMJJBY, for beneficiaries of all government sponsored schemes, who gets a total amount government assistance of Rs. 60,000 or above in a year in the form of pension, subsidy or grant. Yearly renewal (with the procedure of filling up the form) of PMJJBY shall be discontinued and the same shall be linked to payment of government benefits in Basic Savings Bank Deposit Account (BSBDA).
- The Government of India shall make it mandatory to enroll under PMSBY or PMJJBY for availing Employee"s State Insurance Corporation (ESIC) benefits. Employers

must deduct the amount and arrange enrollments in ESIC. Principal employers must verify active enrollment of its outsourced staffs under PMSBY/PMJJBY before approving payment to outsourced vendors, as part of compliance.

- State governments shall bring encouraging policies to incentivize private sector employers of unorganized sectors for paying monthly premiums of APY as social benefit to its employees.
- State governments may tie-up with telecom companies to provide financial awareness as well as handholding people to make them convenient with use of mobile banking in local languages, by way of launching language specific toll- free numbers.

Conclusion

It is noted that if workforce is given assurance of social security, they could result higher productivity leading to the core objectives of SDG. This in turn can enhance aggregate demand in an economy through higher purchasing power of vast population of the country engaged in the unorganized sector. Policy makers shall formulate appropriate strategies to engage the vast youth population through digital and social media platforms so as to make them aware about various employment generation schemes, their rights and processes to follow. local government institutions shall treat youth as key stakeholders and forerunners in rebuilding rural India, and not just treat them as beneficiaries.

The foundation agenda have been addressed successfully within the country. The Government of India, regulator and private sectors players have got suitable scope to step forward for building a superstructure for economic prosperity and inclusive development in the nation. India has world"s largest share of young people. The soaring ambition of this young population is no longer satisfied with the status-quo. Thus, an aggressive agenda towards financial inclusion must be at the core of India"s economic strategy to meet these aspirations. The country demands that political leadership, local government institutions and non-government organizations to join hands in close coordination for the all-round development of rural India.

Keywords

Sustainable development goals, social security, inclusive development, financial inclusion.

NOTES

1. Available at: https://www.ilo.org/global/lang—en/index.htm
2. Ref: www.nrega.nic.in
3. Ref: https://pib.gov.in/PressReleaseIframePage.aspx?PRID=1922622
4. Household Consumption Expenditure Survey (HCES): 2022-23; NSSO, Government of India.

REFERENCES

Amitabh, S. (2009). *10 Obstacles for MFIs Launching Alternative Channels: And What Can Be Done.* The Centre for Financial Inclusion.

Anant, N.J. & B. Aashish, (2008, Jan). *Linking Financial Inclusion with Social Security Schemes.* Working Paper Series No. 22, Institute for Financial Management and Research, Centre for Microfinance.

Anupama, S. & K. Sumita (2013). "An Analytical Study: Relevance of Financial Inclusion for Developing Nations Research Inventry." *International Journal of Engineering and Science, 2*(6): 15-20 .

Arunachalam, R. S. (2008). *Scoping Paper on Financial Inclusion.* The United Nations Development Programme.

Asli Demirguc-Kunt, L.K. (2014). *Global Findex Database, Measuring Financial Inclusion Around the World.* Retrieved from WorldBank: http://pubdocs.worldbank.org/en/681361466184854434/2014-Global-Findex-Report-DKSV.pdf

Bappaditya, M. (2011). "Role of MFIs in Financial Inclusion." *Review of Market Integration, 3.*

Borio, C. & P. Disyatat (2011). *Global Imbalances and the Financial Crisis: Link or no Link?* Monetary and Economic Department. Switzerland: Bank for International Settlements. Retrieved from https://www.bis.org/publ/work346.pdf

Census (2011). *Census Report.* Government of India.

Central Registry of Securitisation Asset Reconstruction and Security Interest of India (n.d.). Retrieved from CERSAI: https://www.cersai.org.in/CERSAI/home.prg

Centre for Law & Policy Research (1950). *Constitution of India.* Retrieved on September 2020, from https://www.constitutionofindia.net/: https://www.constitutionofindia.net/constitution_of_india/directive_principles_of_state_policy/articles/Article%2041

Chakrabarty, D.K. (2013). "Two Decades of Credit Management in Banks: Looking Back and Moving Ahead." *BANCON 2013.* RBI.

Chakravarty, S.R. & R. Pal (2010). *Measuring Financial Inclusion: An Axiomatic Approach.* Indira Gandhi Institute of Development Research. Chen, M. & D. Snodgrass (2001). *Managing Resources, Activities, and Risk in Urban India: The Impact of SEWA Bank.* Washington, D.C: USAID. Retrieved from https://www.wiego.org/publications/managing-resources-activities-and-risk-urban-india-impact-sewa-bank Chidambaram (2007). *Union Budget Speech.*

CRISIL (2011). *CRISIL Inclusix Index.* CRISIL. Retrieved from https://www.crisil.com

CRISIL (2013). *CRISL Inclusix.* An Index Measure India"s Progress on Financial Inclusion, MoFIN and RBI. Retrieved from https://www.crisil.com/content/dam/crisil/our-analysis/publications/crisil-inclusix/CRISIL-Inclusix-An-index-to-measure-indias-progress-on-financial-inclusion-vol1-june2013.pdf

CRISIL (2018 February). *CRISIL Inclusix Report.* Vol 4. Retrieved from https:// www.crisil.com/content/dam/crisil/our-analysis/reports/Research/ documents/2018/march/crisil-inclusix-financial-inclusion-surges-driven- by-Jan-Dhan-yojana.pdf

D. Subbarao, R. (2009 September). *Financial Stability: Issues and Challenges.* Debt Recovery Appellate Tribunal (2002). *The Securitisation and Reconstruction of Financial Assets and Enforcement of Security Interest (SARFAESI) Act.* Retrieved from http://www.drat.tn.nic.in/: http://www.drat.tn.nic.in/Docu/Securitisation-Act.pdf

Demirguc-Kunt, A.A. (2011). *Global Financial Inclusion (Global Findex) Database.* World Bank. Retrieved from World Bank: https://microdata.worldbank.org/index.php/catalog/1097/study-description

Demirguc-Kunt, A. & L. Klapper (2011). *Measuring Financial Inclusion: The Global Findex Database.* Development Research Group, Finance and Private Sector Development Team. World Bank. Retrieved 2012 from http://documents1.worldbank.org/curated/en/453121468331738740/ pdf/WPS6025.pdf

Demirguc-Kunt, A., L. Klapper, & D. Randall (2013). *The Global Findex Database: Financial Inclusion in India.* Development Research Group Finance and Pvt Sector. World Bank. Retrieved from World Bank Group: http://documents.worldbank.org/curated/en/445021468042252014/The-Global-Findex-database-financial-inclusion-in-India

Demirguc-Kunt, Asli & Leora Klapper (2017). *Measuring Financial Inclusion: Global Findex Database.* World Bank. Retrieved from World Bank: http://documents1.worldbank.org/curated/en/453121468331738740/ pdf/WPS6025.pdf

Department of Financial Services, MOF, GOI (2019). "Overview and Progress on Financial Inclusion: PMJDY." *Overview of Financial Inclusion.* Ministry of Finance. Retrieved from https://financialservices.gov.in/sites/default/files/Financial%20Inclusion_annual%20report_material31.3.2019. pdf

DFS. (2012 April 4). Master Circular on Strategy and Guidelines on Financial Inclusion. 26. New Delhi: Department of Financial Services, MoF, GoI. Retrieved from https://financialservices.gov.in/sites/default/files/21132009-FI%20%28Vol%20II-Pt.%29.pdf

DFS. (2014). *Department of Financial Services.* Retrieved from https://financialservices.gov.in/financial-inclusion

DFS. (2019). "Overview and Progress on Financial Inclusion: PMJDY." *Overview of Financial Inclusion.* India: Department of Financial Services, Ministry of Finance, GoI. Retrieved from https://financialservices. gov.in/sites/default/files/Financial%20Inclusion_annual%20report_ material 31.3.2019.pdf

DFS. (2020). Retrieved from Ministry of Finance, GoI: https://financialservices.gov.in

DFS. GoI (2014 August 28). *PMJDY.* Retrieved from Department of Financial Services: https://www.pmjdy.gov.in/scheme

Drèze, J. & A. Sen (2011 September). "Public Action for Social Security: Foundations and Strategy." *Social Security in Developing Countries.* doi:10.1093/acprof:oso/9780198233008.003.0001

Economic Survey 2019-2020 (n.d.). *State of the Economy,* Vol. 2. Retrieved from India Budget: https://www.indiabudget.gov.in/economicsurvey/doc/vol2chapter/echap01_vol2.pdf

Elisabeth, R., G. Anita & L. David (2009). *Mexico"s Prospects for Full Financial.* A White Paper from the Financial Inclusion 2020 Project.

Finance Department, Government of West Bengal (n.d.). Retrieved from Directorate of Registration and Stamp Revenue: https://wbregistration.gov.in/(S(3wokbsjbxdp5uw0tsirx2ooy))/index.aspx

Fondeville, N., E. Őzdemir, & T. Ward (2010). *Social Situation Observatory: Income Distribution and Living Conditions.* ISER—University of Essex (UK) and Tárki (HU) , European Centre for the European Centre for Social Welfare Policy and Research. Applica: European Commission.

Garg, C.C. & A.K. Karan (2009). "Reducing Out-of-Pocket Expenditures to Reduce Poverty: A Disaggregated Analysis at Rural-Urban And State Level In India." *Health Policy and Planning, 24*(2): 116-28. doi:https://doi. org/10.1093/heapol/czn046

GoI. (2008). *Committee on Financial Inclusion.*

GoI. (n.d.). Retrieved from Data.Gov.in: www.gov.in

Hannig, A. & S. Jansen (2010). *Financial Inclusion and Financial Stability: Current Policy Issues.* Asia Development Bank. Retrieved from https://papers.ssrn.com/sol3/papers.cfm?abstract_id=1729122

H.R. Khan, D.G. (2004). *Khan Commission Report.* Reserve Bank of India. Hussain, A. & A. Liu (1989). "Compedium of Literature on the Chinese Social Security System." *Development Economics Research Programme.*

London School of Economics.

ILO. (1984). International Labour Standards on Social security. International Labour Organization. Retrieved from https://www.ilo.org/global/standards/subjects-covered-by-international-labour-standards/social-security/lang—en/index.htm

ILO. (1984a). Social Security. Introduction to Social Security. Geneva.

ILO. (1984b). Into the Twenty First Century: The Development of Social Security. Geneva.

ILO. (1997). *The Cost of Social Security.* Basic Table 1990-1993. Retrieved from http://www.ilo.org/public/english/110secso/css/cssintro.htm

ILO. (2001). "Social Security Issues, Challenges and Prospects." *International Labour Conference 89th Session , Report VI.* Geneva.

ILO. (2002). "Decent Work and the Informal Economy." *International Labour Conference, 90th Session* (p. Report VI). Geneva.

ILO-International Labour Organization (2014). *World of Work Report 2014: Developing with Jobs.* Research Department. Geneva: International Labour Office. doi:13.01.3

India Brand Equity Foundation (n.d.). Retrieved from IBEF: https://www.ibef.org/

Indian Institute of Banking & Finance (2012). *Advanced Bank Management* (Vols. Module-D). Macmillan Publishers India Ltd.

Kamath, R. & S. Ramanathan (2015). *Informal Businesses and Micro-Credit: Evidence from Financial Diaries: A Study in Ramanagaram,* India. IIMB Management Review, Indian Institute of Management Bangalore, Bangalore. doi:10.1016/j.iimb.2015.05.002

Kempson, E. (2006). *Policy Level Response to Financial Exclusion in Developed Economies: Lessons for Developing Countries.* University of Bristol, The Personal Finance Research Centre. Washington DC: Financial Sector Team, Policy Division, Department for International Development.

Kempson, E. & C. Whyley (1999). *Kept Out or Opted Out?: Understanding and Combating Financial Exclusion.* UK: The Policy Press. Retrieved from http://www.bris.ac.uk/media-library/sites/geography/migrated/documents/pfrc9902.pdf

Khan, H.R. (2011). "Financial Inclusion and Financial Stability: Are They Two Sides of the Same Coin." *BANCON.* Chennai: Indian Bankers Association and Indian Overseas Bank.

Krishnan, T. (1999). "Access to Health and the Burden of Treatment in India: an Inter-State Comparison." M.R. (ed.), In: *Disinvesting in Health: The World Bank"s Prescriptions for Health.*

Kumar, N. (February 2012). "An Empirical Analysis of Financial Inclusion Across Population Groups in India." *The IUP Journal of Bank Management, XI*(1). Retrieved from http://ssrn.com/abstract=2150111

Lakshmi, K. (2012). *"Financial Inclusion' Research Initiative.* IMFR. IMFR. Land & Land Reforms and Refugee Relief and Rehabilitation Department Government of West Bengal. (n.d.). *Act & Rules.* Retrieved from Banglarbhumi: https://banglarbhumi.gov.in/BanglarBhumi/Home.action

Leliveld, A. (1991). *Social Security in Developing Countries.* Retrieved from https://research.vu.nl/en/publications/social-security-in-developing-countries

Leyshon & Thrift. (1995). "Geographies of Financial Exclusion: Financial Abandonment in Britain and the United States." *Transactions of the Institute of British Geographers, 20* (New Series): 312-41.

Mas, I. (2012). Payments in Developing Countries: Breaking Physical and Psychological Barriers. *Transaction World Magazine.*

MDG 2000. (2000 September). *Millennium Development Goals.* New York: United Nations Development Programme. Retrieved from https://www.undp.org/content/undp/en/home/sdgoverview/mdg_goals.html

Micro, S.A. (2006). *MSMED Act 2006.* Government of India. Mihasonirina, A. (2010). *ICT, Financial Inclusion, and Growth: Evidence from African Countries.* Draft, African Development Bank.

Ministry of Finance, GoI. (n.d.). *Department of Financial Services, MoF, GoI.* Retrieved from https://financialservices.gov.in: https://financialservices.gov.in/circular-financial-inclusion-archive?field_tags_tid=All&title=&field_start_date_value%5Bmin%5D&field_start_date_value%5Bmax%5D&page=6

Ministry of Finance, GoI. (2019). *Jan Dhan Se Jan Suraksha*. Retrieved from Department of Financial Services: https://jansuraksha.gov.in

Ministry of Rural Development. (1995). *National Social Assistance Programme*. Retrieved July 2020 from https://nsap.nic.in/

Mishra, J. (2020, July). "Agriculture and Social Security." *Kurukshetra (A Journal on Rural Development), 68*(9): 16-21.

MoFin, GoI. (n.d.). *Department of Financial Services*. Retrieved from https://financialservices.gov.in/financial-inclusion

Mohan, R. (2006 March). "Agricultural Credit in India: Status, Issues and Future Agenda." *Economic and Political Weakly*, pp. 1013-23.

Morgan, P. & V. Pontines (2014). *Financial Stability and Financial Inclusion*. Tokyo: Asian Development Bank Institute. Retrieved from http://www.adbi.org/working-paper/2014/07/07/6353.financial.stability.inclusion/

NABARD. (1992). *Micro Credit Innovation*. Retrieved from NABARD: https://www.nabard.org/contentsearch.aspx?AID=225&Key=shg+bank+linkage+programme

NABARD. (1992). *Micro Credit Innovation*. Retrieved from NABARD Website: https://www.nabard.org/contentsearch.aspx?AID=225&Key=shg+bank+linkage+programme

National Commision on Labour (2007). Retrieved from https://www.prsindia.org: https://www.prsindia.org/sites/default/files/bill_files/bill150_20071205150_National_Commission_on_ Labour_2_Chapter_7_unorganised_sector_Part_A_1.pdf

Nazuk, K. (2011). "Half a Nation!: Financial Inclusion Lessons for India." *URGHS, 2*.

Noponen, H. & P. Kantor (2004). "Setbacks and Chronic Problems: The Determinants of Economic Stress Events among Poor Households in India." *Journal of International Development, 16*: 529-45.

NPCI. (n.d.). *AePS Product Overview*. Retrieved from National Payments Corporation of India: https://www.npci.org.in/what-we-do/aeps/product-overview

NPCI. (n.d.). *AePS Product Review*. Retrieved from NPCI: https://www.npci. org.in/product-overview/aeps-product-overview

NSS. (1986-87). *India-Persons Aged 60 Plus Survey*. NSS 42nd Round Schedule 27. Retrieved from http://www.icssrdataservice.in/datarepository/index.php/catalog/36

NSSO. (2000). *Employment and Unemployment in India 1999-2000*. Ministry of Statistics & Programme Implementation, GoI. New Delhi: National Sample Survey Organisation. Retrieved from http://mospi.nic.in/sites/default/files/publication_reports/455_final.pdf

NSSO. (2006). "Morbidity, Health Care and the Condition of the Aged." In N.S. Organisation (Ed.), *NSSO 60th Round, January: June 2006.* New Delhi: Ministry of Statistics and Programme Implementation, Government of India.

NSSO. (2011). *Employment and Unemployment Situation in India (2009-10).* NSS Report No. 537(66/10/1) . Retrieved from http://mospi.nic.in/sites/default/files/publication_reports/NSS_Report_No_537.pdf

Paul, S. (2015). *Rural Development: Concept and Recent Approaches.* New Delhi: Concept Publishing Company (Pvt) Ltd.

PIB. (2012 May 21). "'Swabhimaan': Transforming Rural India Through Financial Inclusion." *Press Information Bureau.* Chandigarh: Media & Communications Officer.

Planning Commision of India (1999). *Human Development Report.* Planning Commision. Retrieved from http://hdr.undp.org/sites/default/files/reports/263/hdr_2002_en_complete.pdf

Planning Commission, GoI. (2001 October). *Report of the Working Group on Social Security.* Retrieved from NITI Ayog: https://niti.gov. in/planningcommission.gov.in/docs/aboutus/committee/wrkgrp/ wg_soclscty.pdf

Raghuram, R. (2009). *A Hundred Small Steps.* Report of the Committee on Financial Sector Reforms, RBI.

Rajan, D.R. (2014). "Finance and Opportunity in India." *Twentieth Lalit Doshi Memorial Lecture* (p. https://www.rbi.org.in/scripts/BS_SpeechesView. aspx?Id=908). RBI. Retrieved from RBI: https://www.rbi.org.in/scripts/ BS_SpeechesView.aspx?Id=908

Ramanan, R. & M. Yadav (2021 January). "Adopting a Holistic Approach towards Rural Development." *Kurukshetra, 69*(3): 5-8.

Ramu, N. (2010 April-September). "Financial Exclusion: Need for Financial Inclusion." *The Alternative, IX*(2): 5-14.S. Retrieved from http://ssrn.com/abstract=2207506N

Rangarajan, C. (2008). *Report of the Committee on Financial Inclusion.* Reserve Bank of India.

RBI. (2007 July 4). *UCBs: IT-enabled Financial Inclusion.* Retrieved from RBI Notification: https://www.rbi.org.in/scripts/NotificationUser.aspx?Mode=0&Id=3695

RBI (2014). *Committee on Comprehensive Financial Services for Small Business and Low Income Households.* Rural Planning and Credit Department, RBI. Mumbai: Reserve Bank of India. Retrieved from https://rbidocs.rbi.org. in/rdocs/PressRelease/PDFs/IEPR1367CCF0114.pdf

RBI. (2020 March 31). *List of Banks in India.* Retrieved from RBI Website: https://m.rbi.org.in/CommonPerson/english/scripts/banksinindia.aspx

RBI. (2020 September 4). *Master Directions: Priority Sector Lending (PSL): Targets and Classification.* Reserve Bank of India. Retrieved from https:// www.rbi.org.in/Scripts/BS_ViewMasDirections.aspx?id=11959

RBI. (2020 January 10). *National Strategy for Financial Inclusion (NSFI): 2019-2024.* Retrieved from Reserve Bank of India: https://www.rbi.org.in/Scripts/PublicationReportDetails.aspx?UrlPage=&ID=1154

RBI. CSES (2013). *How the Poor Manage their Finances: A Study of the Portfolio Choices of Poor Households in Ernakulam District, Kerala.* Centre for Socio-economic and Environmental Studies (CSES), Development Research Group's Project. Kochi: Reserve Bank of India.

Report of the Committee on Medium-term Path on Financial Inclusion (2008). *RBI Reports.* Retrieved from Reserve Bank of India: https://www. rbi.org.in/scripts/publicationreportdetails.aspx?Id=836

Reserve Bank of India (n.d.). Retrieved from RBI Website: www.rbi.org.in Reserve Bank of India (2005 August 23). *Annual Policy Statement.* RBI. Retrieved from https://www.rbi.org.in/Scripts/NotificationUser.aspx?Id=2460&Mode=0

Reserve Bank of India (2005). *Financial Inclusion Taskforce: Report on Progress Towards the Shared Goal.* RBI.

Reserve Bank of India (2014). Report of the Committee to the Review Governance of Boards of Banks in India.

Reserve Bank of India (2016 July 7). *Master Circular on PSL.* Retrieved from RBI: https://m.rbi.org.in/Scripts/BS_ViewMasDirections.aspx?id=10497

Sangwan (2006). "Financial Inclusion and Self Help Groups." *e-Journal, NABARD.*

Santiago, E.G. (2005). "Financial Inclusion". In *Palgrave* (Studies in Banking and Financial Institutions ed., p. Molyneux). Macmillan.

Sarkar, S. (2019). "Approaches Towards Sustainable Development & Financial Stability Through Financial Inclusion among Rural Women." In *Women & Development.* New Delhi: Empire Books International.

SDG Summit (2019). *High-level Political Forum (HLPF) on Sustainable Development under the Auspices of the General Assembly.* New York.

Sen, A. (2000). *Development as Freedom.* New York: Anchor Books.

Serrao, M. & S. Vincent (2012). *Designing a Methodology to Investigate Accessibility and Impact of Financial inclusion.* Retrieved from http://dx.doi.org/10.2139/ssrn.2025521

Shanmugalingam, K. (2012). *The Impact of Financial Inclusion on Economic Development.* Master's Thesis, The University of Queensland, School of Economics.

Singh, C., A. Mittal, A. Goenka *et al.* (2014). *Financial Inclusion in India: Select Issues.* Working Paper: 474, Indian Institute of Management Bangalore, Economics & Social Science, Bangalore.

Singh, C., A. Sanyal, & B. Kanchan (2 December 2015). *Social Security Schemes: A Case for Universalisation*, 498 edn.

SP, S. (2011). "Financial Exclusion: An Introductory Survey." *Centre for Research in Socially Inclusive Services.* Heriot-Watt University, Edinburgh.

Subbarao, D.D. (2009). *Financial Inclusion : Challenges and Opportunities.* Kolkata: RBI.

Supravat Bagli, P.D. (2008). "A Study of Financial Inclusion in India." *Economic and Political Weakly, 1*(8): 1637-48. doi:35.19

Thorsten, B., A. Demirgüç-Kunt & R. Levine (2007 March 6). "Finance, Inequality and the Poor." *Journal of Economic Growth, 12*: 27-49.

Toor, N. (2017). *Handbbook of Banking Information,* 45 edn. Skylark Publication.

UIDAI (n.d.). Retrieved from https://uidai.gov.in/ *United Nations Economic and Social Council* (2012). Retrieved from https:// www.un.org/ecosoc/en/home

Unni, J. & U. Rani (2004). "Technical Change and Workforce in India: Skill Biased Growth?" *The Indian Journal of Labour Economics, 47*(4): 683-92.

Usha Thorat, D.G. (2007 June 19). "Financial Inclusion Conference." In HMT-DFID (Ed.), *Financial Inclusion: The Indian Experience.* Whitehall Place: Reserve Bank of India. Retrieved from https://rbidocs.rbi.org.in/rdocs/Bulletin/PDFs/78680.pdf

Wadhwa, M. (2020 July). "Social Security: Issues Challenges and Initiatives." *Kurukshetra, A Journal on Rural Development, 68*(9): 11-15.

World Bank (2008). *Albania Access to Finance for Enterprise Sector.* Working Paper.

World Bank (2017). *Global Findex Database.* Retrieved from Global Findex: https://globalfindex.worldbank.org/#GF-ReportChapters

World Bank (2018). *Global Financial Inclusion (Global Findex) Database.* Retrieved from the Little Data Book on Financial Inclusion: https://openknowledge.worldbank.org/bitstream/handle/10986/29654/LDB-FinInclusion2018.pdf?sequence=1&isAllowed=y

17

Cross-border Smuggling

Livelihood and the Question of Sustainable Development in the Indo-Bangladesh Border

Riya De and Arkadeep Goswami

India's economic stability relies significantly on agriculture, with nearly 70 per cent of the rural population engaged in agricultural activities. This paper will primarily examine the agricultural issues prevalent in the Cooch Behar district of West Bengal. The district is located in the Sub-Himalayan plains and belonging to the Terai-Agro climatic zone of West Bengal. Out of 3345 sq. km geographical area of the district, 2353 sq. km (70.3% of geographical area) is under cultivation. The district experiences a typical sub-tropical pre-humid climate with high annual rainfall (higher than 3000 mm), high relative humidity (average maximum and minimum of 95 per cent & 65 per cent respectively) and moderate temperature. Tobacco,

Maize and Jute are the major cash crops of Cooch Behar. Beside that paddy, vegetables are also cultivated here.

Putting forth their concern about cross-border smuggling and national security along the densely populated Indo-Bangladesh border, the district administration, as per the suggestions of the

Border Security Force (BSF), has enforced Section 144 of the Code of Criminal Procedure (Chowdhury, 2023). This means that movement and agricultural activities are tightly regulated in the area.

Farmers living along the border face tough restrictions. They are not allowed to grow crops taller than three feet, and they can't easily access their own lands for farming. Instead, they have to rely on the BSF to open the gates in the fencing whenever they need to work on their land.

Adding to their challenges, there's a lack of irrigation system near the border, making it even harder for farmers to grow their crops. In addition, with climate change, the weather in places like Cooch Behar has become more unpredictable, making farming even more difficult.

SDG-1 aims to eliminate poverty in all its manifestations worldwide. It seeks to eradicate extreme poverty globally, ensuring universal access to essential needs such as food, water, shelter, health care, and education. However, human-made challenges often exacerbate the hardships faced by the farmers, making their lives miserable. Consequently, these challenges also affect the well-being of future generations of those particular area, perpetuating the cycle of suffering and deprivation. All these issues combined have a really negative impact on agriculture in the region, making it difficult for farmers to make a living from their land.

Under these peculiar circumstances, the local population has opted for unconventional economic options. To be very specific, they were taking up unsafe migration to other states in search of a job. Many of them have opted for even a dangerous option like cross border smuggling.

SDG-8 emphasizes the importance of promoting inclusive and sustainable economic growth, along with decent work for all individuals. Regrettably, there have been challenges in ensuring hassle-free agricultural activities for impoverished farmers in bordering villages, where both state and central governments' efforts have fallen short. In addition, the United Nations also talks about ensuring the rights of peasants and other people working in rural areas.

The chapter examines the primary factors contributing to the current situation in the study area and to explore potential alternatives aimed at resolving or mitigating these issues.

Objectives

The objectives of this study are:

- To identify the hindrances to the agricultural activities for the villagers residing near the Indo-Bangladesh border in Cooch Behar district of West Bengal.
- To explore potential strategies to address and alleviate these challenges.
- To solicit input and recommendations from various stakeholders, including farmers, BSF personnel, *panchayat*s, and the district administration, in order to formulate comprehensive and inclusive measures.

Through these objectives, we aim to develop a holistic understanding of the issues faced by border communities and propose actionable steps towards sustainable agricultural development and improved livelihoods in the region. This is expected to keep the community from putting their lives at peril by undertaking unsafe migration and other dangerous and illegal employment options.

About the Study Area

Cooch Behar district is located in the north-eastern part of West Bengal, bordered by Alipurduar district to the north and north-west, and Jalpaiguri district to the north-west. To the east, lies the state of Assam. Notably, the district shares a lengthy international border (549.45 km) with Bangladesh to the south-west, south, and south-east. Additionally, Cooch Behar district was home to a total of 110 erstwhile enclaves, which were integrated into the Indian mainland following the Land Boundary Agreement of 2015.

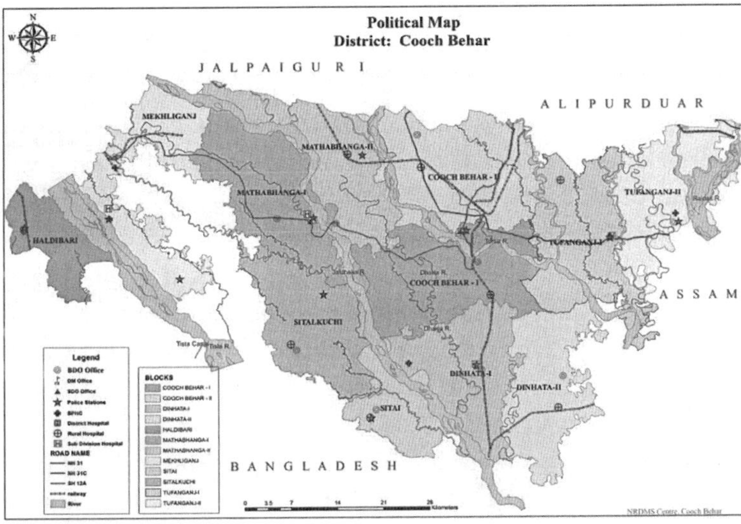

Cooch Behar district comprises of 12 blocks, namely Cooch Behar I, Cooch Behar II, Dinhata I, Dinhata II, Mathabhanga I, Mathabhanga II, Sitai, Sitalkuchi, Tufanganj I, Tufanganj II, Mekliganj, and Haldibari. The district is enriched by the presence of several rivers running through its land. The main rivers are Dharla, Dudua, Gadadhar, Ghar gharia, Jaldhaka and Kalijani.

Total population of Cooch Behar is estimated to be 39,74,912 (estimates as per Aadhar data in 2024). As per 2011 census, Cooch Behar has a population of 28,19,086 out of which 14,51,542 were male and 13,67,544 were female. Among the total population, about 18,50,504 are literates out of which 10,28,733 are male and 8,21,771 are female. In Cooch Bihar, 11,27,977 are workers that includes 8,45,308 men and 2,82,669 women. Among the workers, 3,12,014 depend on agriculture that includes 2,83,599 men and 28,415 women. About 2,72,435 persons work as agricultural labourers which includes 2,12,822 men and 59,613 women. Sex ratio in Cooch Behar is 942 females per 1,000 of males. (India Growing, n.d.).

Literature Review

Availability of secondary data related to border areas was very scarce due to the limited number of studies conducted in these domains. In addition, gathering data from the border areas was very challenging. One of the biggest difficulties of dealing with any issue related to the questions of Indo-Bangladesh border is the unavailability of literature. Thus, the authors had to use whatever limited literature has been available in the public domain. Jamwal has dealt with the question of border management, but the human condition has been off the focus (Jamwal, 2004). Datta has worked on the question providing us with a better understanding of the situation (India Quarterly, 2018).

But, the study posed us a big challenge as the authors had to travel in a solo path. The contradiction between the question of livelihood and the question of national security in the study area was another major factor. All these forced the authors to proceed with the limited secondary data and rely more on the data gathered from the field.

In "Bangladesh-India Border: Issues and Management", Col. Mahbub-ul Alam confirms as:

> The identical Bangladesh-India border gave rise to number of issues such as cross border smuggling, terrorist activities, border fencing, human and drug trafficking, border killing, etc. that often vitiated friendly relations between the two neighbours. More importantly, millions of people living in the border continue to suffer economic hardships and physical restrictions due to frequent incidents along the border. Currently, it has become a common phenomenon that Bangladeshi people are harassed, tortured and even killed by the Border Security Force (BSF) of India. Moreover, the BSF asserts that its personnel fires at smugglers and hostile migrants of Bangladesh, but Bangladesh argues that BSF personnel kills innocent people.

This very statement can be a great entry point in the study. Though limited availability of relevant literature posed a significant challenge, the availability of government policy papers, reports, etc. could provide several useful inputs for the study. The sections related to Indo-Bangladesh border from the report of the Parliamentary Standing Committee was especially of significance. The initiatives like Border Area Development Programme (BADP), and Border Haats will have a significant role to play in the sustainable development of the border area.

Methodology

This study aims to uncover the underlying issue and explore mutually beneficial solutions for all parties involved in the border area management. As part of the study, efforts were made to gather multiple perspectives, dimensions, and dynamics of cross-border struggling as well as to seek a balanced outcome that benefits the key stakeholders.

Cooch Behar district in West Bengal was identified for the study as issues of persons engaged in agrarian activities near Indo-Bangladesh border was quite varied and significant to examine. The villages within close proximity to the Indo-Bangladesh border fence were included in the sample to capture the localized challenges faced by agricultural communities. Specifically, the focus was on Balabhut, Jhaukuthi, and Krishnapur in Tufanganj I block; Rajar Bari and Gadopota in Sitalkuchi block; and Notun Basti, Hemkumari, Dorjipara, and Sardarpara in Haldibari block, as well as Paschim Sahebganj, Purba Sahebganj, and Kalmati in Dinhata II block. All these villages are situated within a 5-km radius of the border fence.

Due to financial constraints and time limitations, the focus was given to the areas accessible via public transport where the mentioned issues are prevalent. Sitalkuchi is particularly sensitive politically and socially, and it is prone tò illegal activities, including cattle smuggling. The survey included 300 households in Tufanganj I block. Additionally, twelve focus group discussions (FGDs) across all the aforementioned villages were also held. Primary source of data was made by conducting FGDs. Through separate meetings with both male and female farmers organized in villages, the challenges confronting agricultural activities in the border region were the focus of the discussions. These sessions served as a platform for participants to share their first-hand experiences and insights. Importantly, at the culmination of each FGD, participants collabouratively formulated actionable suggestions aimed at addressing the identified issues.

Due to the sensitive nature of the issues involving national security and bureaucratic processes, the researchers relied on informal discussions with various government authorities, including BSF personnel. The data collection process was completed within fifteen days. Most of the FGDs were conducted in the evening, while daytime was dedicated to filling out the baseline survey format through door-to-door visits. Structured observation techniques enabled the researchers to cross-verify the data collected through other sources.

Discussions

FGDs enabled the authors to delve deep into the challenges confronting agricultural activities in the study area. To grasp the core issues of the area, it is imperative to consider the geographic layout of the villages. As previously mentioned, all the villages are located within a 5-km radius from the Indo-Bangladesh border. However, there is a crucial point. The barbed wire fencing has not been positioned directly on the actual border line. Instead, there is a gap between the International Border Pillar and the barbed wire fence, ranging from approximately 150 m to 500 m. Remarkably, in some areas, this gap exceeds even 1 km or more.

(a) Security-related Issues

Within this expanse between the barbed wire fence and the International Border Pillar lie vast hectares of Indian land, owned by the local community. There is a serious misconception among the populace that this area constitutes the "no man's land". However, in reality, these lands belong to the farmers of the bordering villages. Towards accessing these lands for farming activities, the farmers are to travel through the fencing gates, which are regulated by the BSF personnel. Generally, there are designated times for operating these gates, including morning slots from 7:00 a.m. to 9:00 a.m., from 11:00 a.m. to 1:00 p.m., and 3:00 p.m. to 4:00 p.m. However, there are instances where the gate timings could not be maintained due to inadequate staffing within the BSF.

Especially during the winter season, when visibility is impaired by fog, the BSF may refrain from opening the gates for the morning slot. This inconsistency in gate operations further complicates farmers' access to their lands and exacerbates the challenges they face in managing agricultural activities along the border region.

Furthermore, due to the persistent visibility challenges, the BSF personnel, in collabouration with the district authorities, impose certain restrictions on farmers regarding the cultivation of crops exceeding a height of 3 ft. Consequently, farmers are prohibited from cultivating cash crops such as jute or maize, despite the district's favourable weather and soil conditions for these crops. This restriction further affects agricultural productivity and deprives the local farmers of the opportunity to capitalize on crops that could potentially enhance their economic prospects. This pattern of "prohibition" extends not only to the land situated between the International Border Pillar and the barbed wire fence but also to the lands adjacent to the barbed wire fence within the "main territory". Cultivating crops exceeding a height of 3 ft, including jute or maize, is strictly forbidden in these areas. This blanket restriction severely limits farmers' choices and options for crop cultivation, regardless of their land is located within the border region.

As per the national security protocols, these farmers are required to obtain written permission for the transportation of agricultural equipment and vehicles within the specified area. However, navigating the bureaucratic process to obtain such permissions poses numerous challenges to farmers, adding unnecessary hassles to their daily activities.

(b) High Input Cost for Agriculture

As expressed, the agricultural land located between the International Border Pillar and the border fence face significant challenges related to irrigation. In many cases, there are either inadequate or no irrigation facilities available for cultivation in the area. Compounding this issue, these lands lack access to electricity, thereby necessitating the use of diesel-operated pumps for irrigation. Relying on diesel pumps not only adds to the operational costs but also contributes to environmental concerns as well as bring additional financial burden to the farmers. Consequently, the overall cost of agricultural production in these areas escalates significantly, placing additional strain on the livelihoods of farmers who are already grappling with various restrictions and limitations. Moreover, to combat cross-border smuggling activities, the BSF imposes restrictions on the transportation of fertilizers, pesticides, and seeds. Though these restrictions are being made in line with the concerns of border security, such measures limit the application of these essential inputs for agricultural production at the "right time". As a result, farmers face considerable difficulties in procuring vital supplies, hindering their ability to effectively cultivate their lands and sustain their livelihoods.

There is no doubt that the national security of our homeland cannot be compromised. At the same time, it is important to address the adverse impacts of such security measures/restrictions on the farmers in carrying out the agricultural activities in the border areas.

(c) Ecosystem Imbalance Factors

Positioning of search light masts near the fencing are made to enhance surveillance, which also leads to certain difficulties to the farmers. The intense and dazzling light emitted by these searchlights can severely affect crops, often resulting in burns or complete destruction of the produce. Moreover, the continuous illumination throughout the night disrupts the local ecosystem. Insects are attracted to these bright lights, leading to infestations that ravage crops in the surrounding areas. This ecological imbalance further exacerbates the already challenging conditions faced by farmers in border regions.

Balancing the imperative of national security with the need to mitigate the unintended consequences on agricultural livelihoods is very much essential. Exploring measures to minimize the adverse effects of these searchlights in the productivity of agricultural crops while maintaining effective border surveillance is essential for fostering sustainable development in these border areas.

(d) Illegal Trespass

The distance between the International Border Pillar and the border fence leads to another serious issue. The inhabitants of the neighbouring country illegally traverse the border and encroach upon Indian territory unhindered until they reach the fencing. This unrestricted access poses serious challenges for Indian farmers residing in the border areas.

Farmers lament that instances of crop destruction in the border areas is a routine matter. Bulk movement of cattle from the neighbouring country often leads to extensive damage to the standing crops in the farm land. Compounding these issues, farmers find themselves unable to safeguard their land effectively due to restricted access during scheduled times for the opening of fencing gates. Due to the presence of an international treaty, neither the BSF nor the State Police wish to take strict action in such instances.

(e) Diplomatic Issues

The personnel stationed outside the fence for border security, within Indian territory, are unable to intervene effectively to protect the crops of Indian farmers. This regulatory constraint further enhances the vulnerability of the farmers to incursions and damages perpetrated by individuals from across the border.

Addressing these challenges necessitates a comprehensive approach that includes bolstering border security measures, enhancing surveillance, and facilitating timely interventions to safeguard the interests of Indian farmers and protect agricultural lands from encroachment and destruction.

(f) Lack of Information

The farmers are not well aware of the modern techniques of agricultural activities. They are even unaware of the different government schemes which are available for them to develop agricultural productivity.

All these challenges have compelled many farmers to seek alternative livelihoods, often resorting to inappropriate or unsustainable means of income generation. Faced with dwindling agricultural prospects, coupled with the inability to protect their lands and sustain their livelihoods, farmers are left with few viable options. In some cases, this dire situation pushes individuals towards unsafe migrations in search of better opportunities, increasing their vulnerability and perpetuating cycles of poverty and instability.

Findings

Due to operational restrictions for carrying out agricultural activities in the border areas that resulted in reduction of livelihood opportunities and sources of income, the farmers from the bordering villages have been changing their professions. Sometimes, they get themselves engaged with certain jobs due to the pressure. Without considering the consequences, they move to different parts of India with very little information about the job providers or the risk factors of the job. Many of them have no clue about the basic safety measure, if they met with an accident or face certain difficulties away from their home. Even the Public Distribution System (PDS) facilities, medical facilities and many other basic amenities are not available to them. The education of the children of these migrant labourers are being hampered to a large extent as they accompany the adult family members who migrate in search of alternate livelihood opportunities. There are several incidents where the migrant workers could not get their wages properly. As they go to the informal sector to work, they could not receive any social security cover or get any legal support on several occasions at their workplace.

To understand the gravity and extent of unsafe migration issues and the response of the state, the authors communicated with the district administration. Visit to the local government offices in the border areas revealed that the *panchayat*s do not keep any records related to migration. They even do not have any idea about which part of India the people of their areas are going to. To deep dive into the matter, the authors tried to collect some basic information about the migration status of the district through RTI. Unfortunately, none of the authorities could provide us with a single data about migration. All the authorities agreed about the seriousness of the issues but did not have any plan or understanding to mitigate the issue.

All the key stakeholders including government agencies who deal with the long-term and day-to-day activities in the border areas could play a crucial role in mitigating this issue. A core committee shall be formed where BSF personnel, District Magistrate; elected representatives from local government, legislative assembly and parliament; office of the Assistant Director of Agriculture; office of the irrigation and waterways department; office of the labour commissioner of distinct, representatives from farmers and other major stakeholders. Such a step is very important to protect the rights of the farmers as well as ensure the national security of the country. The interests of all the parties shall be taken care properly so that they are not forced to change the profession or the place of work and pushed away from their native/social moorings.

Due to bureaucratic procedures, there is very limited scope for interaction between the farmers and the BSF personnel. Although the Border Security Force of each Border Out Post (BOP) arranges a meeting for the farmers once in a month, it does not result in any fruitful discussions, as gathered about the past experiences. Many factors contribute in this direction. First, the people living in the border areas have a discomfort to attend any meeting in restricted places like BOPs. Though the BSF personnel try to make the environment of the meeting very comfortable by offering water and snacks, people still do not feel comfortable when the security personnel attend the meeting with live firearms. The language used in the meeting is another problem. In Cooch Behar district, very few farmers understand Hindi language. On the other hand, most of the BSF officials are not able to understand Bengali language as they are drawn from different parts of India. Women of the villages do not participate in the meetings as the meetings are held at BOPs and the timing of the meetings is also inappropriate for the women. Keeping the seriousness of national security in mind, BSF personnel restrict access to the border gate. However, this restriction can create challenges for farmers to conduct agricultural activities.

As visibility issues persist in the border area, BSF personnel restrict the cultivation of crops exceeding 3 ft in height.

Suggestions

It is suggested that the monthly meeting of all stakeholders in the border areas shall be held inside the village, maybe in the local school, local club premises or community halls. It can give enough confidence to the villagers to attend the meeting. The BSF personnel shall avoid carrying live firearms to the venue for the meeting. Participation of the women farmers shall be ensured by revising the timing of the meeting accordingly. Among the BSF personnel, those who can speak the local language shall be engaged to represent their views during the meeting or else a neutral translator may be engaged to do the translation. Such an attempt will enable to make the environment friendlier so that free and frank discussion could be held. It will lead to informed decision-making, after detailed deliberations among all those present in the meeting.

Timings for opening and closing of the gate shall be fixed by the BSF personnel in consultation with the farmers, considering the suitability of timings for agricultural activities. If possible, the gate can be left open by regulating the movement from 7:00 a.m. to 4:00 p.m.

Agriculture department shall take the initiative to introduce alternative cash crop cultivation that are less than 3 ft in height in the border areas, keeping in view the security measures (PIB., n.d.). Proper guidance is required for farmers to conduct agricultural activities scientifically. The office of the Assistant Director of Agriculture (ADA) office can play a role in this (Dash, 2024). If possible, low-yield maize or jute seeds can be introduced through proper testing. The office of the ADA can also take responsibility for conducting extensive awareness camps to make the farmers aware of the different government schemes available for the farmers and guide them to avail of those schemes. In this context, it is pertinent to note that

> active involvement and participation of youth in agriculture with enabling policy and programmes will rejuvenate the "Agro Eco System" in the country, in line with its strides towards reaching the Sustainable Development Goals, earlier than anticipated. (Gireesan, 2020)

Irrigation and waterways department shall take necessary initiatives such as setting up solar pump machines, maintaining the water bodies to enhance their storage capacity, etc. to ensure adequate water supply for agricultural activities. In this context, it is suggested that "water budgeting" in the border areas shall be undertaken by the state government of West Bengal which aims to ensure sustainable water management in the area.

> Water budgeting is the process of managing water resources effectively in a given area. It involves assessing water availability, estimating usage for various needs like agriculture and industry, and promoting efficient use and conservation practices. (Gireesan, 2023)

This will enable the farmers and other stakeholders to optimize the utilization of water, modify the agricultural practices and if necessary, diversity the agricultural crops.

As those areas are situated close to the India-Bangladesh border, the Government of Bangladesh has a crucial role to play in mitigating the issues where the Bangladeshi people or cattle are involved. Regular flag meeting between the security personnel from both the sides shall be made to address the issues of illegal trespass of human or cattle.

A programme must be implemented with a balanced attitude towards national security as well as the strengthening of local economy. Hence, it is important to mention that before taking up any development initiative in the border areas, deliberations with the all stakeholders shall be made. A special working group may be formed with representation from state government, BSF, local government institutions, etc. to implement such programmes. NGOs working in the field of holistic development can also be consulted and be entrusted with specific tasks during its operationalization.

Conclusion

The international border between India and Bangladesh is significant for several reasons. It is a contiguous border where people residing on either side have been socially, economically and culturally connected for centuries till the demarcation of border took place in 1947. This is a major factor to be kept in mind, while addressing various needs, concerns, issues and problems in the border areas. As discussed in this article, the life and livelihood of the people in the border areas have been caught in a standstill. The stagnancy in the local economy forced many persons to take up illegal option like cross-border smuggling or undesirable and unhealthy option like unsafe migration, to earn a livelihood. It will not only socio-economically emancipate the people of these villages, it will also curb the tendency of looking for alternative economic sources of livelihood by resorting to illegal, undesirable and unhealthy options and extra-economic activities. The generation of income and creation of local markets can be a positive approach to deal with the peculiarities in the area.

The authors wish to advocate for the initiation of a specific policy for the border areas, especially in the Indo-Bangladesh border, leading to the comprehensive development of the region, without compromising the national security, foreign relations and considering the burning livelihood issues of the local community.

Acknowledgements

The authors thank all of those who supported them in this work. They specially thank the government officials, elected representatives of local governments, and the local community residing in the India-Bangladesh border areas in Cooch Behar, West Bengal who provided their inputs for the study. The authors also thank the president, secretary and other members of the centre for Inclusive Development Charitable Trust for their support for undertaking this study.

REFERENCES

Agencies. (2017 August 8). *Government Creating Buffer Zone Near Indo-Bangla Border to Combat Wheat Blast.* MillenniumPost | No Half Truths.

Cooch Behar District Population 2024. *India Growing.* (n.d.). https://www.indiagrowing.com/West_Bengal/Cooch_Behar

Chowdhury, S.K. (2023). "Guarding Border: Bodies and Dichotomy In Gendered Control Over Mobility in a Borderland of Bangladesh." *Gender, Place & Culture, 30*(11): 1594-1616. https://doi.org/10.1080/0966369x.2023.2200475

Dash, D.K. (2023 November 10). *Now Senior Officials to Spend at Least One Night in Border Villages to Assess Challenges There | India News—Times of India. The Times of India.* https://timesofindia.indiatimes.com/india/now-senior-officials-to-spend-at-least-one-night-in-border-villages-to-assess-challenges-there/articleshow/105131827.cms?from=mdr

Gireesan K. (2020 September 30). *Youth in Agriculture: Opportunities, Challenges and the Way Forward in the Post-COVID-19 Scenario | Gireesan | IAHRW International Journal of Social Sciences Review.* i-Scholar. https:// www.i-scholar.in/index.php/IIJSSR/article/view/208662

Gireesan K. (2023). "Water Budgeting for Sustainable Development: A Micro Level Study on Climate-resilient Agriculture." *The Palgrave Handbook of Socio-ecological Resilience in the Face of Climate Change*, pp. 257-76. https://doi.org/10.1007/978-981-99-2206-2_16

Jain, B. (2023 November 12). *Bee Warriors' to Help BSF Keep Intruders, Smugglers at Bay on Indo-Bangla Border | Delhi News—Times of India. The Times of India*. https://timesofindia.indiatimes.com/city/delhi/bee-warriors-to-help-bsf-keep-intruders-smugglers-at-bay-on-indo-bangla-border/articleshow/105159337.cms

Vibrant Village Programme (n.d.). *Press Information Bureau*. https://pib.gov.in/PressReleaseIframePage.aspx?PRID=1942876

18

Exploring the Sociocultural Livelihood of the Santhal Tribe and Its Implications for SDGs

A Study in Bankura District

Sanjoy Karmakar

Indigenous communities around the world possess diverse cultural identities and socio-economic structures that have evolved over centuries, often harmonizing with the natural environment. One such indigenous group, the Santhal tribe, residing in the Bankura district, stands as a living testament to this rich tapestry of traditions, rituals, and sociocultural practices. The author selected Chhatna block of Bankura district, West Bengal as the study area. The research study embarks on an exploration of the sociocultural livelihood of the Santhal tribe, aiming to unravel the complexities of their unique way of life.

Bankura district, nestled in the eastern part of India, hosts the Santhals, an indigenous community with a distinctive cultural heritage deeply rooted in their connection to nature, agricultural cycles, and spiritual beliefs. As globalization and modernization increasingly influence the lives of such communities, there is a growing need to understand the dynamics of their sociocultural livelihood and its implications on broader development goals. This research sets out to investigate the intricate interplay between tradition and adaptation within the Santhal tribe, shedding light on the rituals, festivals, and performances that form the core of their cultural identity. The significance of festivals like "Sohorai" and "Karam" in expressing the Santhals' reverence for nature and aspirations for prosperity will be explored in detail. In addition, this study places the sociocultural livelihood of the Santhal tribe within the global context of Sustainable Development Goals (SDGs). By examining how their practices align with SDG objectives related to poverty alleviation, gender equality, and environmental sustainability, the research seeks to contribute insights that can inform more inclusive and culturally sensitive development strategies.

Objectives

The major objectives of the study are: to understand the sociocultural livelihood of the Santhal Tribes in the study area; to assess the environmental impact of Livelihood Practices of Santhal Tribes; and, to assess their alignment with the SDGs.

Literature Review

Puttaraja and Heggade (2012) highlighted the significant role women play in the social, cultural, economic, and religious aspects of tribal societies. These women are viewed as valuable economic assets within their communities. However, despite their pivotal role, they still face substantial challenges in areas such as education, employment, health care, and economic empowerment. The term "empowering" is used to denote the process of enabling disadvantaged groups, particularly impoverished tribal women, to attain and wield power and resources. Verma (1960) extensively explored the sociocultural organizations of the Sanria Paharias, Mai- Paharias, and Kumarbhag. The community is also known as Santals or Shantals. According to Ahmad (2002), the name is a corruption of "Saontar", which the Santals adopted during their residence in the Saont area of the Midinipur district in West Bengal. The term "Santal" is an English word borrowed from Hindi, aligning with "Saontar" as used by Bengali-speaking population. Typically, they refer to themselves as *hor* (man). Another analogous term is *hor*, which signifies the way or means. A *hor* (man) is engaged in seeking the *hor* (way or means), and the endeavor persists until a satisfactory outcome is achieved. Pradhan *et al.* (2017) in his paper challenges the legitimacy of discerning stratification patterns among Indian tribes through the lens of caste hierarchy, "Sacred" hierarchy, or class-based divisions. His scrutiny is contextualized within the tribes of Gujarat.

Methodology

This study relies on a combination of primary and secondary data sources, with a predominant focus on primary data gathered through field surveys conducted by the researcher. A random sample of 120 households has been selected from the study areas. Secondary data have been sourced from the books, journals, Internet and others. For this study, a multifaceted approach combining qualitative and quantitative methods was adopted. The database encompasses demographic data such as population distribution and livelihood specifics including occupation profiles, income levels, and access to government schemes. Sociocultural data delves into cultural practices, social organization, and infrastructure availability. Methodologically, the study undertakes a literature review to contextualize existing knowledge, followed by field surveys and qualitative research techniques like participant observation and key informant interviews to capture the nuances of Santhal culture and livelihoods. Quantitative analysis complemented this qualitative data, with statistical methods used to identify correlations between sociocultural factors and development outcomes. Stakeholder consultations ensured that the local perspectives are integrated ethically, and the findings are synthesized into a comprehensive report, offering insights and recommendations for sustainable development planning aligned with SDG goals in Bankura district.

Study Area

The study focuses on investigating the sociocultural livelihood of the Santhal tribe within Bankura district, situated in the south-western region of West Bengal, India.

Fig: 18.1: Key Map of the Study Area

Bankura district, encompassing diverse landscapes ranging from hills to fertile plains, is renowned for its rich cultural heritage and heterogeneous population. Home to the Santhal tribe, one of the prominent indigenous communities, the district offers an ideal setting to delve into the socio-economic dynamics and cultural nuances shaping the livelihoods of indigenous peoples. By examining the sociocultural fabric and livelihood patterns within this context, the research seeks to uncover insights crucial for advancing sustainable development goals, particularly in addressing sociocultural inequalities and fostering inclusive growth strategies aligned with the Sustainable Development Goals (SDGs). Chhatna block of Bankura district in West Bengal has been selected as the study area (Fig. 18.1).

Discussions and Analysis

(a) Historico-anthropological Introduction

The Santhals, constituting the largest Adivasi community in India, are predominantly found in states such as Jharkhand, Bihar, West Bengal, Madhya Pradesh, Assam, Tripura, and Odisha, with some of them reside in the neighbouring countries like Bangladesh, Bhutan, and Myanmar, particularly along the border areas. Anthropological history reveals significant findings in the Shiwalik foothills of the north-western Himalayas, where evidence of Ramapithecus, possibly the earliest species in the hominid lineage dating back approximately fourteen million years, has been unearthed. Subsequent investigations suggest the presence of Australopithecus-like species in India around two million years ago, indicating a substantial evolutionary gap following Ramapithecus. The migratory sequence to India, post-Negritos, is believed to have included the arrival of the "Proto-Australoids" or "Austrics" group, foundational to the region's diverse populace and potentially instrumental in the development of the Indus Valley Civilization. The Santhal people's historical origins trace back to migrations from various Indian states, particularly Bihar, Jharkhand, West Bengal, and Odisha, with oral accounts suggesting economic constraints as a significant driver of migration, leading to settlements in regions such as Nepal, notably Jhapa and Morang districts.

(b) Society and Social/Political Practices

To analyse the aspect of "Society and Social/Political Practices" through the lens of this study, the author examines how the Santhal tribe's societal structure, social practices, and political engagement intersect with their sociocultural livelihood and the broader framework of SDGs.

Societal Structure and Social Practices of the Santhal Tribe: This study delves into the intricate societal structure of the Santhal tribe, including their kinship systems, traditional governance mechanisms, and communal practices. It may explore how social cohesion and solidarity within the Santhal community contribute to their sociocultural livelihood strategies, such as collective farming, mutual assistance networks, and cultural rituals that reinforce social bonds. Understanding these social practices is crucial for comprehending the resilience and adaptive capacity of the Santhal tribe in navigating socio-economic challenges.

Political Engagement and Governance Dynamics: This study may shed light on the political engagement of the Santhal tribe within the governance framework of Bankura district. This includes examining their representation in local government institutions, advocacy efforts for land rights and cultural preservation, and interactions with mainstream political structures. Understanding the political agency of the Santhal tribe is essential for assessing their ability to influence policies and programmes that impact their sociocultural livelihoods and contribute to achieving SDG goals related to social inclusion, indigenous rights, and participatory governance.

(c) Implications for SDG Goals

Through the study's findings, the paper discusses the implications of the Santhal societal practices engagement for SDGs, particularly those related to poverty alleviation, gender equality, education, and sustainable communities. For instance, it may highlight how traditional Santhal practices of collective resource management align with SDG-1 (No Poverty) and SDG-2 (Zero Hunger) by promoting food security and economic empowerment. Additionally, it may underscore the importance of recognizing indigenous knowledge and cultural heritage in achieving SDG-4 (Quality Education) and SDG-10 (Reduced Inequalities). Overall, the analysis of "Society and Social/Political Practices" in the context of this paper offers insights into the intricate dynamics shaping the sociocultural livelihoods of the Santhal tribe and underscores the significance of incorporating indigenous perspectives and community participation in SDG implementation strategies within Bankura district and beyond.

The rich social-cultural tapestry of the Santhal tribe, as described, intersects with several SDGs in significant ways:

Gender Equality (SDG-5): The transition of leadership to female members in the absence of male figures within Santhal families reflects a degree of gender equality. Additionally, the freedom experienced by Santhali women and their participation in communal activities suggest progress toward gender empowerment.

Reduced Inequalities (SDG-10): The erosion of caste distinctions and the casteless nature of Santhal society demonstrate a commitment to reducing social inequalities. Granting individuals equal status regardless of birth contributes to a more inclusive and equitable society.

Sustainable Communities (SDG-11): The communal living and strong sense of community fostered within Santhal villages promote sustainable communities. The well-organized system for managing social and judicial matters ensures community cohesion and effective governance.

Responsible Consumption and Production (SDG-12): The meticulous construction of Santhal homes from locally-sourced materials like bamboo, paddy straw, wood, and mud aligns with the principles of sustainable consumption and production. This promotes the efficient use of resources and reduces environmental impact.

Peace, Justice, and Strong Institutions (SDG-16): The structured system for managing social and judicial matters, led by the "Majhi Hadam" and supported by various office bearers, contributes to peace, justice, and strong institutions within Santhal society. This ensures the fair resolution of conflicts and effective governance.

Cultural Preservation (SDG-17): The adherence to distinctive customs related to birth, death, and marriage, as well as the celebration of cultural festivals like "Sohrai", showcases the Santhal tribe's commitment to preserving their cultural heritage. This aligns with the goal of promoting the diversity of cultures and traditions.

Overall, the sociocultural practices of the Santhal tribe described in the passage contribute to various SDGs by promoting gender equality, reducing inequalities, fostering sustainable communities, encouraging responsible consumption and production, ensuring peace and justice, and preserving cultural heritage.

(d) Village Administration

The Santhal community thrives as a democratic society, rooted in principles of equality and enduring cohesion. Santhal villages, characterized by robust social and political structures, prioritize social organization and harmonious relationships over wealth accumulation. Unlike mainstream "Pahadiya" culture in Nepal, Santhal clans stand on equal footing, devoid of class distinctions based on status or occupation. Typically, Santhal villages comprise diverse clans governed by a well-established political organization called "Punchayati", led by a secular headman known as the "Majhi". The village council, or "Atu Mone Hor" (Punchayati), includes essential roles such as the "Jag Majhi", "Paranik", "Gudit", "Jag Paranik", "Naike", and "Kudam Naike", with each family represented in the council. This institution serves as the paramount authority for resolving disputes and upholding customs and laws governing various aspects of Santhal community life. During village council meetings, the "Majhi" presides over discussions and acts as a representative in inter-village disputes, supported by the "Paranik" and "Gudit" in succession scenarios. The "Jag Majhi" plays a crucial role in youth oversight and intergenerational knowledge transfer, while the religious heads "Naike" and "Kudam Naike" oversee religious ceremonies and rituals. Majhi Than a sacred place made in the open space little away from residential area (Fig. 18.2).

Fig. 18.2: Majhi Than

(e) Judicial System

The Santhals maintain a well-organized judicial system, crucial for managing and resolving internal challenges within their community, reflecting their commitment to justice and social cohesion. Their governance system, known as "Majhi Parganna", aligns with principles of local self-governance, facilitating community decision making and socio-economic restructuring. Led by the "Majhi Hadam", supported by various office bearers like the "Paranik", "Jag Majhi", "Jagparanik", "Naike", and "Gudit", this system addresses diverse challenges and ensures equitable solutions. The hierarchical structure, with positions like "Disham Majhi" and "Diheri", demonstrates a commitment to fair and hierarchical justice. Santhals, preferring clustered communities near natural resources, organize into twelve groups or "Thars", each specializing in distinct roles like priesthood, business, rulership, judiciary, music, and defence. This organizational structure, including village, *parganna*, and highest councils, ensures inclusive decision making and community representation. This adherence to justice, community cohesion, and social organization aligns with various SDG goals, including Reduced Inequalities (SDG-10), Peace, Justice, and Strong Institutions (SDG-16), and Sustainable Communities (SDG-11), contributing to inclusive governance and equitable development.

(f) Life-Cycle Ceremonies

Birth Ceremony: The traditional practices surrounding the birth of a Santhal child underscore cultural norms and religious rituals within the community. Despite the ceremonial impurity attributed to the mother and parents during the initial five days post-birth, these practices reflect the community's adherence to longstanding customs and spiritual beliefs, contributing to the preservation of cultural heritage. The offering of a special dish to "Marang Buru", the primary deity, symbolizes reverence for spiritual entities and the importance of spiritual connections within the community, fostering a sense of belonging and identity.

Furthermore, the naming convention, which honours ancestors and reflects familial lineage, emphasizes the significance of familial ties and intergenerational connections. While these practices may appear to conflict with contemporary notions of gender equality and individual autonomy, they highlight the importance of cultural diversity and the preservation of indigenous traditions, contributing to the achievement of SDG-16 (Peace, Justice, and Strong Institutions) by promoting inclusive and culturally sensitive approaches to community development and governance.

Marriage: The division of the Santhal community into twelve distinct clans underscores the importance of cultural identity and social cohesion within the community, contributing to the preservation of traditional values and customs.

Fig, 18.3: Celebrating Baha Parab

The avoidance of intermarriage within the same clan reflects a commitment to maintain familial lineage and prevent potential conflicts arising from close kinship ties. The prevalence of arranged marriages, as well as the recognition of various types of marriages delineated in the book *Mechi Dekhi Mahakali*, highlights the diversity of marital practices within the Santhal community. While these practices may appear to restrict individual autonomy in marriage, they also ensure the continuity of cultural heritage and social stability within the community, aligning with SDG-16 (Peace, Justice, and Strong Institutions) by promoting inclusive and culturally sensitive approaches to family and community governance. Additionally, by valuing traditional marital practices and familial relationships, the Santhal community contributes to the achievement of SDG-5 (Gender Equality) by fostering respect for gender roles and promoting harmonious familial relations.

Death Rituals: The funeral rituals observed by the Santhal community upon the passing of an individual reflect cultural traditions aimed at honouring the deceased and ensuring a peaceful transition to the afterlife, contributing to the preservation of cultural heritage and social cohesion within the community. The use of white cloth for enshrouding the body and the procession to the final resting place symbolize reverence for the deceased and the importance of respecting ancestral traditions.

The scattering of unhusked rice and cotton seeds at crossroads demonstrates a belief in spiritual protection and the mitigation of potential obstacles, fostering a sense of spiritual well-being and community solidarity. Additionally, the provision of meals to mourners during the mourning period signifies a gesture of appreciation and support, promoting social cohesion and solidarity within the community. These funeral rituals align with SDG- 16 (Peace, Justice, and Strong Institutions) by fostering cultural sensitivity, social harmony, and the preservation of traditional values and practices within the Santhal community, contributing to inclusive and equitable community development.

(g) Proximity to Nature

The Santhal ethnic communities' deep-rooted connection with nature, as depicted in the passage, aligns with several SDGs by promoting sustainable practices, cultural preservation, and community cohesion:

Life on Land (SDG-15): The Santhal's settlement choices and resource utilization demonstrate a harmonious relationship with the natural environment. By residing near forests and rivers and engaging in hunting and fishing, they showcase a sustainable lifestyle that respects biodiversity and ecosystems.

Good Health and Well-being (SDG-3): The Santhals' preference for traditional hunting and fishing practices and their culinary preferences, such as pork, reflect a cultural appreciation for natural, locally-sourced foods, contributing to healthy dietary habits and overall well-being within the community.

Gender Equality (SDG-5): Rituals such as the symbolic venture into hunting for young Santhali individuals symbolize rites of passage that may involve both genders, emphasizing equal opportunities for personal growth and responsibility within the community.

Climate Action (SDG-13): The Santhal community's deep reverence for nature, as expressed through their festivals and rituals honouring seasonal cycles and agricultural practices, promotes awareness of climate change and the importance of preserving environmental sustainability.

Cultural Preservation (SDG-11): Santhali festivals, cultural customs, and mythological narratives serve as powerful mechanisms for preserving indigenous knowledge, traditions, and cultural heritage, contributing to the resilience of their cultural identity amidst changing times.

Partnerships for the Goals (SDG-17): The Santhal community's close-knit social structure and collective efforts in celebrating festivals and practising sustainable agriculture exemplify the importance of community partnerships and collabouration in achieving common goals, including environmental conservation and cultural preservation.

Overall, the Santhal community's intimate bond with nature, as depicted in the passage, embodies a holistic approach to sustainable development, wherein cultural traditions, environmental stewardship, and community well-being are interconnected and mutually reinforcing, contributing to the achievement of various SDGs.

In the case of the Santhal community, their cultural practices, including hunting, naming ceremonies, marriage, and death rituals, are deeply intertwined with nature. They thrive within the niche of nature, living in close proximity to it and considering it an integral part of their lives. Unlike those from more civilized and scientific societies who often view nature with detachment, Santhals immerse themselves in it, embodying a unique culture inherently intertwined with the natural world.

Another aspect of this paper involves evaluating how the traditional livelihood practices of the Santhal tribe in Bankura district impact the environment. It delves into understanding the ecological footprint of activities such as agriculture, hunting, gathering, and other customary practices carried out by the Santhals. By assessing the environmental impact, the aim is to identify potential areas of concern, such as deforestation, habitat degradation, soil erosion, water pollution, or loss of biodiversity, resulting from these livelihood practices. Understanding the environmental impact is crucial for devising strategies to promote sustainable resource management and mitigate adverse effects on the ecosystem, aligning with broader goals of environmental conservation and sustainable development.

Besides, this paper focuses on examining how the sociocultural livelihood practices of the Santhal tribe align with the United Nations' SDGs. It involves analysing the extent to which the Santhals' way of life contributes to achieve specific SDGs related to poverty alleviation, gender equality, health and well-being, education, sustainable agriculture, clean water and sanitation, climate action, and other relevant areas. By assessing alignment with SDGs, researchers seek to identify areas where Santhal practices positively contribute to sustainable development objectives and areas where there may be gaps or opportunities for improvement. This analysis helps in formulating targeted interventions and policies that support the Santhals' sociocultural livelihoods while advancing broader sustainable development goals at the local, national, and global levels.

Conclusion

This chapter has provided valuable insights into the sociocultural livelihood practices of the Santhal tribe in Bankura district and their implications for SDGs. Through a comprehensive exploration of Santhal traditions, customs, and economic activities, we have gained a deeper understanding of the intricate relationship between the Santhals and their environment. The study has highlighted the rich cultural tapestry of the Santhal community, characterized by unique social structures, religious beliefs, and traditional livelihood practices such as agriculture, hunting, and gathering.

The analysis has underscored the importance of considering indigenous knowledge and practices in the context of sustainable development. By assessing the environmental impact of Santhal livelihood practices, the author has identified areas where traditional wisdom aligns with SDG objectives, such as promoting biodiversity conservation, sustainable land management, and community resilience.

It is imperative to foster partnerships between policymakers, local communities, and other stakeholders to ensure inclusion of indigenous perspectives in development planning and implementation. By recognizing the rights and contributions of indigenous communities like the Santhals, one can work towards achieving more inclusive and sustainable development outcomes. Ultimately, this research serves as a call to action for promoting cultural diversity, environmental stewardship, and social equity in pursuit of a more just and sustainable future for all.

Keywords

SDGs, santhal's livelihood, tribal people, socio-economic condition, social practices.

REFERENCES

Ahmad, A. (2002). *Social Geography*. Rawat Publisher.

Ambasht, N.K. (1970). *A Critical Study of Tribal Education*. Chand, Delhi.

Ayyanar, M., S. Ignacimuthu, & R. Rajendran (2005). "Traditional Knowledge of Kani Tribals in Kouthalai ofTirunelveli Hills, Tamil Nadu, India." *Journal of Ethnopharmacology, 102*(3): 319-26.

Census Commission of India (2001). *West Bengal: Data Highlights the Scheduled Tribes*. Census of India. Retrieved January 10, 2010.

Das, A.K. (1991). "Scheduled Tribe: A Socio-Economic and Cultural Profile in West Bengal." *Bulletin of C.R.I.*, Kolkata.

Jana, S.K. (2001). "Christianity and Tribal Identity: A Case Study of the Santals of Bhimpore in the District of Midnapore, West Bengal." *Man and Life, 7*(3-4).

Hoel, P. G. & R.J. Jessen (1977). *Basic Statistics for Business and Economics*. Wiley.

Pradhan, P., L. Costa, D. Rybski, W. Lucht, & J.P. Kropp (2017). "A Systematic Study of Sustainable Development Goal (SDG) Interactions." *Earth's Future, 5*(11): 1169-79.

Puttaraja, K., & O.D. Heggade (2012). Economic Empowerment of Tribal Women in Karnataka: A Case Study in Mysore and Chamarajanagara Districts." *Studies of Tribes and Tribals, 10*(2): 173-81.

Verma, P. (1960). *Sociocultural Organizations of Tribals*. Metro Publishers, Rajasthan.

19

Microfinance and Its Role in Achieving the Sustainable Development Goals with Reference to Indian Microfinance Sector

Saibal Paul

Development is inevitable as the strategic and coordinated development is necessary to put a dent on underdevelopment.

In order to bring convergence in the multifarious development, United Nations Development Programme (UNDP) developed the Sustainable Development Goal (SDG) which shall be viewed as "Global Goals" to engage in the endeavour to end poverty, protect the planet, and ensure that by 2030, to bring peace and prosperity by all people on earth. The SDGs aim to put an end to discrimination against women and girls, hunger, AIDS, and poverty. The significant focus of SDGs is to bring convergence between different arrays by aiming to bring equilibrium between social, economic, and environmental sustainability. Nations are committed to accord the highest priority to the nations with the least development.

Contribution of economics is inevitable in bringing equilibrium between the trinity of social, economic, and environmental aspects of development. In the seventeen SDGs, at least seven goals are linked with finance and economics. As these goals are mostly to address the unnoticed areas of development and uplift the unserved population, we need to understand the importance and scope of social development finance, known as microfinance, to achieve the goals.

Microfinance is not a new concept. Microfinance has a long history, with Irish loan funds dating back to 1720 and later regulated by strong regulations, courtesy goes to Jonathan Swift. Credit cooperatives were established in Germany in the 1850s to serve those whom traditional banks were hesitant to serve. Various forms of microfinance, such as Susus in Ghana, Tandas in Mexico, Cheetu in Sri Lanka, Hui in China, and Chit Funds and Maroops in Manipur, have been providing credit to the underserved population for generations. While these initiatives have helped to meet the credit needs of the poor, there has always been a focus on the purpose of the loan and repayment strategies. Nobel Laureate Muhammad Yunus has restructured it, taken a step ahead, and made it a movement for reinventing mainstream economics to create a world with three zeros: zero unemployment, zero poverty, and zero net carbon emissions. Microfinance has gone far beyond microcredit. It is a bouquet of products designed for the poorer population, including micro credit, micro savings, micro leasing, micro insurance, and micro pensions.

Benefaction of Microfinance

To examine the linkages of microfinance to SDGs, we need to assess the influence of microfinance on the lives of the borrowers. This secondary data-based analysis of the impact of microfinance, on a global scale, along with other sources, will review a primary data set that has been compiled by Sa-Dhan to identify the impact of the microfinance sector on the various parameters of the SDGs.

Kasali's 2020[1] study analysed the impact of microfinance loans on poverty alleviation in South-West Nigeria through primary research. The results revealed that while microfinance loans positively contributed to poverty alleviation in the region, government aid is still needed. The author recommended that governments support microfinance institutions with low-interest funds to disburse. A comprehensive study by Donou-Adonsou and Sylwester[2] of 85 developing countries found that microfinance lending significantly increases total factor productivity (TFP) and promotes economic growth. Furthermore, evidence suggests that microfinance positively impacted economic growth in Nigeria and Bangladesh. Notably, the relationship seems two-way in Bangladesh. Analysing data graphically, Ekpenyong and Nnamocha[3] determined microfinance loans positively influenced Nigeria's GDP and various economic sectors. Tarozzi, Desai, and Johnson[4] conducted a study examining the effects of microfinance access in rural Ethiopia, focusing on areas like agriculture, animal husbandry, self-employment, labour supply, education, and women's empowerment. Despite increased borrowing, they found limited socio-economic improvements overall.

> The Impact assessment studies conducted by the Institute of Development Studies (IDS) in the United Kingdom in association with three Universities in the UK—Bath, Sheffield and Sussex have indicated that three out of four (76.8 per cent) of the clients of Share Microfin (SHARE) have experienced significant reduction in poverty, and half of them are no longer meagre. Women are able to solve their social problems and with increased opportunities coming their way, they are eager to look for better prospects in life.[5]

A study conducted by the UNDP on "Microcredit and Women Empowerment through SHARE" has come out with the following observations: There is a sign of significant poverty reduction and it has been found that women have better control over income, assets, and expenditure; Women have started to break social barriers by interacting with other people in society, using their collective strength to address village issues more openly and boldly even before bureaucrats; Significant decrease in child labour has been noticed and the importance of education among both boys and girls is felt.[6] In case of Cashpor microcredit "Significant reduction in PPI score at loan cycle 3-4".[7] Banerjee, Breza, Duflo, and Kinnan[8] found in randomized evaluation of a group-lending microcredit programme in Hyderabad, India, that microcredit access increased investment and profits for small businesses.

Contribution of Microfinance to Achieve SDG-1 (End Poverty) and SDG-8 (Create Decent Work and Economic Growth)

Microfinance industry serves the marginalised population that has been excluded by the traditional financial system, deeming them un-bankable and unsuitable for business due to high opportunity costs. This sector is evolved to assist individuals in poverty, who require financial assistance to pursue their entrepreneurial aspirations. While it is essential to provide support for basic needs such as health care, education, and housing, microfinance has proven its value not only in normal circumstances but also during crises like the pandemic. Governments have utilized this channel to inject funds into the households of the poor for survival and recovery. Therefore, microfinance plays a crucial role in reducing poverty. An in-depth study in Uttar Pradesh on impact of urban microfinance narrates

> Urban microfinance has a considerable impact on poverty reduction, the standard of living, social well-being, empowerment and entrepreneurship in the urban poor, according to the findings.[9]

Sa-Dhan's independent impact study[10] illustrates

> ....before joining an MFI, more than half of the respondents (54%) relied on a single income source. However, this percentage decreased to one-fourth (25%) during the survey. In terms of the main income earners in their households, more than three-fifths of the respondents (61%) mentioned experiencing over thirty days without work before joining an

> MFI, whereas the current percentage stands at 50 per cent. Furthermore, just less than four-fifth of the respondents (79%) indicate having some monthly household savings, which is an increase from the previous figure of 54 per cent before obtaining their first MFI loans. Almost all the respondents (99%) reported experiencing at least some improvement in their economic and financial condition after joining an MFI, with more than half of them noting a significant improvement. It shows that microfinance contributes significantly to achieve decent work and economic growth.

Microfinance's Contribution to Achieve SDG-2 (End Hunger)

"End Hunger" can only be achieved if the support goes to the population who is hungry. The government has to be contributing in this segment significantly. However the major challenge is the reach. Microfinance sector has that reach which can be used by development initiatives. However, as noted from the earlier discussions, microfinance facilitates the increase in income. A study in Bankura district[11] portrays

> . . . This means that with other variables held constant, that if income of the households increases by a unit, on an average the estimated logit increases by about 0.0016 units. This implies that the probability of food security is likely to increase with family income.

The study in Gazipur and Mymensingh districts of Bangladesh[12] narrates that

> microcredit intervention made a significant contribution to increase the household food consumption expenditure of the borrowers.

Though zero hunger is a big target and all the ecosystem contributors need to be working in tandem but microfinance sector has definitely put a dent on the hunger through its interventions.

Microfinance's Contribution to Achieve SDG-5 (Achieve Gender Equality)

Around 95 per cent of microfinance beneficiaries are women, they are the sources of finance for the development of the family. Second, by virtue of going out of the regular social circle, the women are also source of information for the family. Both of these situations are making them empowered and in many cases compelling the society to accept the women as equal partner of the community. Sa-Dhan's microfinance impact study[13] describes

> ...approximately 44 per cent of participants experienced a substantial boost in confidence when communicating with individuals outside their usual circle after engaging with an MFI. An additional 55 per cent mentioned that their confidence had slightly improved. In terms of independent movement, 46 per cent reported a significant increase in their confidence while navigating on their own. Approximately 45 per cent felt that their social standing had notably risen following their collabouration with an MFI. In general, 43 per cent observed a considerable rise in awareness regarding literacy and education. Another 43 per cent highlighted that their skills in reading, writing, and arithmetic had significantly improved. Knowledge about government welfare initiatives varied, with 81 per cent being aware of Prime Minister's Awaas Yojana (PMAY), 79 per cent knowing about the Mid-Day Meal scheme, 40 per cent for NPS, and 52 per cent for old age pensions. From the discussions, it can be clearly indicated that going out of the regular domain and participating in the larger discussions infuse self-confidence, self reliance and strong information base on women.

Microfinance's Contribution to Achieve Other SDGs

The microfinance sector provides loans primarily for the goal of generation of income, but it also supports non-income purposes where ever possible. In March 2023, microfinance sector had gross loan portfolio of Rs. 1,79,855 cr, of which 95 per cent was for income generation purposes.

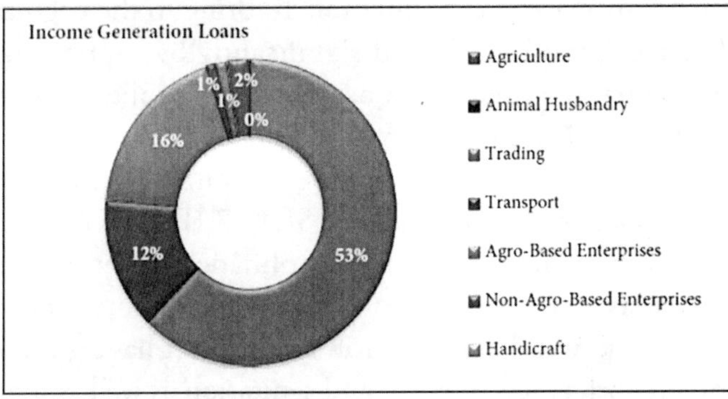

Source: Bharat Microfinance Report 2023

Fig. 19.1: Loans for Income Generation Purposes

Above chart (Fig. 19.1) is explaining the areas where microfinance loans are used by the end borrowers of India. If we remove the portion of agriculture which is 53 per cent then 47 per cent of the portfolio has been extended for promotion of enterprises. Some of them are also part of downstream enterprises of large industry. Overall it shows microfinance sector is contributing to the SDG-9 with promotion of industry.

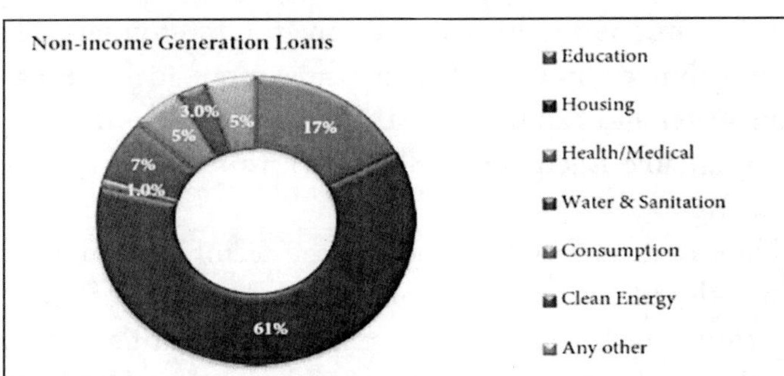

Source: Bharat Microfinance Report 2023

Fig. 19.2: Loan for Non-Income Generation Purposes

As narrated earlier, microfinance sector also extends loans for non-income generation purposes. The borrowers also access loans for water and sanitation, which addresses the SDG-6, Improve Clean Water and Sanitation. To bring to the cognizance microfinance sector contributed significantly by supporting the upfront money required for constructing the toilets, to access Swachh Bharat Mission's contribution of government. The borrowers also access loans for buying amenities of clean energy, which is supporting to promote the SDG-7 (Ensure Affordable, Clean and Sustainable Energy). Microfinance sector also caters their borrowers with loans for health which is a support to establish good health and well-being. Microfinance sector has significantly contributed both access of water and sanitation as well as usage of clean energy in the life of poor people by giving them door step access to the finance.

Conclusion

The main objective of SDG is to set a target of development in front, build-up collabourative alliances and joint monitoring to keep the designed interventions focussed toward goals. Out of seventeen SDGs, microfinance sector has significant contribution to four, i.e. SDG-1 (End Poverty), SDG-2 (End Hunger), SDG-5 (Achieve Gender Equality), and, SDG-8 (Create Decent Work and Economic Growth). In addition, the microfinance sector also contributed towards achieving three more goals, i.e. SDG-6 (Clean Water and Sanitation), SDG-7 (Ensure Affordable, Clean and Sustainable Energy) and SDG-3 (Ensure Good Health and Well-being).

The spectacular contribution of the sector is to support and advance the unreached, those who have been out of the ambit of development historically. The phenomena can be understood from the outreach. The Economic Survey data from January 2023 highlights the crucial position of rural India in the country's economic picture, considering 65 per cent of the population lives in rural areas. Though rural regions account for around

45 per cent of India's gross domestic product (GDP), there is a stark imbalance as only 11 per cent of total banking deposits and 9 per cent of overall credit belonged to rural areas, as on December 2022. This discrepancy can be ascribed to insufficient banking infrastructure, restricted financial knowledge, investment behaviours, and a shortage of formal identification in rural regions. While contributing significantly to GDP, rural India lags regarding access to banking services and credit, pointing to the need for greater financial inclusion. However, 74 per cent of the borrowers of microfinance sector are from rural areas.

It is noteworthy that microfinance is reaching out to the unreached population, achieving the parameters of SDGs which possibly no one can do. According to Bharat Microfinance Report 2023, the Compound Annual Growth Rate (CAGR) of last ten years, of reaching to the end borrowers, was 6.82 per cent; in March 2023 microfinance sector was serving to 532 lakh poor people. In case of Gross Loan Portfolio (GLP), the CAGR of last ten was 21.50 per cent; in March 2023 microfinance sector was having GLP of Rs. 179,855 crore. Keeping the same CAGR, in 2030, microfinance sector will cater to 844 lakh poor people with GLP of Rs. 7,03,002 crore (US$ 83691 million).

> The global market for microfinance estimated at US$200 billion in the year 2022, is projected to reach a revised size of US$506 billion by 2030, growing at a CAGR of 12.3 per cent over the analysis period 2022-30"[14].

The number is massive, the support for achieving SDG will be substantial and moreover development of the population of any country brings equality in the country.

In any country, if the unreached population is not catered and strategically brought out of poverty, the country will be always lagging behind to achieve the SDGs. From the detailed discussions, it can be pronounced that microfinance is one of the strongest tool to bring changes in the life of the bottom of the pyramid. Both local and international lenders and investors should support this segment with financial resources to flourish.

Keywords

Microfinance, micro enterprise, sa-dhan, sustainable development goals, MFI, UNDP.

NOTES

1. https://www.mdpi.com/1911-8074/15/9/393#:~:text=The%20study%20revealed%20that%20microfinance,disbursed%20at%20concessionary%20interest%20rates—"The Impact of Microfinance Institutions on Poverty Alleviation", Collin Chikwira, Edson Vengesai, Petronella Mandude.
2. https://www.sciencedirect.com/science/article/abs/pii/S1062976916301260 "Growth effect of banks and microfinance: Evidence from developing countries" Ficawoyi Donou-Adonsou, Kevin Sylwester.
3. http://doisrpska.nub.rs/index.php/actaeconomica/article/view/7484—"The Impact of Microfinance Institutions Oneconomic Growth in Nigeria", Orok Bassey Ekpenyong, Patrick Nwaeze Nnamocha.
4. https://www.aeaweb.org/articles?id=10.1257/app.20130475—"The Impacts of Microcredit: Evidence from Ethiopia", Alessandro Tarozzi, Jaikishan Desai, Kristin Johnson.
5. https://www.sharemicrofin.com/Impact/ImpactAssessment
6. https://www.sharemicrofin.com/Impact/ImpactAssessment Impact Assessment of Share Microfin by IDS
7. https://sptf.info/images/outcomes-wg-brief-cashpor-20151124-english.pdf
8. https://www.aeaweb.org/articles?id=10.1257/app.20130533—"The Miracle of Microfinance? Evidence from a Randomized Evaluation", Abhijit Banerjee, Esther Duflo, Rachel Glennerster, Cynthia Kinnan.
9. https://www.emerald.com/insight/content/doi/10.1108/JEAS-09-2021-0175/full/html—"Evaluating the Role of Microfinance Institutions in Enhancing the Livelihood of Urban Poor", Nazia Hasan, Anjani Kumar Singh, Manoj Kumar Agarwal, Bijay Prasad Kushwaha.

10. https://www.sa-dhan.net/wp-content/uploads/2023/05/Report-IMPACT-OF-MICROFINANCE_compressed.pdf—"Independent Study on IMPACT OF INDIAN MICROFINANCE SECTOR" by Sa-Dhan.
11. https://www.inspirajournals.com/uploads/Issues/1234814742.pdf—"Impact of Microfinance on Food Security: Some Evidences from the District of Bankura in West Bengal".
12. https://www.researchgate.net/publication/353923570_Role_of_Microcredit_in_Improving_the_Food_Security_Status_of_the_Rural_Poor_Women_Evidence_from_Bangladesh,—"Role of Microcredit in Improving the Food Security Status of the Rural Poor Women: Evidence from Bangladesh", Shejuti Haque.
13. https://www.sa-dhan.net/wp-content/uploads/2023/05/Report-IMPACT-OF-MICROFINANCE_compressed.pdf—"Independent Study on Impact of Indian Microfinance Sector" by Sa-Dhan.
14. https://www.fintechfutures.com/techwire/global-microfinance-strategic-market-report-2023-2030-how-microfinance-can-live-up-to-expectations-unlock-a-promising-narrative/—"Global Microfinance Strategic Market Report 2023-2030: How Microfinance Can Live Up to Expectations & Unlock a Promising Narrative?", Report of Research Market.

Index